English G 21

D1

Differenzierende
Ausgabe

Cornelsen

English G 21 • Band D 1

Im Auftrag des Verlages herausgegeben von
Prof. Hellmut Schwarz, Mannheim

Erarbeitet von
Susan Abbey, Nenagh, Irland
Barbara Derkow Disselbeck, Köln
Allen J. Woppert, Berlin
sowie Laurence Harger, Wellington, Neuseeland

unter Mitarbeit von
Wolfgang Biederstädt, Köln
Joachim Blombach, Herford
Helmut Dengler, Limbach
Martina Schroeder, Stedtlingen
Jennifer Seidl, München
Udo Wagner, Voerde
Mervyn Whittaker, Bad Dürkheim
Herbert Willms, Herford

in Zusammenarbeit mit der Englischredaktion
Kirsten Bleck (Projektleitung);
Dr. Eva Grabowski (verantwortliche Redakteurin);
Susanne Bennetreu (Bildredaktion); Julie Colthorpe;
Dr. Philip Devlin; Bonnie S. Glänzer; Mara Leibowitz;
Anne Linder; Kathrin Spiegelberg; Uwe Tröger;
Klaus G. Unger *sowie* Britta Bensmann

Beratende Mitwirkung
Walter Droste, Spenge; Manuela Feierabend-Vonhausen, Rossfeld; Birgit Heinemann, Neu Wulmstorf; Ivette Huxol, Wiedemar; Bernd Jost, Salzbergen; Dr. Dieter Krohn, Hannover; Gabriele Rotter, Wiesbaden; Karl Starkebaum, Diekholzen

Illustrationen
Graham-Cameron Illustration, UK: Fliss Cary, Grafikerin
sowie Roland Beier, Berlin

Fotos
Rob Cousins, Bristol

Layoutkonzept und technische Umsetzung
Aksinia Raphael; Korinna Wilkes

Umschlaggestaltung
Klein und Halm Grafikdesign, Berlin

Für die freundliche Unterstützung danken wir der Cotham School, Bristol.

www.cornelsen.de
www.EnglishG.de

1. Auflage, 4. Druck 2007/06

Alle Drucke dieser Auflage sind inhaltlich unverändert und können im Unterricht nebeneinander verwendet werden.

Druck: CS-Druck CornelsenStürtz, Berlin

ISBN: 978-3-06-031316-7 – broschiert
ISBN: 978-3-06-031366-2 – gebunden

Inhalt gedruckt auf säurefreiem Papier aus nachhaltiger Forstwirtschaft.

Dein Englischbuch enthält folgende Teile:

Hello/Welcome	Einstieg in das Buch
Units	die sechs Kapitel des Buches
Topics	besondere Themen – z.B. „Weihnachten in Großbritannien“
Skills File (SF)	Beschreibung wichtiger Lern- und Arbeitstechniken
Grammar File (GF)	Zusammenfassung der Grammatik jeder Unit
Vocabulary	Wörterverzeichnis zum Lernen der neuen Wörter jeder Unit
Dictionary	alphabetische Wörterverzeichnisse zum Nachschlagen

Die Units bestehen aus diesen Teilen:

Lead-in	Einstieg in das neue Thema
A-Section	neuer Lernstoff mit vielen Aktivitäten
Practice	Übungen
Text	eine spannende oder lustige Geschichte

In den Units findest du diese Überschriften und Symbole:

I can ...	Hier kannst du zeigen, was du auf Englisch schon sagen kannst.
Looking at language	Hier sammelst du Beispiele und entdeckst Regeln.
STUDY SKILLS	Einführung in Lern- und Arbeitstechniken
DOSSIER	Schöne und wichtige Arbeiten kannst du in einer Mappe sammeln.
ACTIVITY	Aufgaben, bei denen du etwas vorspielst, malst oder bastelst
GAME	Spiele für zwei oder für eine Gruppe – natürlich auf Englisch
GETTING BY IN ENGLISH	Alltagssituationen üben; Sprachmittlung
LISTENING	Aufgaben zu Hörtexten auf der CD
Now you	Hier sprichst und schreibst du über dich selbst.
POEM / SONG	Gedichte/Lieder zum Anhören und Singen
PRONUNCIATION	Ausspracheübungen
REVISION	Übungen zur Wiederholung
WORDS	Übungen zu Wortfamilien, Wortfeldern und Wortverbindungen
Checkpoint	Im Workbook kannst du dein Wissen überprüfen.
Extra	Zusätzliche Aktivitäten und Übungen
	Partnerarbeit/Gruppenarbeit
/	Nur auf CD / Auf CD und im Schülerbuch
	Textaufgaben
//	parallele Übungen auf zwei Niveaus
○ ●	leichtere Übung/schwierigere Übung

Inhalt

Inhalt

Hello!

My name is Polly.
Pretty Polly! Pretty Polly!
What about you?

I'm from
What about you?

My mum
and dad are
from

I'm
What about you?
My favourite
colour is
My favourite song is
'If you're happy and
you know it,
clap your
And I like
and
What about you?
What about
you?

Welcome

I can …

… talk to my partner in English.

Hi! My name is … What's your name?
I'm … years old. How old are you?
I'm from … Where are you from?

Talk to different partners. Take notes.

…

… name?	… old?	… from?
Simon	11	…
…		

Now meet Jack, Ananda, Sophie, Dan and Jo from England:

This is *Sophie Carter-Brown*.
She's new in Bristol. She's 11 years old.

This is *Jack Hanson*.
Jack is 11 years old.
He's from Bristol.

This is *Dan Shaw* – with his twin brother *Jo*.
They're 12 years old. They're from Bristol.

This is *Ananda Kapoor*.
She's 11 years old. She's from Bristol too.

I can …

… talk about my partner in English.

This is …
He's/She's … years old.
He's/She's from …

Tell the class about your partners.

…

▸ *WB 1–2 (pp. 3–4)*

1 Welcome to Bristol

Bristol is in England. It's a great place!

a) *What can you see in the photos?*
I can see ... in photo number 1.
I can see ... in photo number ...

a band • a boat • boys •
a football • girls • a kite •
a skateboard • trees • water

b) *Now listen and act.*

▸ *WB 3 (p. 5)*

1

2

3

4

2 Welcome to Cotham Park Road

17 Cotham Park Road is a big, old house in Bristol.

a) *Is the house empty? Listen and find out.*

b) *Complete the sentences. Listen and check.*

When the house is empty, Prunella is ...
When the house is full, Prunella is ...

happy • not happy

3 SONG Prunella's song

Sing and act out the song.

Prunella's song

I'm Prunella the poltergeist,
Hee, hee, hee!
I close things and I open things,
I push things and I pull things,
I drop things
And then I laugh:
Hee, hee, hee!

I'm Prunella the poltergeist,
Hee, hee, hee!
I can see you, you can't see me.
You look, but you can't find me,
I drop things
And then I laugh:
Hee, hee, hee!

Prunella the poltergeist,
That's me.
Prunella the poltergeist,
Hee, hee, hee!

4 Sophie and Prunella

a) Listen. Who's in the pictures?

Picture 1: Sophie, Sophie's mum, ...

Picture 2: ...

Sophie • Sophie's mum • Sophie's dad • Emily • Toby • baby Hannah • Sheeba • Prunella

b) Discuss your answers.

A: I think that's Sophie. *B:* Yes, I think that's right. / No, I think that's Emily. / ...

c) Match the numbers and letters. Then listen and check.

A: I think 1 is B.

B: No, I think it's ... /
Yes, I think that's right.

A: This is very nice!

B: You can take baby Hannah, Emily.

C: Sophie, you can help me in here.

D: Oh! Who are you?

E: That's your room there.

F: What? You can see me?!

▸ WB 4 (p. 5)

5 Welcome to Hamilton Street

The twins Dan and Jo Shaw live at 7 Hamilton Street, Bristol, with their father. Today is the last day of the summer holidays.

Mr Shaw — Sorry I'm late, boys.
Jo — OK, Dad.
Dan — I've got the shopping list.
Mr Shaw — Thank you, Dan. Let's look at the list ... School bag. Jo, you need a school bag, right?
Jo — Yes, Dad.
Dan — Me too, Dad.
Mr Shaw — Pencil case. Dan, you need a pencil case, right?
Dan — Yes, Dad.
Jo — Me too, Dad.
Mr Shaw — OK, OK. Two bags, two pencil cases, two ... rubbers, two pencil sharpeners, two pens – felt tips?
Jo — Yes, Dad.
Mr Shaw — Two exercise books, two rulers, two glue sticks, two MP3 players ... hey, what's this?!
Jo — We need MP3 players, Dad.
Mr Shaw — Not for school! This is a school shopping list. Let's go, you two!

▸ *WB 5 (p. 6)*

I can ...

... say what's in my classroom.

I can see a ...

Draw your classroom network. Swap networks. Say what's in your partner's network.

I can see a ...

...

I can …

… talk about colours in English.

A: What colour is your rubber/…?
B: It's red/pink/purple …

Talk to different partners.

…

6 My favourite colour

Dan My favourite colour is blue.
The blue school bag for me, please.
Jo And the red school bag for me.
Mr Shaw OK. What about pencil cases?
Jo Orange for me, please.
Dan The blue pencil case for me.
And I need a rubber. The green rubber, please.
Jo Ugh! A green rubber!
Yellow for me.
Mr Shaw Right … pencil sharpeners …
Dan A blue pencil sharpener, please.
Jo Black for me, please.
Dan And we need the glue sticks.
Jo And the MP3 players!

> *Is it Jo's? Is it Dan's?*

7 Now you

Make dialogues with your favourite colours.

A: The green rubber, please
B: Ugh! A green rubber?! Yellow for me.
And the blue pencil, please.
A: Ugh! A blue pencil?! Black for me.
And …

8 SONG Prunella's plates

Listen. Then sing and act out the song.

I like red,
Red, red, red.
Here's my red plate.
Ooops!
Crash! Bang! Wallop!
Aaaaw. Oh well …

I like green,
Green, green, green.
Here's my green plate.
Ooops!
Crash! Bang! Wallop!
Aaaaw. Oh well …

I like brown,
…

▸ *WB 6–7 (pp. 6–7)*

9 Welcome to Paul Road

The Kapoors have got a shop at 13 Paul Road in Bristol. They live in a flat over the shop.

Ananda — Well, is my new school uniform OK?
Mrs Kapoor — Very nice, Ananda, very nice.
Dilip — Monday today, Tuesday tomorrow ... the big day for my baby sister ... first day at the new school ...
Mrs Kapoor — It's a nice school, Ananda.
Dilip — It's a *big* school, Ananda.
Mrs Kapoor — Stop that, Dilip! You can go to the shop and help your father.
Dilip — OK, OK, Mum. But why me? It's the last day of my holidays too.

10 POEM The days of the week

a) *Listen. Then write down the poem in your exercise book.*

The days of the week

Day one of the week is ...,
Two ..., three ..., OK?
Then ... and ... and then: Hooray!
..., ... : we can play.

b) *Read the poem to your partner.*

▸ WB 8 (p. 7)

11 Two newspapers for number 19

Mark Good morning, Mr Kapoor.
Mr Kapoor Good morning, Mark.
You need the newspapers for …?
Mark Cotham Park Road, Mr Kapoor.
Mr Kapoor Right … Cotham Park Road: one 'Times' for number 2, one for number 3, one for number 8, two for number 19 … Ah, Dilip! Very good. You can help Mark now. And I can have breakfast.

12 The numbers

1	one	11	eleven	21	twenty-one
2	two	12	twelve	22	twenty-two
3	three	13	thirteen	30	thirty
4	four	14	fourteen	40	forty
5	five	15	fifteen	50	fifty
6	six	16	sixteen	60	sixty
7	seven	17	seventeen	70	seventy
8	eight	18	eighteen	80	eighty
9	nine	19	nineteen	90	ninety
10	ten	20	twenty	100	a hundred

13 Telephone numbers

14 POEM Numbers

Say and act out the poem.

Numbers

One, two, three,
I can see.

Four, five, six,
I can do tricks.

Seven, eight,
Oh, I'm late!

Nine, ten,
Goodbye, then.

► *WB 9–10 (p. 8)*

15 Welcome to the Pretty Polly Bed and Breakfast

Mary, Peter and Jack Hanson (and Polly, the parrot) welcome you to

The PRETTY POLLY Bed & Breakfast

28 Cooper Street Bristol BS6 6PA
(0117) 969 22 00

Wheelchairs | Families | Pets

It's Monday.
Mrs Hanson is at work.
Mr Hanson is at work too.
He's at work in the Pretty Polly Bed and Breakfast.

Jack — Morning, Dad.
Mr Hanson — Morning? It's 12.15, Jack!
Polly — 12.15! 12.15!
Jack — Well, it is the last day of the holidays, Dad.
Mr Hanson — Yes, half past seven tomorrow, Jack!

I can ...

... say what the time is.

It's eleven o'clock

It's quarter past ...

It's half past ...

It's quarter to ...

It's eleven o'clock.

It's eleven fifteen.

It's eleven thirty.

It's eleven forty-five.

It's eleven o nine.

It's eleven twenty-five.

It's eleven thirty-seven.

It's eleven fifty-two.

16 Now you

a) What's the time?
6.05, 9.15, 4.25, 7.45, 3.40, 8.30, 12.18, 10.55, 2.36, 5.00

b) Draw five clocks.
Listen and fill in the correct times.

Swap clocks with a partner.
Listen again and check.

▸ *WB 11–13 (p. 9)*

c) Draw five clocks with five different times.
Your partner asks:
A: Excuse me, what's the time, please?
B: It's ...
A: Thank you.
B: You're welcome.

Then you ask your partner.

17 Good luck!

Mrs Schmidt Excuse me, can I say goodbye?
Mr Hanson Oh, Mrs Schmidt ...
Mrs Schmidt Your B&B is great. Thank you, Mr Hanson, and goodbye.
Polly Goodbye. Goodbye.
Mrs Schmidt Goodbye, Polly. And goodbye, Jack.
Jack Goodbye ... and a nice trip back to Germany, Mrs Schmidt.
Mrs Schmidt Thank you, Jack. And good luck with your new school.
Mr Hanson Thank you, Mrs Schmidt.
Polly Good luck! Good luck!

DOSSIER ***About me***

Make a first page for your dossier.

My name is ...
I'm ... old. I'm from ...
My favourite colour is ...
My telephone number is ...

New school, new friends

I can ...

... say lots of things in English.

What can you see in the photos?
– I can see a comic in photo B.
– There's an apple in photo ...
– There are books in photo ...
...

D

A

B

C

1 In the morning

It's the first day of the new school year.
It's 8 o'clock in the morning in Bristol.

a) *Copy the chart.*

	Ananda	Dan + Jo	Jack	Sophie
Photo				
Words				

b) *Listen. Match the photos and the names.*

c) *Listen again.*
Match words from the box to the names.

apple • banana • book • CD • clock • comic • cornflakes • lamp • milk • mobile phone • money • pencil case • sandwich box • school bag

► *P 1–2 (p. 25) • WB 1–2 (pp. 10–11)*

2 Extra GAME

Draw one thing from the box in **1c**.
Who can guess what it is?
A: Is it a comic?
B: Yes, it is. / No, it isn't.

DOSSIER ***My school bag***

Draw and label lots of things.

In my school bag there's a ... / there are ...

1 Before lessons

Put the pictures in the right order.

It's 8.30 and the new students are at school.

Dan Look, Jo. Room 14!
Jo OK. – You're nervous, right?
Dan Me? No! You're nervous.
Jo No, no.
Dan OK. Then you go first.
Jo No, you go first.
Dan No, you.
Jo No, you.
Dan Oh, OK.

Ananda Hi! Oh, you're twins!
Dan Hi. Yes, we're Dan and Jo. I'm Dan, the clever twin. He's Jo, the mad twin.
Jo Don't listen to Dan. *He's* the mad twin.

Ananda Come and sit with me and Jack. – Hey, Jack! Here are Dan and Jo. They're twins. This is ... er ...
Dan It's OK. I'm Dan and he's Jo.
Jack Well, *I'm* Jack. And *she's* Ananda.

2 ACTIVITY

Write your name on a piece of paper. Put all the papers in a box.
Take a piece of paper. Make one or two sentences about the student.

Anton I've got Max. He's 11 years old. / ... from Bonn. / ... clever.
Max Yes, that's right. I've got Ina. She's ...
Ina No, that's wrong. I'm ...

Looking at language

Copy and complete.

I'... Dan, the clever twin.

Yes, we'... Dan and Jo.

You'... nervous, right?

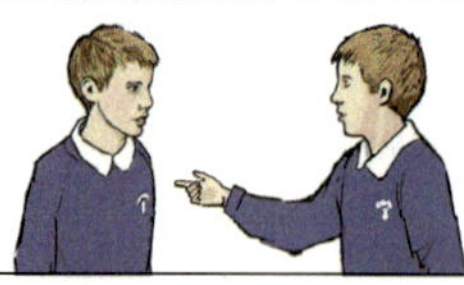

You'... twins!

He'... Jo, the mad twin.
She'... Ananda.
It'... 8.30.

They'... twins.

▸ GF 1–2a: Personal pronouns/Verb (to) be (pp. 131–132) • P 3–4 (p. 26) • WB 3–6 (pp. 11–12)

3 Ananda is a nice name

Dan Ananda is a nice name. Is it Indian?
Ananda Yes, it is.
Jo Are your mum and dad from India?
Ananda No, they aren't. My mum is from Bristol. My dad is from Uganda.
Jack And how old are you?
Ananda I'm 11. What about you, Jack? Are you 11 too?
Jack Yes, I am.
Jo We aren't 11. We're 12.
Jack And you're from Bristol, right?
Dan Yes, that's right.
Ananda Are your mum and dad from Bristol?
Dan Our dad, yes. But our mum ...
Jo Our mum isn't here. She's in New Zealand with her new partner. Our mum and dad aren't together.
Jack Oh, I'm sorry.
Dan I'm sorry too.
Ananda Oh look. Here's the teacher.

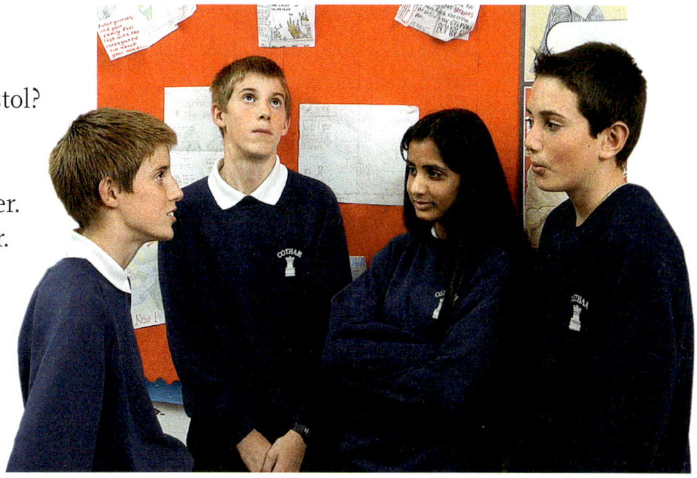

Who are they?
– Her dad is from Uganda.
– Their mum is in New Zealand.

4 ACTIVITY

Make a mobile or a poster for your classroom.

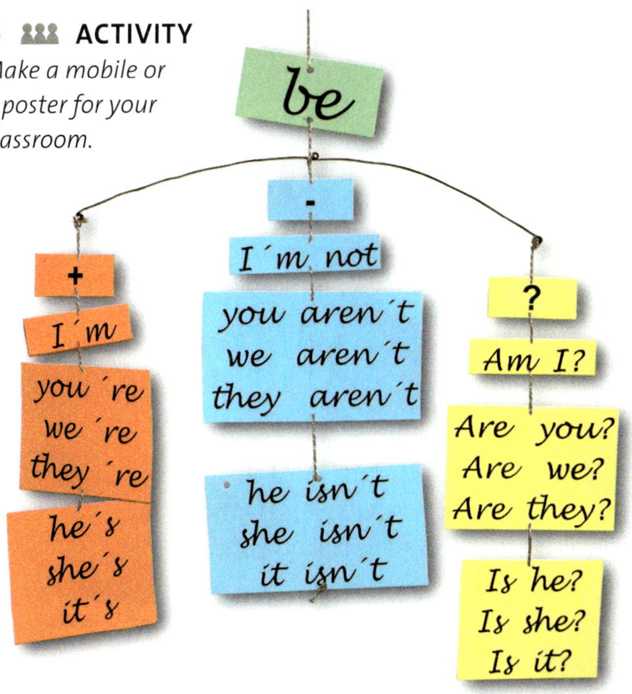

5 GAME

Mime things from the box. Can your group guess?
A: Are you a dog/...?
B: Yes, I am. / No, I'm not.

a baby • a dog • happy • a house • a kite • mad • nervous • a parrot • a poltergeist • a teacher • a tree

▸ GF 2b–c: Verb (to) be (p. 132) • P 5–7 (pp. 26–27) • WB 7–8 (p. 13)

6 Meet Mr Kingsley

Who can play football? Ananda – Sophie – Jo?

Mr Kingsley — Good morning. Welcome to Cotham School. I'm your form teacher *and* your English teacher. My name is Paul Kingsley, K–I–N–G–S–L–E–Y. And you're Form 7PK: P for Paul, K for Kingsley. And now please tell me your names. Oh, and can you play football? I'm your PE teacher too! – Yes, you please.

Ananda — I'm Ananda Kapoor. I can't play football, but I can play hockey.

Mr Kingsley — Thank you, Ananda. Now you.

Sophie — My name is Sophie Carter-Brown.

Jo — Carter-Brown? One name isn't enough?

Form 7PK — Ha ha ha.

Mr Kingsley — Quiet, please. – And who are you?

Jo — I'm Jo. Jo Shaw.

Mr Kingsley — Can you play football, Jo?

Jo — Yes, I can, Mr Kingsley.

Mr Kingsley — Good. Football is good. Jokes about names are bad. Can you remember that, Jo?

Jo — Yes, Mr Kingsley.

► *GF 3: can (p. 133) • P 8 (p. 27)*

7 Now you

Talk to your partner.

A: Can you play football/tennis/...?
B: Yes, I can. And I can play ... too. / No, I can't. But I can play ...

badminton • basketball • football • hockey • tennis

Tell the class:
My partner can't play football or tennis. But he/she can play hockey.

8 SONG Alphabet rap

A B C D E F G
Throw a ball, climb a tree.

H I J K L M N
Write your name, drop your pen.

O P Q R S T U
Yes, that's right. Do what I do.

V W X Y Z
Enough, enough, your face is red.

9 Now you

A: Can you spell your name, please?
B: It's Lilli Schröder. L–I–double L–I. New word: S–C–H–R–O with two dots –D–E–R.

► *WB 9–11 (p. 14)*

10 Timetable time

Mr Kingsley — OK, quiet please. Now, take out your exercise books. Listen and write down the timetable for today, Tuesday.
At 8.45 on Tuesday it's English with me, here in Room 14.
Then it's Geography in Room 16.

Jo — Mr Kingsley? I'm sorry. Can you spell 'Geography', please?

Mr Kingsley — That's OK, Jo. I can write it on the board: G–E–O–G–R–A–P–H–Y.

Jo — Thank you, Mr Kingsley.

Mr Kingsley — You're welcome, Jo. After the morning break it's …

11 Form 7PK's timetable

a) *Copy the timetable. Look at the subjects. You can find the words in the Vocabulary.*

Drama • Maths • Music • PE • RE • Science

b) *Now listen and complete the timetable.*

c) *Swap timetables with your partner. Listen again and check.*

▸ GF 4: Imperatives (p. 134) • P 9–11 (pp. 28–29) • WB 12–15 (pp. 15–17)

Timetable, Form 7PK

TUESDAY

Time	Subject	Room
8.45	English	14
9.40	Geography	16
10.35	Morning break	–
10.50	…	…
11.45	…	…
12.40	Lunch break	–
1.40	…	…
2.35	…	…

STUDY SKILLS Wörter lernen

Das Vocabulary (ab S. 150) gibt dir viele Informationen zu den neuen Wörtern einer Unit und hilft dir, diese Wörter zu lernen.

Schau dir Seite 158 an. Welche Schulfächer findest du dort? Mehr Tipps zum Lernen der Wörter findest du ab S. 122.

▸ SF 1 (pp. 122–123) • P 12 (p. 29) • WB 16–17 (pp. 17–18)

12 Extra SONG Wonderful World

a) *Copy the subjects from the board.*

b) *Listen and tick the school subjects.*

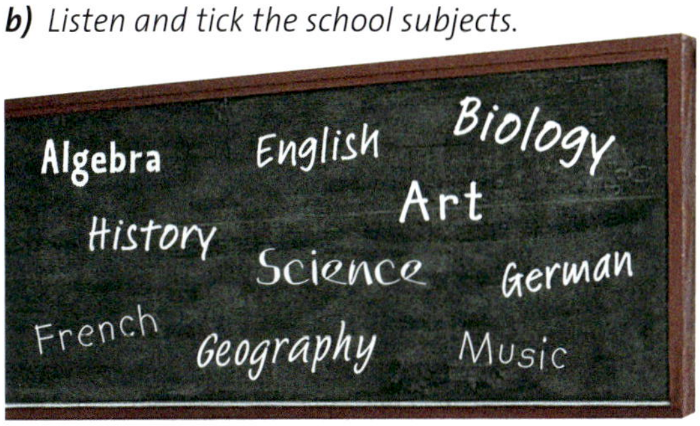

13 Lunch break

Ananda Let's sit here.
Sophie OK.
Jack Hi! Can we sit with you?
Ananda Yes, you can.
Jo Is the food OK?
Sophie Mmm, I've got the lasagne. It's OK.
Ananda I've got the pizza. It's really good.
Dan Oh, I haven't got a chair.
Ananda Look, there's an empty chair at that table.
Sophie Jack, do you like the Geography teacher?
Jack The bank robber?
All What?!
Ananda Mr Barker isn't a bank robber!
Jack Well, no, but he has got a face like a bank robber. I can see him on a poster: 'Wanted: bank robber'.
Sophie Your ideas are really mad, Jack!
Jo Hey, what have we got next?
Sophie Music, and then Maths.
Ananda Oh, I like Maths.
Dan/Jo You're mad!

14 My lunch break

a) *Prepare a dialogue. You can use ideas from **13**.*

A: Can I sit with you?
B: Yes, ...

A: Do you like ...?
B: He's/She's very nice/boring/...
A: He's/She's OK.

A: What have we got next?
B: ...

A: Is the food OK?
B: It's OK/great/ really good.

A: Oh, I like ...
B: You're mad. I like ...
A: Oh, I like ... too.

b) *Practise your dialogue and act it out in class.*

DOSSIER ***My school***

My school
My school is ...
I'm in Class ...
My class teacher is ...
My friends are ...
My favourite subjects are ...
I like ...

Extra *Make a timetable with your subjects. Put it in your DOSSIER.*

▸ *GF 5: have got (pp. 134–135) • P 13–15 (pp. 29–30) • WB 18–21 (pp. 18–20)*

1 WORDS Two pictures – what's different?

a) *Partner A: Look at picture A. Partner B: Look at picture B. Write sentences about your picture.*

There's one ... / There are two/three ...

b) *Work with a partner. What's different?*

A: There are three ... in picture A.
B: There are three ... in picture B too.

B: There are two ... in picture B.
A: There's one ... in picture A.
That's different.

a) *Partner B: Write sentences about your picture.*

There's one ... / There are two/three ...

b) *Work with a partner. What's different?*

A: There are three ... in picture A.
B: There are three ... in picture B too.

B: There are two ... in picture B.
A: There's one ... in picture A.
That's different.

2 PRONUNCIATION 'a' or 'an'?

a) *Listen and read:*

An apple, a green apple, an English apple,
a red English apple, an old apple,
a brown apple: Ugh!

b) *Say and write these words with **a** or **an**:*

rubber • English teacher • blue ball • orange chair • pencil case • felt tip • happy mum • exercise book • old house • student • empty box • uniform • MP3 player

c) *Listen and check your answers.*

Looking at language

– ***a*** *vor b, c, d, f, g, ... (Konsonanten)*
– ***an*** *vor a, e, i, o, u (Vokalen)*

Vorsicht! Es kommt darauf an, wie man ein Wort ausspricht, nicht wie man es schreibt. Deshalb: ***an*** MP3 player *und* ***a*** uniform.

3 Photos (Personal pronouns)

a) *Complete the sentences with:* I • you • he • she • it • we • they

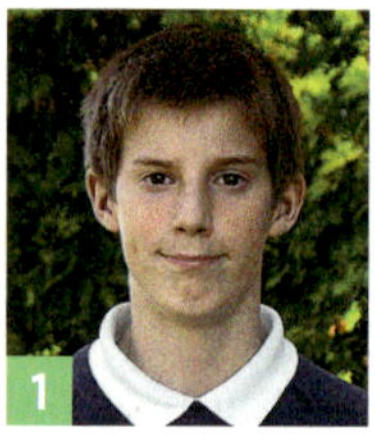

1 This is Jo. He's in my form.

2 This is Dan. ...'s in my form too.

3 This is Dan with Jo. ...'re twins.

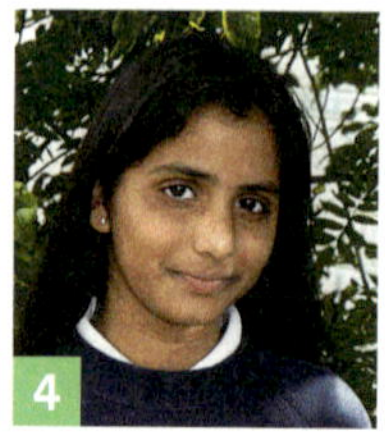

4 This is Ananda. ...'s very nice

5 This is my school. ...'s very big.

6 This is me. ...'m at school here.

7 This is me with Ananda. ...'re friends.

8 And this is you, Dad. ...'re with Polly!

b) **Extra** *Draw pictures of students in your class. Talk to your partner.*

A: This is ... I'm/He's/She's/We're/They're ...
B: Who's that? Is that ...?

4 The new school (be: positive statements)

Complete the sentences with: 'm • 's • 're

1 The new school is in Bristol. It's a good school.
2 Dan and Jo are at school. It... the first day. They... nervous.
3 Ananda is at school too. She... in the classroom.
4 Jack is in the classroom too. He... with Ananda.
5 *Jo:* Hi, I... Jo. This is my brother, Dan. We... twins.
6 *Dan:* I... the clever twin. He... the mad twin.
7 *Jo:* Dan, you... nervous.
8 *Jack:* Dan and Jo, you... mad!

5 Prunella isn't a parrot (be: negative statements)

a) *Write sentences.*

1 Prunella		a parrot.
2 Polly		a poltergeist.
3 I	'm not	from Bristol.
4 Mr and Mrs Hanson		Sophie's mum and dad.
5 Sophie and Emily	isn't	twins.
6 Dan and Jo Shaw		sisters.
7 Jack	aren't	12 years old.
8 Bristol		in Germany.
9 My friend and I		teachers.

b) **Extra** *Correct the sentences.*

Prunella isn't a parrot. She's a poltergeist.

6 Yes, he is. / No, she isn't. (be: questions and short answers)

Match the questions and answers.

a) 1 *Is Dilip Ananda's brother?* — Yes, they are.
2 Is the school a big school? — *Yes, he is.*
3 Are the Carter-Browns new in Bristol? — Yes, I am.
4 Are you a student? — Yes, it is.

b) 1 *Is Mrs Hanson in a wheelchair?* — No, they aren't.
2 Is 17 Cotham Park Road empty now? — No, we aren't.
3 Are the twins from London? — *No, she isn't.*
4 Are you and your family from Bristol? — No, it isn't.

7 About you (be: questions and short answers)

Answer the questions. Then write two more questions and ask a partner.

1 Are you 12? — Yes, I am. / No, I'm not.
2 Are you clever? — Yes, I ... / No, ...
3 Are your English books in your school bag? — Yes, they are. / No, they aren't.
4 Are your mum and dad from Bristol? — Yes, they ... / No, ...
5 Are you and your friend from Germany? — Yes, we are. / No, we aren't.

6 Is your mum 42? — Yes, she is. / No, she isn't.
7 Is your father a teacher? — Yes, he ... / No, he ...
8 Is your English teacher from England? — Yes, he/she ... / No, ...
9 Is your school big? — Yes, it is. / No, it ...

8 Can Ananda play hockey? (can/can't)

a) *Ask and answer questions about the pictures. Use words from the box. Take turns.*

do tricks • find their school things • open and close things • play football • play hockey • play tennis • sing • talk

1

Can Ananda ...?
– Yes, she ...

2
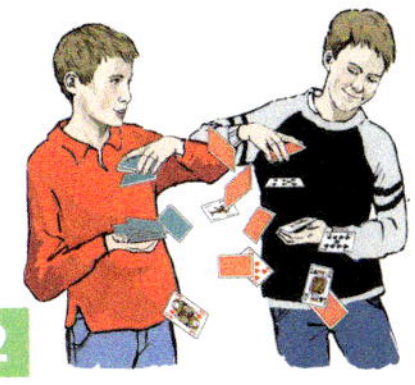
... the twins ...?
– No, they ...

3

... Prunella ...?
– ...

4

... Dilip ...?
– ...

5

Can the baby ...?
– No, she ...

6

... Mr Kingsley ...?
– Yes, ...

7

... Sophie and Emily...?
– ...

8

... Jack ...?
– ...

b) *Now ask your partner questions.* A: Can you ...? B: Yes, I can. / No, I can't.

9 WORDS Classroom English

a) *Read the phrases in the box.*

Quiet, please! • What's that in English? • Can I open the window, please? • Sorry, I haven't got my exercise book. • Look at the picture on the worksheet. • What page are we on, please? • Sorry? • It's your turn. • Can I go to the toilet, please? • Can we work with a partner? • Can you help me, please? • What's for homework? • Can we go now, please?

Listen. When you hear the phrases in the box, put up your hand.

b) *Make a chart. Who says what?*
Listen again and check your answers.

	teacher	student
Quiet, please!	✓	
What's that in English?		✓
Can I open the window, please?		
...		

c) *Which phrases can teachers and students say?*

d) *What can you say in English? Use phrases from the box.*

1 Es ist heiß in der Klasse.
2 Es ist zu laut in der Klasse.
3 Du möchtest eine Aufgabe nicht allein lösen.
4 Du findest die richtige Seite nicht.
5 Dein Partner/Deine Partnerin ist jetzt an der Reihe.
6 Du hast deinen Partner/deine Partnerin nicht verstanden.
7 Du suchst ein Wort auf Englisch.
8 Du hast nicht gehört, was ihr als Hausaufgabe aufhabt.

10 ACTIVITY DOs and DON'Ts (Imperatives)

The teacher uses lots of dos and don'ts in the classroom, for example:
Dos: Be quiet. Look at the board.
Don'ts: Don't talk to your partner now. Don't look out of the window.
Make a list of ***dos*** *and* ***don'ts*** *for your classroom.*

Dos	Don'ts
Open your books.	Don't shout in the classroom.
Listen to your partner / the teacher.	Don't forget your felt tips.
Help your partner.	Don't write on your desks.

11 WORDS The new timetable

a) *Partner B: Look at p. 114.*
Partner A: What lessons aren't in your timetable? Ask your partner.

A: What's lesson 1 on Monday?
B: Maths.

b) *Now answer your partner's questions.*

	Monday	Tuesday	Wednesday	Thursday	Friday
1	...	German	...	...	...
2	Science	Geography	Maths	Maths	Drama
3	Science	RE	English	English	Science
4	Drama	...	...	PE	PE
5	...	PE	Geography	PE	Music
6	English	Music	...	German	Maths

c) **Extra** *Write your dream timetable for Friday. Don't show your partner! Can you guess your partner's timetable?*

A: Is your lesson 1 Maths?
B: No, it isn't. Is your lesson 1 PE?
A: Yes, it is. Is your lesson 1 History?

12 STUDY SKILLS Das Vocabulary

a) *Finde im Vocabulary (S. 150–155) folgende Informationen heraus.*

1. Welches Wort benutzt man mit „welcome" (S. 8) für das deutsche „willkommen *in*"?
   to ► S. 150: „Welcome (to Bristol). Willkommen (in Bristol)."
2. An welcher Stelle des Satzes steht „too" (S. 8)?
3. Wie sagt man auf Englisch „auf dem Foto" („photo", S. 9)?
4. Was ist das Gegenteil von „empty" (S. 10)?
5. Welches Lautschriftzeichen steht für die Aussprache von „th" im Wort „think" (S. 11)?
6. Wo liegt die Betonung bei „exercise book" (S. 12)?
7. Welches Wort benutzt man mit „work" (S. 16) für deutsch *„bei* der Arbeit"?

b) **Extra** *Partner/in A: Schreib drei Fragen zu den Vocabulary-Einträgen zu den Seiten 18–19.*
Partner/in B: Schreib drei Fragen zu den Vocabulary-Einträgen zu Seite 20–21.
Stellt euch gegenseitig die Fragen.

○ 13 Jo has got a twin brother (have got/has got)

a) *Make sentences with:* ***have got • has got***

1. Jo *has got* a twin brother.
2. The twins *have got* a great dad.
3. ...

b) *Say what you have got. Make five sentences.*

1. Jo
2. The twins
3. Sophie
4. Prunella
5. The Kapoors
6. Jack
7. Ananda
8. Mr and Mrs Hanson

- a nice name.
- a shop.
- a parrot.
- a twin brother.
- a B&B.
- a great dad.
- a nice room.
- two sisters.

14 What have they got? (have got/has got)

a) *Say what they've got (✓) and what they haven't got (✗).*

	brother	sister	pet
Jack	✗	✗	✓
Ananda	✓	✗	✗
Dan	✓	✗	✓

Jack *has got* a pet. But he *hasn't got* a brother.
And he ... a sister.

b) **Extra** *What have the students in your class got? Ask questions.*

A: Have you got a brother?
B: Yes, I have. / No, I haven't.

Then tell the class.

Jenny *hasn't got* a brother.
But she *has got* a sister. And she ...

15 GETTING BY IN ENGLISH New friends

a) *What is it in English?*
(The answers are on these pages.)

1 Ich bin Dan. (p. 20)
2 Komm und setz dich zu mir. (p. 20)
3 Danke.
– Gern geschehen. (p. 23)
4 Magst du den Erdkundelehrer? (p. 24)
5 Du bist verrückt. (p. 24)
6 Ich mag Musik. (p. 24)

b) *Make a dialogue with words from a).*

A: Grüße B und sag, wie du heißt.
B: Grüße zurück und sag, wer du bist.
A: Schlag vor, dass ihr zusammensitzt.
B: Bedanke dich.
A: Frag B, wie alt er/sie ist.
B: Antworte und frag dasselbe.
A: Antworte und frag, ob er/sie Englisch mag.
B: Sag, dass du Englisch magst, aber dass dein Lieblingsfach Mathe ist.
A: Sag, dass er/sie verrückt ist.

c) *Act out your dialogue for the class.*

STUDY SKILLS Stop – Check – Go

*Manchmal solltest du kurz anhalten (**Stop**) und dich fragen, was du gelernt hast (**Check**). Und überlege, wie es am besten weitergeht (**Go**). Also etwa so:*

Stop *Einmal pro Unit, z.B. jetzt für Unit 1.*

Check *Kenne ich wirklich die Vokabeln aus Unit 1? (Lass dich zehn abfragen!)*
Kann ich die Grammatik von Unit 1? Kann ich z.B. jemandem sagen, was ich tun kann und was nicht?
Kann ich einen Dialog zum Thema „New friends" schreiben?

Damit du nicht vergisst, dich zu „checken", wirst du am Ende jeder Unit daran erinnert: **Checkpoint** ▸ *im Workbook*

Go *Tipps, was du tun kannst, wenn etwas noch nicht so „sitzt", findest du auf Seite 124.*

▸ SF 2 (p. 124)

Checkpoint 1 ▸ WB (p. 23)

How's the new school?

It's 3.30 and it's the end of school for today.

7
They're great! Jo and Dan are twins – they're very nice, and you really can't see who is Jo and ...
Ananda, how was the first day at your new school?
8
Good, thank you, Mrs Smith.
Hello, Mrs Smith. 'Computer World'?
I like the uniform! Thank you, Mrs Kapoor. See you.
9
Well, go on, go on. Jo and Dan and ...?
Then there's Jack. He's very nice and his mad ideas are great!
10
A packet of mints, please. Oh, your little girl is at Cotham now!
Yes, first day today.
Bye, then.
11
Bye, Mr Brown, and thank you. Now, Ananda, tell me more: Are there girls in your form too?
Little girl, tell Mum everything!
12
There's a very nice girl. Her name is Sophie. Her sister Emily isn't nice, but she's very pretty and Dilip likes her ... a lot!

13

14

Working with the text

1 Who says it?

a) *Match the speech bubbles to the photos.*

b) *Put the speech bubbles in the right order.*

Mrs Kapoor

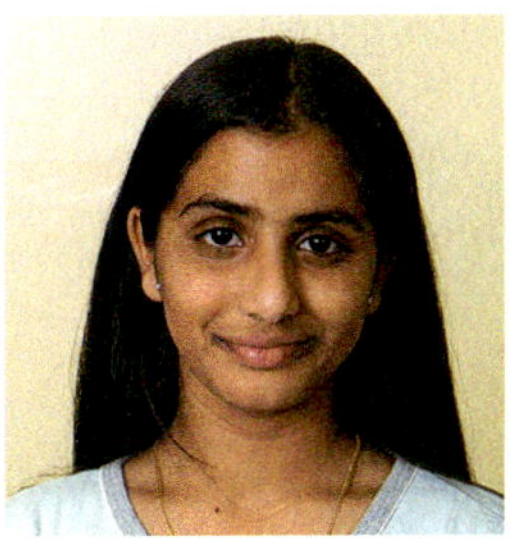
Ananda

A He's very nice too.

B Jo and Dan are twins. – Then there's Jack.

C Hi, Mum. I need my tea.

D Are there girls in your form too?

E And the teacher?

F First tell me about your classmates.

G The form is nice.

H There's a very nice girl.

I Tell me about school.

2 After the first day at school

a) *Write a dialogue for Jack and his dad. Use the ideas in the box.*

Mr Hanson	How's your new school?
Jack	...
Mr Hanson	...
Jack	Mr Kingsley. He's nice too.
Mr Hanson	...
Jack	There are two nice girls, Ananda and Sophie.
Mr Hanson	Are there nice boys in your class too?
Jack	Yes, ...
Mr Hanson	That's great! I need my tea now.
Jack	Good idea, Dad!

Well, the form is very nice.

Dan and Jo are twins. They're clever.

Tell me about your classmates.

And who is your form teacher?

b) **Extra** *Write a dialogue for Sophie and Prunella, or for Dan, Jo and their dad.*

c) *Act out your dialogue for the class.*

► WB 22–23 (pp. 20–21)

Make a birthday calendar

I can ...

... say when my birthday is.

My birthday is in May.
When's your birthday?
...

1 Months of the year

a) Write the months in the right order.

b) Compare with your partner.
A: What's the first month?
B: January. What's the next month?

Then mark where the words are different from the German words. January, ...

c) Listen to the CALENDAR SONG and check your order. Say the months in English.

d) Complete the sentences.
1 My birthday is in ...
2 My mum's/dad's birthday is in ...
3 My brother's/sister's/friend's birthday is in ...
4 Christmas is in ...
5 Valentine's Day is in ...
6 Halloween is in ...

e) **Extra** *Draw a picture for your favourite month. Can your partner guess the month?*

2 Dates

You write	You say
9th April	**the** ninth **of** April
on 31st May	on **the** thirty-first **of** May
1998	nineteen ninety-eight
2005	two thousand and five

a) Listen. Then read the numbers out loud.

1st	first	12th	twelfth
2nd	second	13th	thirteenth
3rd	third	14th	fourteenth
4th	fourth	...	
5th	fifth	20th	twentieth
6th	sixth	21st	twenty-first
7th	seventh	22nd	twenty-second
8th	eighth	23rd	twenty-third
9th	ninth	...	
10th	tenth	30th	thirtieth
11th	eleventh	31st	thirty-first

b) Say these dates.
12th February, 18th July, 20th May, 30th December, 14th January, 3rd April, 19th August, 22nd September, 2015, 15th June, 1986
the twelfth of February, ...

c) **Extra** *Talk to a partner.*
A: What's the date today?
B: It's the ...
What's the date tomorrow/next Monday/ ...

▸ WB 24–26 (p. 22), Activity page 1

3 Extra ACTIVITY Make a calendar for your class

You can make a birthday calendar or a year planner for the class.

A birthday calendar

Each student can make a card for the class birthday calendar.

A year planner

a) *What can you put in your year planner? Discuss in class. You can use the ideas in the box. Add your own ideas.*

What about …?
That's a good/great idea.
What date is …?

Christmas • Easter • Halloween • holidays • Valentine's Day • the next class test • project week • birthdays • a school party/disco • back to school • …

b) *Work in groups. Each group can make a page for one month.*

A weekend at home

I can …

… talk to my partner about my home.

- I live in a house/flat.
- There are … rooms in my …
- We have/haven't got a garden …
  What about you?

- I've got a big/small room.
- I share a room with my …
- In my room there's …/there are …
  What about your room?

•••

Homes for people …

1 House or flat?

a) *Can you remember?*

I think …
the Shaws live in a …
the Kapoors live in a …
the Hansons live in a …
the Carter-Browns live in a …

b) **Extra** *Listen and check.*

DOSSIER ***My room***

You can bring a picture or a photo of your room to school. Label the picture and put it in your DOSSIER.

▸ *WB 1–2 (p. 24)*

… and homes for pets

2 Where are the pets?

a) Say where they are.

The rabbits are in …

The dog is in …

cat • dog • hamster • parrot • rabbit

A a hutch in the garden

D a basket in the kitchen

b) Partner B: Look at p. 114.

Partner A: Copy the chart.

Listen. Tick the right boxes.

	Photo				
	A	B	C	D	E
Sheeba					
Hip and Hop					
Harry					
Polly					
Bill and Ben					

c) Talk about the pictures.

Sheeba is in photo … She's a …

Hip and Hop are in photo … They're …

Sophie has got … pets.

… hasn't got a pet.

Dan and Jo have got …

d) **Extra** *Write sentences about the Bristol pets.*

B a cage in the living room

C a cage in the living room

E a basket in the bedroom

3 Now you

Talk about pets.

budgie • fish • guinea pig • horse • mouse • tortoise • …

I've got a pet.

My grandma/friend has got …

He/She has got a basket in the …

I/We haven't got a pet.

We can't have … in our house/flat.

We haven't got a garden.

► *P 1 (p. 42) • WB 3–4 (p. 25)*

I can …

… sing and act the song 'This is the way I …'
Sing and act.

This is the way I clean my teeth,
Clean my teeth, clean my teeth.
This is the way I clean my teeth,
Early in the morning.
…

… wash my face …
… eat my toast …
… go to school …

1 Friday afternoon

Ananda — Have you got plans for the weekend?
Jack — Well, we've got that essay for Mr Kingsley: 'A day in the life of …'
Jo — Oh, that's easy! Listen: 'A day in the life of Jo Shaw. I get up at 7.15 every morning. Then I clean my teeth.'
Dan — No, no, no. I get up at 7.15, you sleep. I clean my teeth, you sleep. I wash my hands and face, you sleep. You get up at 7.45.
Jo — OK, OK. 'We go to the kitchen and have breakfast. Then we go to school.' The end.
Jack — You two write boring essays. – Oh, there's my bus! Bye!
All — Bye, Jack.

Look at the mind map. Is it Jo's day or Dan's day?

▸ GF 6: Plural (p. 135) • P 2–3 (p. 42) • WB 5–6 (p. 26)

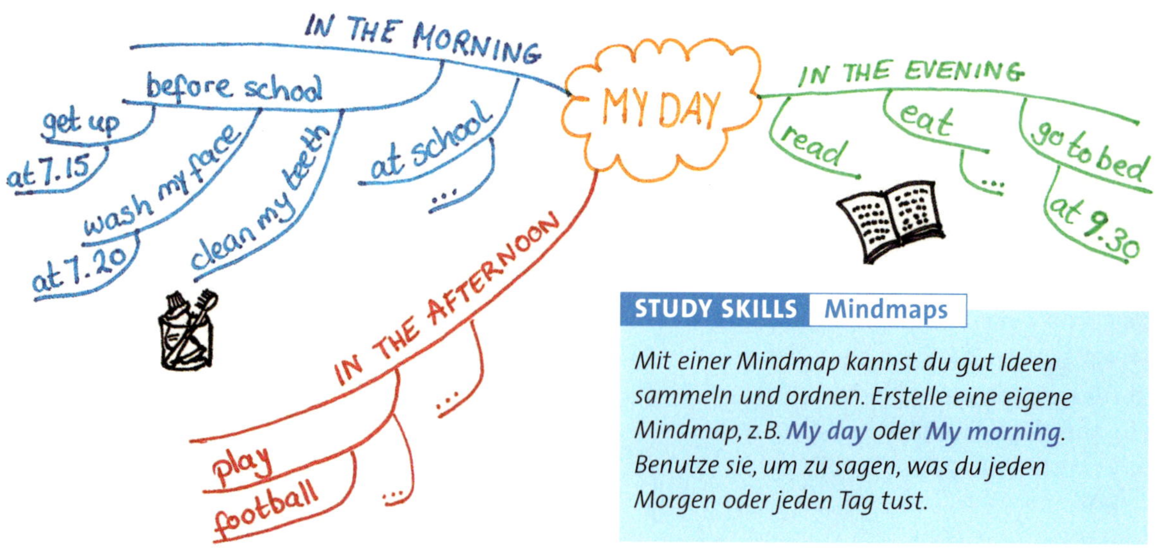

STUDY SKILLS Mindmaps

Mit einer Mindmap kannst du gut Ideen sammeln und ordnen. Erstelle eine eigene Mindmap, z.B. **My day** *oder* **My morning**. *Benutze sie, um zu sagen, was du jeden Morgen oder jeden Tag tust.*

▸ SF 3 (p. 125) • P 4 (p. 42) • WB 7 (p. 27)

2 On Saturday mornings

On Saturday mornings Sophie gets up at 9 o'clock. She gets dressed. Then she gives the pets their breakfast.
First she feeds Sheeba, the dog. Sheeba eats meat. Sophie gives her water too.
Then she goes to the living room and feeds Harry, the hamster. He likes toast and carrots and water. Toby watches. Then he tries to help Sophie. He cleans the cage and puts hay in it.
After that Sophie goes to the rabbit hutch. It's in the garden. Sophie feeds Hip and Hop. They like rabbit food, carrots and water.
Then Sophie has *her* breakfast.

Copy and complete the chart. Add more pets.

pet	eats	drinks
a dog		
a hamster		
…		

Looking at language

a) *Complete the sentences from **1** and **2**.*

Singular		Plural	
I	I … up at 7.15 every morning.	*we*	Then we … to school.
you	You … up at 7.45.	*you*	You two … boring essays.
he/she/it	Sophie … up at 9 o'clock.	*they*	They … rabbit food, carrots and water.

b) *What's different with **he, she, it**? Find more examples.*

► *GF 7a–b: Simple present (pp. 136–137) • P 5–7 (pp. 43–44) • WB 8–10 (pp. 27–28)*

3 POEM My fish Wanda

My fish Wanda

My fish Wanda, she's OK.
She lives in a bowl and she plays all day.
She eats fish food and drinks and drinks.
I really wonder what she thinks.

Listen. Then practise the poem. Read it to the class.

4 Now you

Write a poem about a pet. You can put your poem in your DOSSIER.

My	dog hamster …	Hasso Flecki …	he's she's	OK.

He She	lives in	our house a cage …	and	he she	sleeps plays …	all day.

He She	eats	meat carrots …	and drinks and drinks.

I really wonder what	he she	thinks.

► *P 8–9 (pp. 44–45)*

5 Saturday afternoon

Prunella — Can I help you with your homework, Sophie?
Sophie — No thanks, Prunella. I don't need your help.
Prunella — You don't like me.
Sophie — Of course I like you, Prunella. But I really don't need your help.
Prunella — Well, can I see your essay?
Sophie — Yes, here you are.
Prunella — 'A day in the life of the Carter-Brown family.' Hmm ... This is all wrong, Sophie.
Sophie — Wrong? Why?
Prunella — Look here: 'My sister Emily and I sometimes argue.' Sometimes? You don't argue sometimes – you argue all the time.
And here: 'My brother Toby does judo on Saturdays.' He doesn't do judo on Saturdays – he plays football on Saturdays.
And here: 'My mum and dad go to bed early.' They don't go to bed early. They watch TV till 11.30 every night! Sorry, Sophie. This isn't very good.
Sophie — No?
Prunella — No. Let's write a new essay. We don't need the old essay.
Sophie — No?
Prunella — No!

6 GAME My friend Nora

Play the game in teams.

Team 1
A: Our name is Nora. My friend Nora likes numbers. But she doesn't like letters.
B: My friend Nora likes November. But she doesn't like December.
C: Sorry. I can't go on.

Team 2
A: OK. Two points for your team. It's our turn. Our name is Patrick.
B: My friend Patrick likes ...

Looking at language

a) *Complete these sentences from* **5**.
I *don't* need your help.
You ... like me.
He ... do judo on Saturdays.
We ... need the old essay.
You ... argue sometimes.
They ... go to bed early.

b) *Which sentence is different?*

▸ *GF 7c: Negative statements (p. 137) • P 10–12 (pp. 45–46) • WB 11–14 (pp. 28–30)*

7 Sunday afternoon: Tea at the Shaws' house

Find Dan and Jo on the family tree. Is their dad Michael or Harry? Is their mum Elizabeth or Catherine?

Grandma Well boys, here's your family tree. Look. Your grandparents are at the top: Grandpa and me, and your Grandpa and Grandma Shaw.
Dan And the cross is there because Grandpa Shaw is dead, right?
Grandpa Right.
Grandma And here are our children: one son, two daughters.
Jo Oh yes, here's Uncle Harry, Mum's brother. And here's Aunt Elizabeth, her sister. And here's our mum, Catherine.
Grandpa Yes, Jonah.
Grandma And Harry is married to your Aunt Jane, and here are your cousins, Anne and Mark.
Dan And you're their grandparents too. So you've got five grandchildren.
Grandpa Yes: all one big happy family.
Dan One big happy family?
Grandpa Yes, Daniel: children and parents – married, single or divorced – they're all family.
Dan A family without a mum!
Jo We've got a mum. She just isn't here.
Dan Yeah, right.

▸ GF 8–9: Possessive determiners, possessive form (p. 138) • P 13–16 (pp. 46–47) • WB 15–18 (pp. 30–32)

8 Extra Now you

a) *Collect photos of your family. It can be your real family or your dream family. Then make your family tree and label it. You can put it in your DOSSIER.*

b) *Talk about your family tree.*

Is that your ...?
This is my ...
That's ...
What's his/her name?
Who's that?

▸ P 17 (p. 47)

1 REVISION Bristol people and pets (Personal pronouns)

Match these sentences.

1 *'My name is Polly!*	We've got two cats – Bill and Ben.'
2 Ananda hasn't got a pet.	You're a good dog!'
3 Sophie has got two rabbits.	*I'm a parrot.'*
4 'Dan and I like pets.	You aren't in your basket.'
5 'Bill and Ben, where are you?	They're in a hutch in the garden.
6 Sheeba has got a nice basket.	She can't have pets in her flat.
7 'Come here, Sheeba!	It's in the kitchen.

2 PRONUNCIATION Plurals

Is the '-s' like this?

Or is it like this?

Or is it like the word 'is'?

a) *Listen and say the words.*

b) *Copy the chart. Listen and complete it with words from the box.*

[-s]	[-z]	[-ɪz]
boats	*beds*	*boxes*

beds • boats • books • boxes • boys • budgies • cats • cages • colours • dogs • friends • hutches • months • pages • pencil cases • plans • raps • shops • streets • things

c) *Swap charts. Listen again and check.*

3 Weekends (Simple present: positive statements)

a) *Make sentences.*

I	play football	
My friends	go to the park	
My friends and I	write e-mails	every weekend.
Dan and Jo	get up late	every Saturday.
We	make the beds	every Sunday.
They	listen to CDs	
My mum and dad	do boring things	

b) **Extra** *Write four sentences about your weekends.*

4 STUDY SKILLS Pets (Mind maps)

a) *Make a mind map with these words. You can look at page 37 and 39 for more ideas.*

cage • cat • do tricks • dog • fish • guinea pig • hamster • homes • hutch • milk • pets • play • rabbits • what they do • what they eat/drink • ...

b) *Talk about your mind map.*

We've got lots of pets in our class.
There are dogs and ... and ...
Rabbits/dogs ... live in/sleep in ...
Hamsters eat/drink ...

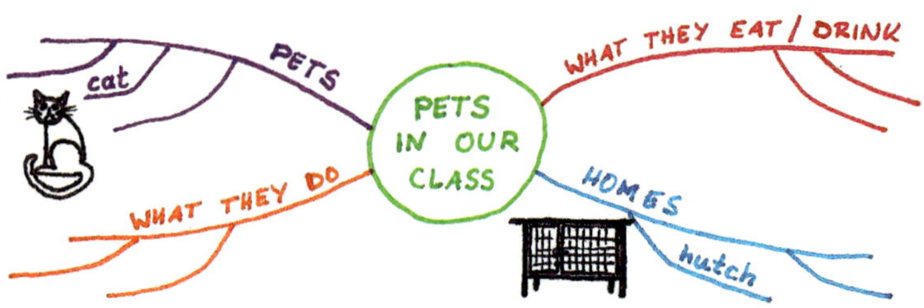

5 Extra PRONUNCIATION The '-s' in the simple present

a) Listen to the poem. Then read it out loud.

b) Copy the poem. Use different colours for the different '-s' sounds: [-s] [-z] [-ɪz]

c) Listen and check.

She comes and goes,
She sits and thinks,
She watches and listens,
She drops the books,
She drops the pens,
She opens and closes
a window, a bag, ...
Well, she's a poltergeist.

6 Every day after school (Simple present: positive statements)

a) Say what they do every day. Use the verbs in the box.

eat • feed • listen • open • play • read • write

1 Jo *plays* football every day.

2 Jack ... Polly every ...

3 Ananda ... an apple ...

4 Dan ... computer games ...

5 Sophie ... books ...

6 Dilip ... to music ... on his MP3 player ...

7 Jack ... e-mails ...

8 Prunella ... and closes things ...

b) What about you? Work in groups of six.

Timo — I play football every day.
Anna — Timo plays football and I talk to my friends every day.
Lena — Timo plays football and Anna talks to her friends and I ... every day.
...

7 What they do every day (Simple present: positive statements)

a) *Partner B: Go to p. 114.*
Partner A: Look at the chart. What can you say about Jack and Ananda?
A: Jack gets up at 7.15. What about Ananda?
B: Ananda gets up at ... She gets dressed at ... What about Jack?

b) *What about you? Complete a copy of the chart. Talk to your partner.*
A: I get up at ... What about you?
B: I get up at ... I get dressed at ... What about you?

	Jack	Ananda	You	Your partner
get up	at 7.15	...	...	...
get dressed	at 7.30	...	...	...
have breakfast	at 7.45	...	...	
go to school	at 8.10	...		
come home from school	at 4.00			
listen to CDs	at 6.15			
go to bed	at 9.00			

c) **Extra** *Write about your partner's day.*

8 LISTENING At the pet shop

a) *Look at the picture for two minutes. Then close your book. Say what's in the pet shop window.*
A: Three rabbits.
B: A brown dog, and ...

b) *Make a list of the pets in the picture.*
3 rabbits, 2 ...

c) *Look at your list and listen. What's different? Write down the new number.*

d) *Six pets are missing. What are they?*

9 WORDS Clean a sandwich?

Which words can go with the verbs? Which can't?

1 clean | a cage / a sandwich / the board

2 write | an essay / a book / a picture

3 listen to | the teacher / a lamp / a CD

4 go to | the shops / homework / school

5 play | a book / a computer game / football

6 live | in a house / at 13 Paul Road / on a shelf

10 I don't, he doesn't (Simple present: negative statements)

Complete the dialogues with **don't/doesn't** *+ verb.*

a) *Ananda and Dilip*

Ananda I don't like (like) our Drama teacher.
Dilip You … (like) him? But he's nice.
Ananda Well you … (see) him every day.
Dilip That's right, we … (see) him every day. We *see* him on Mondays for football.
Ananda It isn't fair: the girls at Cotham … (play) football.
Dilip Of course you … (play) football. You're girls.
Ananda Dilip! I really … (like) big brothers!
Dilip Ha ha ha.

b) *Bill and Ben*

Bill I like my twin, Dan.
Ben And I like my twin, Jo.
Bill But your Jo doesn't clean (clean) his teeth every morning.
Ben And your Dan … (make) his bed every morning.
Bill Jo … (read) books.
Ben Dan … (write) e-mails.
Bill Jo … (feed) you and me.
Ben No. But he … (sing) in the bathroom.
Bill Dan sings nice songs! He … (play) boring music, like Jo!

11 Can you remember? – A quiz (Simple present: positive and negative statements)

a) *Correct the sentences. Use* **doesn't** *or* **don't** *+ verb.*

1 Mrs Hanson lives in New Zealand.
Mrs Hanson doesn't live in New Zealand.
Mrs Hanson lives in England.
2 The Kapoors live in a flat over a B&B.
The Kapoors don't …
The Kapoors live …
3 Jack and his parents live in London.
4 Jo likes Maths.
5 Polly sleeps in a hutch in the garden.
6 Sophie gets up at 6 o'clock on Saturday mornings.
7 Emily helps Sophie with the pets on Saturdays.
8 Ananda plays football at school.

b) **Extra** *Make a quiz with a partner. Write three wrong sentences about people in the book and three wrong sentences about people in your class. Swap quizzes. Can you correct all the sentences?*

12 WORDS The right word

Complete the sentences with a word from the box.

> about (1x) • at (1x) • in (2x) • over (1x) • to (4x) • with (1x)

1 Please listen ... this CD. Then we can talk ... it.
Please listen to this CD. Then we ...
2 Can I talk ... you? I need help ... my homework.
3 Let's go ... the shops and look ... T-shirts.
4 Welcome ... Cotham. I sing ... the school band.
5 The Kapoors live ... a flat ... their shop.

13 WORDS The fourth word

> aunt • daughter • divorced • do • father • hutch

a) *Find the fourth word.*

1 father – mother
son – *daughter*
2 play – hockey
? – judo
3 Mr and Mrs Hanson – married
Mr and Mrs Shaw – ?
4 mum – mother
dad – ?
5 grandpa – grandma
uncle – ?
6 fish – bowl
rabbit – ?

b) **Extra** *Put the words into groups of four.*

> ball • carrots • climb • close • drink • eat • open • pull • push • throw • tree • water

*1 open – close
push – p...*

2 throw – ...

3 eat – ...

14 Extra WORDS The family tree

Find the missing words.

> aunt • cousin • daughters • dead • divorced • Grandma • married • son

Grandpa and ... Thompson have got one son and two ... The twins' ... is Elizabeth. She's single.
James is Elizabeth's ..., and James is the twins' ...
Their Uncle Harry is ... to Jane. But Dan and Jo's mum and dad are ...
Their dad's dad – Grandpa Shaw – is ...

Look at p. 41 and check your answers.

15 My home, your home (Possessive determiners)

a) *Choose the right word.*

1 The Hansons have got a B&B. *Its/Their* name is the Pretty Polly Bed and Breakfast.
2 They've got five bedrooms in *his/their* house.
3 Jack has got a computer in *his/her* room.
4 Jack: 'Hi, Sophie. This is *your/our* parrot. *My/Her* name is Polly. Is this *your/his* dog?'
5 Sophie: 'Yes, this is *my/their* dog. *My/Her* name is Sheeba. I've got two rabbits too. *Her/Their* names are Hip and Hop.'

b) *Write sentences about your house, your room, your pet(s). Use:* **my • your • his • her • ...**
We live in a flat. Our flat is ... My brother has got a dog. His name is ...

16 Polly's cage – the Shaws' garden (Possessive form)

Follow the lines. Make two lists.

…'s	…s'
Polly's cage	the Shaws' garden
Mr Kingsley's	…

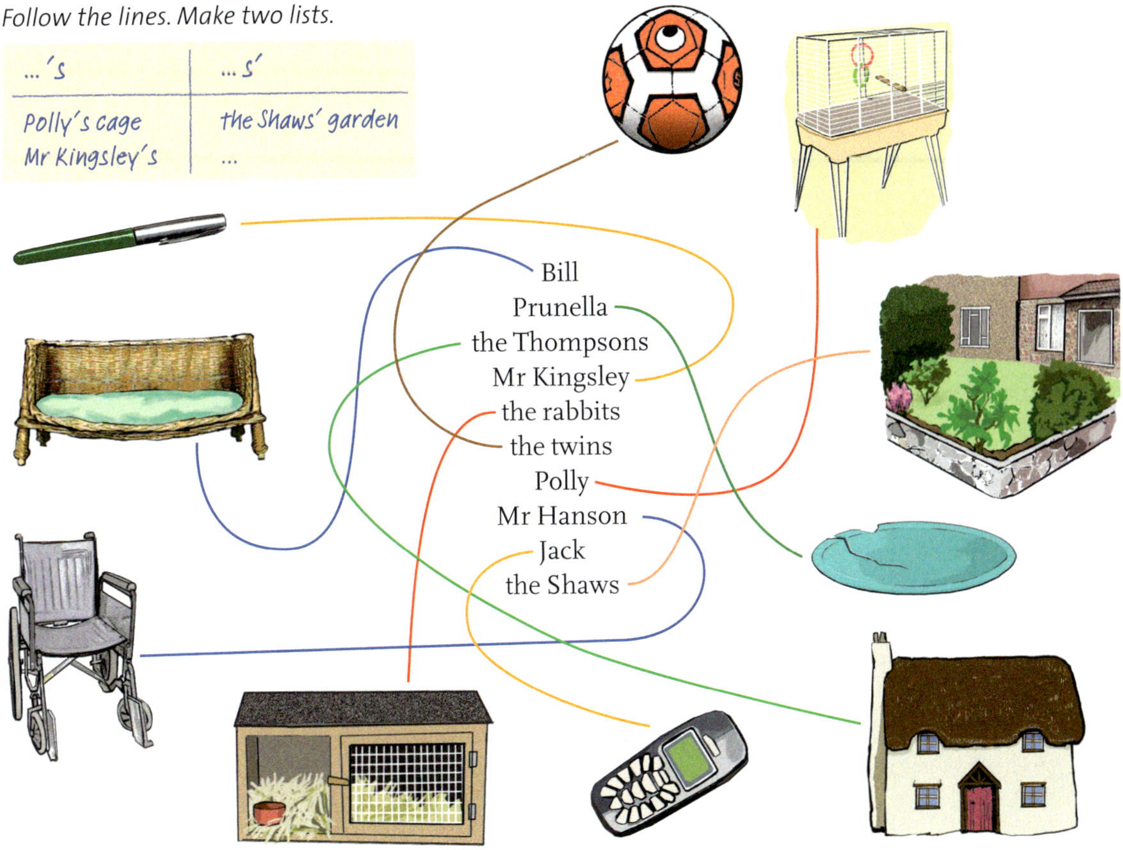

17 GETTING BY IN ENGLISH English guests

a) *What is it in English? (The answers are on these pages.)*

1 Hast du am Wochenende etwas vor? (p. 38)
2 frühstücken (p. 38)
3 Kann ich dir bei deinen Hausaufgaben helfen? (p. 40)
4 Nein danke. Ich brauche deine Hilfe nicht. (p. 40)

● **b)** *Partner A: English guests are at your home.*
Partner B: You and your parents are English guests at Partner A's home.
Make two dialogues with words from a).

Dialogue 1

A: Heiße die Familie willkommen.
B: Sag danke.
A: Frag, ob du ihnen mit ihren Taschen helfen kannst.
B: Sag danke, aber ihr braucht keine Hilfe.

Dialogue 2

A: Frag, ob sie am Wochenende etwas vorhaben.
B: Sag, dass ihr viele Pläne habt.
A: Sag, dass du das großartig findest. Sag, dass ihr samstags um neun Uhr frühstückt.
B: Sag, dass das OK ist.

c) *Practise one dialogue and act it out.*

A day in the life of ...

A day in the life of Jack Hanson

by Jack Hanson

My family has got a bed and breakfast. We get up early every morning. First I make my bed and have my shower. And then I get things ready for breakfast: the table in the kitchen for the family, the table in the living room for the guests. After breakfast I go to school. I'm at home again at 4 o'clock. Then I do my homework, or I help my parents.

Lots of interesting people come to the Pretty Polly B&B: families from other countries, film stars and bank robbers. We've got a new guest, Mr Green. I think he's a bank robber. Or a spy. He wears sunglasses all day! And he doesn't talk to us. It all fits.

After my homework I watch TV. Then I play games on my computer or listen to music or write stories. I go to bed at 9 o'clock.

Extra

A day in the 'life' of a poltergeist

by Prunella the poltergeist

I don't get up in the morning. I don't sleep. I'm a poltergeist! At 1 o'clock in the morning I go to Mr and Mrs Carter-Brown's room. I open the window. At 2 o'clock, Mr Carter-Brown gets up and closes it. Then he and Mrs Carter-Brown argue. 'You open the window every night,' he says. 'You're mad,' she says. Hee, hee, hee!

At 3 o'clock I go to Emily's room. I don't like Emily. She isn't nice to her sister Sophie. Sophie is my friend. I open Emily's school bag. Then I drop it. After that, Emily can't sleep. Hee, hee, hee!

At 7.30 I go to Sophie's room. 'Sophie, get up! It's time for school!' But she can't hear me. She just sleeps and sleeps. Then I push and pull her bed. Or I drop her books. Or her alarm clock. She doesn't need an alarm clock. She has ...t me! Hee, hee, he

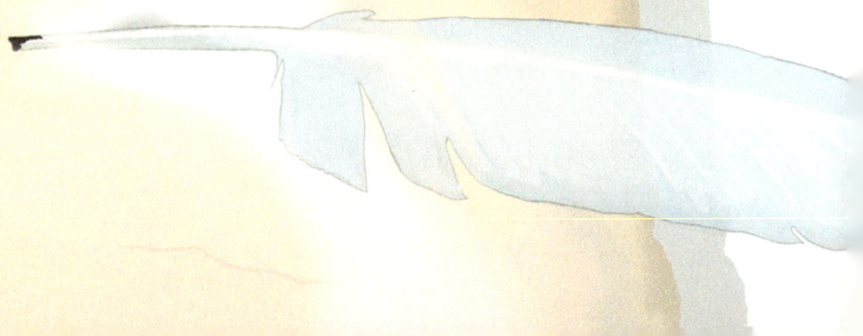

Extra

A day in the life of Bill and Ben

by Daniel Shaw

Bill and Ben are cats. Every morning after breakfast I open the door for them. Then Bill and Ben go out. First the two cats go to the park. They play their favourite game, 'Chase the birds'. After the game, Bill and Ben are hungry and thirsty. They find lots of water in the park, but no food.

Then they go to the shops. Their favourite shop is Mr King's fish shop. Bill and Ben like fish a lot. They watch Mr King. They watch and watch. Then Ben gives the signal. He goes to Mr King and miaows. 'I'm hungry,' he miaows. But Mr King doesn't give Ben a fish. He chases him. Ben runs away. Bill runs too. But he runs to the shop. He takes a fish before Mr King sees him. And then he runs to the park again. Bill and Ben have a great lunch. Then they sleep. And after that they go home and wait for Jo and me.

Working with the text

1 Right or wrong?

Correct the wrong statements.

a) Jack's essay
1. Jack's family has got a shop.
   Wrong. They've got a B&B.
2. Jack doesn't help his parents.
3. The Hansons have got a new guest.
4. Jack thinks Mr Green is a film star.
5. Jack goes to bed at 9 o'clock.

b) **Extra** Prunella's essay
1. Prunella gets up early every day.
2. Mr and Mrs Carter-Brown argue. That makes Prunella happy.
3. Sophie needs a new alarm clock.

c) **Extra** Dan's essay
1. Bill and Ben play 'Chase the dogs' in the park.
2. Mr King likes cats in his shop.
3. After lunch Bill and Ben sleep in the park.

2 Now you

Talk about the essay. Use words from the box.

I think Jack's essay is/isn't very ...

I like/don't like it because it's/it isn't ...

boring • clever • difficult • easy • good • interesting • nice • silly

3 Your essay

a) *Write an essay: 'A day in the life of ...' (you, a friend, a pet, ...). Use words and phrases like:*

First I/he/she ... Then ...

After that .../After breakfast/...

at 9.15, on Saturdays

in the morning/afternoon/evening

Your mind map (from p. 38) can help you.

b) **Extra** *Draw a picture for your essay and put the essay and the picture in your DOSSIER.*

▸ WB 19 (p. 33)

Checkpoint 2 ▸ WB (p. 35)

My dream house

1 The Carter-Browns' house

a) *Look at the picture of the Carter-Browns' house. What can you see?*

b) *Make a mind map. You can use the words in the box.*

armchair • bath • bathroom • bed • bedroom • chair • cooker • cupboard • desk • dining room • dishwasher • fridge • kitchen • lamp • living room • shelves • shower • sink • sofa • stairs • stereo • table • toilet • TV • wardrobe • washing machine

2 Can you remember?

Partner A: Ask your partner about the Carter-Browns' house.

What colour is the kitchen/fridge/...?
Where's the stereo/...?
What's in the ... room?

Close your book. Answer your partner's questions.

Partner B: Close your book. Answer your partner's questions.

I think it's yellow ...

In the ...

I don't know.

A bed/...

Open your book. Ask your partner about the Carter-Browns' house.

3 Prunella's tour of the house

Prunella has got a visitor.

a) *Look at your mind map from* ***1b****.*
Listen to Prunella's tour. Mark these things on your mind map:
- the rooms Prunella goes to
- the things in the rooms

b) *What things are different or interesting for Uncle Henry? Listen again and check.*

the TV • the armchair • the sofa • the fridge • the cooker • the dishwasher • the sink

4 A tour of your dream house

a) *Make a picture of your dream house or your dream room.*

b) *Plan a tour of your house or your room. You can collect words in a mind map.*

c) *Talk to your partner about your picture.*
This is my dream house/flat/room.
It has got ... rooms. I've got a ... in my room.
I/We sit/watch TV/ ... here.
My mum/sister eats/plays/sleeps/... here.
It's very nice/big/...

Answer your partner's questions.
What's that? Have you got a ...?

▸ *WB 20 (p. 34)*

DOSSIER ***My dream house***

You can put your dream house or dream room in your DOSSIER.

Sports and hobbies

I can …

… talk to my partner about sports and hobbies.

A: After school I play football/…
On Mondays I go to … lessons.
What about you?

B: I play … / I read … / I watch … /
I listen to … music /
I meet … in my free time.

…

Form 7PK

Our sports and hobbies

1

2

4

3

5

1 Form 7PK's hobbies

a) *Write the numbers 1–8 in a list. Match phrases from the box to pictures on the poster. Write them next to the numbers.*

collect stamps/cards • go riding • go swimming • go to dancing lessons • make models • play football • play hockey • play the guitar

Listen and check your answers.

b) *Use your list from 1a) and make a chart. Listen again and complete the chart.*

	Jo	Ananda	Dan	Sophie	Jack
1 play football	✓				
2 play hockey		✓			
3 make models					

c) *Check your answers.*

A: I think Sophie goes .../plays .../...

B: Yes, you're right. / No, I think she ...

2 Extra ACTIVITY A class poster

a) *Bring a picture of one of your hobbies to school. You can make a class poster.*

b) *Prepare 3–4 sentences about your picture.*

My picture is number five. I go to ... on Monday afternoons. Here I'm at my ... lessons.
I like ... a lot.

▸ P 1–3 (p. 58) • WB 1–2 (p. 36)

DOSSIER *My sports and hobbies*

Glue pictures or photos onto a page. Write some sentences.

1 The Kapoors at the sports shop

Shop assistant Good afternoon. Can I help you?
Mrs Kapoor Yes, please. We need hockey shoes for my daughter. Size four, please.
Shop assistant Here you are, a size four hockey shoe.
Mrs Kapoor Thank you. Try it on, Ananda. Does it fit?
Ananda Yes, it does.
Shop assistant Does she like the colour?
Mrs Kapoor Do you like the colour, Ananda?
Ananda No, I don't.
Mrs Kapoor No, she doesn't.
Shop assistant What about these red and white shoes? Does she ...?
Ananda I can talk too, you know.
Mrs Kapoor Ananda!
Ananda Can I try them on, please?
Shop assistant Yes, of course. Well?
Ananda Do they look nice, Mum?
Mrs Kapoor Yes, they do. Do you want them?
Ananda Do I want them? Oh yes, I do!
Mrs Kapoor OK, we'll take them.

> *Right or wrong? Ananda likes the red and white shoes.*

2 Now you

Prepare a shopping dialogue. Act it out.

A: Good morning/afternoon. Can I help you?
B: Yes, please. I need ...

a dress • a sweatshirt • a top • a T-shirt

football boots • shoes • shorts • socks • jeans

A: What size?
B: Size four/ten/S/M/L/..., please.
A: Here you are, size ...
B: Thanks.

A: Does it fit?
B: Yes, it does. / No, it doesn't.

A: Do they fit?
B: Yes, they do. / No, they don't.

A: Do you like it?
B: Yes, I do. I'll take it. / No, I don't.

A: Do you like them?
B: Yes, I do. I'll take them. / No, I don't.

Looking at language

*Wie werden in **1** Fragen gestellt, auf die man als Antwort ein **Yes** oder **No** erwartet?*

*Complete the questions from **1**.*

I	... I want them?
you	... you like the colour?
he/she/it	... she like the colour? ... it fit?
they	... they look nice?

► *GF 10a–b: Simple present: questions/short answers (p. 139) • P 4–8 (pp. 59–60) • WB 3–7 (pp. 37–38)*

3 Prunella plays tennis

Prunella — Sophie, come and play with me!
Sophie — I can't. I've got homework. It's an English project: 'What do people do in their free time?'
Prunella — Great, you can ask me!
Sophie — You? Oh … OK. What do you do in your free time, Prunella?
Prunella — I sing, and I play the piano, and I collect plates and I play tennis.
Sophie — You play tennis? Alone?
Prunella — No. I play with Uncle Henry. He hasn't got a head, so I always win.
Sophie — How do you play tennis?
Prunella — With your racket, of course!
Sophie — Oh! And when do you play tennis?
Prunella — At night, when you're all in bed.
Sophie — And where do you play?
Prunella — We play in the garden.
Sophie — But the neighbours …?
Prunella — Oh, they think your family is mad anyway.

Complete the chart about Prunella.

what?	with?	how?	when?	where?
plays tennis				

4 Extra Now you

*Use ideas from **3**.*

A: What do you do in your free time, B?
B: I … and I …
A: You …? Alone?
B: No, I … with …
A: When do you …?
…

Looking at language

*Find all the questions with question words in **3**.*
What do people do in their free time?
…

▸ GF 10c: wh-questions (p. 140) • P 9–10 (pp. 60–61)

STUDY SKILLS Wörter nachschlagen

Wenn du ein Wort nicht kennst und es auch nicht aus dem Zusammenhang erraten kannst, dann sieh im Dictionary ab S. 179 nach.

Schlag diese Wörter im Dictionary nach:
know, neighbour, anyway
Auf welchen Seiten findest du sie?

Nun finde heraus:
– In welcher Reihenfolge stehen die Wörter?
– Welche Informationen gibt es zu ihnen?

Schreib drei Wörter aus dem Dictionary auf. Dein/e Partner/in hat eine Minute Zeit herauszufinden, was sie bedeuten.

▸ SF 4 (p. 126) • P 11 (p. 61) • WB 8–9 (p. 39)

5 An e-mail to Jay

Ananda has got a cousin in New York. She often writes to him.

Send | Save | Attach | Tools

To: jay.gupta@newyork-ny.com

Subject: Your hobbies

Dear Jay

Just a quick e-mail today …
Here are some questions. Can you answer them for me? It's for an English project.
- What are your hobbies?
- How often do you do them?
- Do you go to school matches?
- Have you got a bike? How often do you ride it?

Thanks a lot!

Love
Ananda

The next morning Ananda finds an answer from her cousin.

Hi, Ananda

Here's a quick answer to your e-mail.
- My hobbies are basketball, basketball and basketball.
- I play every day (I play for the school basketball team).
- I sometimes go to school baseball games. But I NEVER go to football games – they're boring! (American football of course!)
- Yes, I've got a bike. But I don't often ride it …
  I usually walk.

Say hi to Dilip for me.

Jay

▸ *GF 11: Adverbs: word order (p. 140) • P 12–15 (pp. 62–63) • WB 10–13 (pp. 40–42)*

6 Now you

Answer the questions in Ananda's e-mail.

My favourite hobby/sport is …

I	always usually often never	play football go to … lessons go to school matches ride my bike …	after school. on Fridays/… in the evening.

7 Extra Lazy Larry

Listen and do what Larry does.

8 I hate sport

On Wednesdays Jack's mum does yoga after work, and his dad plays basketball. Jack has to do his homework.

'At least I don't have to do yoga or play basketball,' Jack says. 'I hate sport!'
'Hate sport, hate sport,' Polly says.
'And now we have to do our English project about free time. And what do most people do in their free time? Sport!'
'Hate sport, hate sport.'
'At least you understand me, Polly. Oh no, it's 5.30. I have to lay the table for dinner. I have to do everything in this house! And why? Because Mum does yoga and Dad plays baskctball!'
'Basketball, basketball!' Polly says. 'Go team! Go team!'
'Oh no, Polly. Not you too!'

9 SONG I have to get up

a) Listen. Make two groups (boys and girls) and sing the song.

b) **Extra** *Make a new song. Here are some ideas:*

players ... play ball

... shout at us

... do sport

trainer ... train us

... go and play

I have to get up

I have to get up, I have to get up,
I have to get up in the morning.

(S)he has to get up, (s)he has to get up,
(s)he has to get up right now.

I have to get dressed, I have to get dressed,
I have to get dressed in the morning.

(S)he has to get dressed, (s)he has to get dressed, (s)he has to get dressed right now.

The teacher has to teach things.

The students have to learn things.

The teacher has to shout a lot.

And then we can all go home.

► *GF 12: (to) have to (p. 141) • P 16–19 (pp. 63–64) • WB 14–16 (pp. 42–43)*

1 REVISION Jo plays football, he doesn't ... (Simple present statements)

a) *Complete the sentences.*

1 Jo (play) football every day after school. He ~~(play)~~ hockey.
Jo plays football every day after school. He doesn't play hockey.
2 Dan and Jo (go) swimming a lot. They ~~(go)~~ riding.
3 Jack sometimes (make) model boats. He ~~(make)~~ model cars.
4 The girls in Form 7PK (play) hockey. They ~~(play)~~ football.
5 Sophie: 'I (go) to dancing lessons. I ~~(go)~~ to music lessons.'
6 Toby (do) judo. He ~~(do)~~ yoga.
7 Ananda (collect) stamps. She ~~(collect)~~ cards.
8 Prunella (like) tennis. She ~~(like)~~ computers.

b) *Write sentences about yourself, your family, your friends or their pets.*
I ..., but I don't ... My dad/mum/brother plays ... He/She doesn't ... My parents ...
Tell your class or different partners.

2 WORDS A word snake

a) *Find ten words about sports and hobbies.*

b) *Find five verbs. Match them to the words in a).*

c) **Extra** *Make a word snake for your partner about your room/pets/your hobbies/...*

3 WORDS A mind map

Copy the mind map. Add to it. Add more words later.

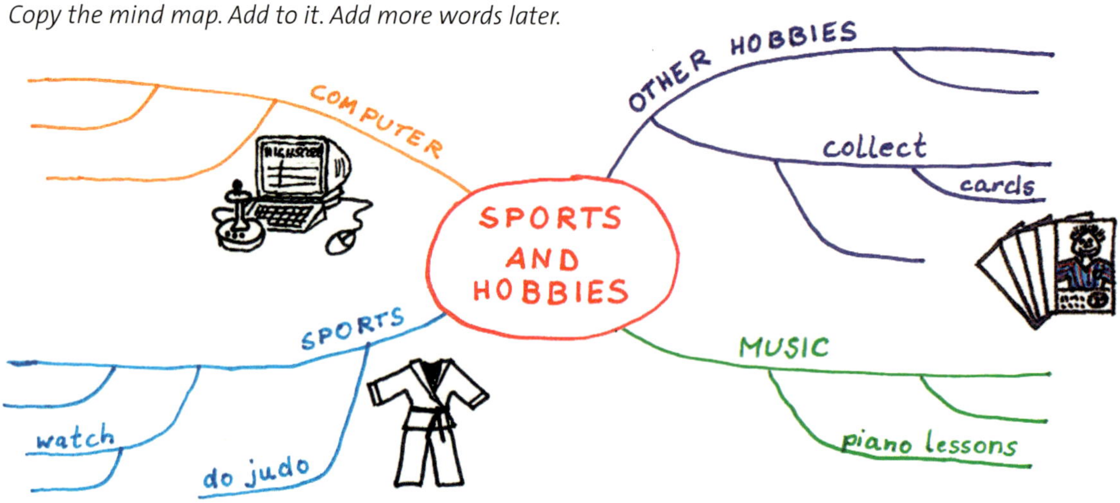

► SF 3 (p. 125)

4 Do you like them? (Simple present: questions)

a) *Complete the questions with:*

Do you   Do they   Do I

Mum Look, these are nice football boots. *Do you* like them?
Dilip Yes, I do, Mum. Can I try them on?
Mum Yes, of course. ... fit?
Dilip Yes, they do. ... look OK?
Mum They look very nice. ... want them?
Dilip ... want them? Yes, I do!

b) *Complete the questions with:*

Does he   Does she   Does it

1 Ananda plays hockey. *Does she* like football?
2 What about Dilip? ... like football?
3 This sweatshirt is too small for Dilip. ... fit Ananda?
4 And Dilip? ... help in the family shop?
5 And Ananda? ... help in the shop too?

5 Does it fit? (Simple present: questions) ▸ D p. 118

Ananda needs more things. Make Mrs Kapoor's questions. Add do or does.

1 *Ananda* The sweatshirt fits.
Mrs K. *Does the T-shirt fit too?*
2 *Ananda* We need white T-shirts for tennis.
Mrs K. ... you need white shorts too?
3 *Ananda* I like the black shoes.
Mrs K. ... you like the red shoes too?
4 *Ananda* I like jeans.
Mrs K. ... your friends like jeans too?
5 *Ananda* The green top looks nice.
Mrs K. ... the black top look nice too?
6 *Ananda* The red shorts fit.
Mrs K. ... the white shorts fit too?

6 Extra Hi Kelly! (Simple present: questions)

Kelly is a new girl in Ananda's form. Complete Ananda's questions with do or does.

1 ... you and your family live in Cotham?
2 ... you live in a flat or a house?
3 ... your big sister go to our school too?
4 ... your sister share a room with you?
5 ... you do sport in your free time?
6 What about your brother? ... he like sport?
7 ... your sister work at the weekend?
8 And you? ... you work at the weekend?

7 A quiz about the families in your English book (Simple present: questions and answers)

Make questions for a quiz. Ask your partner. Answer his/her questions.

Does	Ananda/...	live in a flat?
Do	Sheeba/...	live in a house with a garden?
	he/she	live with the Carter-Browns?
	Mr .../Mrs ...	sleep in a basket?
	Dan/...	do sport? / like music? / ...
	the twins	like his/her brother / ...
	they	get up at 7.15?
		...

8 Do you know your classmates? (Simple present: questions and short answers)

a) *Make appointments with three classmates for 1, 2 and 3 o'clock: Write their names in your list.*
Can we meet at ... o'clock? – Yes, OK. / No, sorry.

My appointments
1 o'clock – Marco
2 o'clock – Sandra
3 o'clock – ...

b) *Copy the chart. Are the sentences below true for you? Then put a tick (✓) in your chart. Not true? Then put a cross (X).*

	me	Marco	Sandra	...
1 I play football in a team.				
2 I make models.				
3 I watch sport on TV.				
4 I go to the shops every Saturday.				
5 I play the guitar.				

c) *Go to your appointments. (Your teacher will tell you when it is 1, 2 or 3 o'clock.) Find out about your classmates. Complete your chart.*
A: Marco, do you play football in a team?
B: Yes, I do. / No, I don't.

d) *Tell your class about your partners. Don't say their names. Can the class guess them?*
This boy plays football in a team.
He doesn't make models, but he ...

9 Sport in different countries (Simple present: wh-questions)

Partner B: Go to p. 115. Partner A: Look at the chart.

Name	Sophie	Yoko	Sanjay	Britta and Lars	Your partner
Where ... come from?	Bristol		Delhi		
What sport ... do?		does judo		play basketball	
When ... do sport?	on Saturdays		every Monday		

a) *Partner A: Ask your partner questions. Write the missing information in your exercise book.*
A: What sport does Sophie do?
B: She goes riding.
A: Where does Yoko come from?
B: She ...
Then answer your partner's questions.

b) **Extra** *Write texts like this:*
Sophie comes from Bristol. She goes riding on Saturdays.
Yoko ...

//○ 10 An interview about hobbies (Simple present: questions) ► D p. 118

a) *Look at the girl's answers. Then write the boy's questions. Don't forget to add* **do** *in each question.*

1 you – like – sport
Do you like ...?
Yes, I like sport a lot.

2 what – sports – you – like
What sports ...?
Well, I like all sports, but I really like basketball.

3 you – play – for a team
...?
Yes, I play for a team – the team at my school.

4 where – you – play
...?
We play at our school or at other schools.

5 when – you – play
...?
We play after school or at weekends.

6 you – do – other things – in your free time
...?
Yes, I do other things in my free time. I collect things.

7 what – you – collect
...?
Well, I collect football cards and stamps.

8 you – like – music
...?
Yes, I like music a lot. I often listen to music in the evening.

b) **Extra** *Make three questions about hobbies for your partner. Interview him or her.*

11 STUDY SKILLS Wörter nachschlagen

a) *Write the words in alphabetical order.*

1 dead, divorced, difficult, different
2 classmate, clever, climb, class
3 plan, place, plate, play
4 week, well, wear, Wednesday
5 think, third, thing, this

b) *Look at the words in the box. Put them in the correct list.*

bowl • at • act • band • activity • because • aunt • all • again • baby • ask • back • bedroom

a – answer	*anyway – bag*	*ball – break*
act	*at*	*bowl*
...	...	...

c) *Find the words in the Dictionary (pp. 179–191) and answer the questions.*

1 ***wardrobe:*** What word comes before it? What word comes after it?
2 ***grandpa:*** What letter don't you say in the word?
3 ***aunt, August:*** How do you say 'au' in the two words?
4 ***get dressed:*** Can you find this under 'get', under 'dressed', or under 'get' and 'dressed'?
5 ***lesson:*** What word comes before it? What word comes after it?
6 ***sunglasses:*** Where can you find this word first in the book? Check the page and find the sentence.

► SF 4 (p. 126)

12 PRONUNCIATION [æ] and [eɪ]

a) Listen to the poem with skate-words. Then practise it.

b) Try this poem with black-words. Listen and practise it.

Happy rabbit in a hat,
Where's the mad black cat?
At the bank?
Bad, bad, bad!

c) Say the words. What is the odd one out?

1	bank	baby	band
2	date	day	dad
3	plan	play	page
4	mad	make	match
5	flat	great	name

Listen and check.

d) Put the words from c) in the chart.

black-words [æ]	skate-words [eɪ]
bank	baby
band	…
…	

13 LISTENING Sport on the radio

a) What sports can you hear? Listen and look at the pictures. Four are right.

b) English and German sports words are often the same. Listen again and try to find some. Can you think of more?

c) **Extra** *Find pictures of different sports. Label them with German-English sports words.*

14 WORDS Opposites

Find nine pairs of opposites.

answer black question go to bed white never empty late right ask wrong work early answer play get up full always

15 Prunella and the computer (Adverbs: word order)

a) *Prunella sometimes mixes up Sophie's e-mails. Correct the sentences.*

Vorsicht! Häufigkeitsadverbien wie ***often***, ***never*** oder ***always*** stehen immer vor dem Vollverb! Also nie ***I go ~~often~~ swimming***.

1 go often swimming. I
I often go swimming.
2 sometimes tennis. plays My brother
3 sport My dad watches always at the weekend.
4 riding. goes never My mum
5 She always in the morning. walks
6 watch school matches. always and I My friends
7 usually goes swimming Our class on Friday.
8 never sport. Our rabbits do.

b) **Extra** *What do you or your friends do? Write three sentences. Use an adverb in each sentence:*
always – usually – often – sometimes – never

c) **Extra** *Make an exercise for your partner. Write the sentences from b) again, but this time mix up the words.*

16 WORDS Link the words

a) *Which nouns from the yellow box go with the verbs from the orange box?*
clean – shoes, teeth

clean • come • do • like • listen to • make • play • write

bed • CDs • computer games • e-mails • home • homework • judo • music • piano • shoes • stories • teacher • teeth • tennis

b) *Complete these sentences.*
1 Jack *cleans* his *teeth* every morning.
2 When he comes ... from school, he does his ...
3 Jack sometimes writes ... after school.
4 In the evening he often sits in his room and ... computer games.
5 He ... music so he sometimes ... CDs in the evening.

17 Who has to wash the car? (have to/has to)

a) *The Carter-Brown family has got a job timetable. Who has to do what this week?*

Week of 4th December

wash the car	Dad
clean the bathroom	Emily and Toby
feed the pets	Sophie and Toby
go shopping	Mum and Emily
make dinner	Dad

Mr Carter-Brown has to wash the car.
Emily and Toby have to ...

● ***b)*** *What's different in this timetable?*

Week of 11th December

wash the car	Emily
clean the bathroom	Mum
feed the pets	Sophie and Toby
go shopping	Dad and Sophie
make dinner	Mum

Mr Carter-Brown doesn't have to wash the car.
Emily has to do it.

18 My partner and I (have to/has to)

a) *Tell your partner what you have to do at home.*

1 make my bed
2 clean my room
3 help in the kitchen
4 help in the garden
5 feed the pets
6 go to bed at eight o'clock

A: I don't have to make my bed in the morning. What about you?
B: Yes. / No. I have to help my parents at home. What about you?

b) *Make sentences about you and your partner.*

I have to ..., and Sven has to ... too.

I have to ..., but Sven doesn't have to.

I don't have to ..., but Sven has to.

19 GETTING BY IN ENGLISH Shopping

a) *What is it in English? (The answers are on these pages.)*

1 Guten Tag. Sie wünschen? (p. 54)
2 In welcher Größe? (p. 54)
3 Größe 4, bitte. (p. 54)
4 Probiere ihn an. (p. 54)
5 Passt er? (p. 54)
6 Magst du die Farbe? (p. 54)
7 Wie wär's mit diesen Schuhen? (p. 54)
8 Kann ich sie bitte anprobieren? (p. 54)
9 Sehen sie gut aus? (p. 54)
10 Ja, natürlich. (p. 54)
11 Vielen Dank! (p. 56).
12 Ja, wir werden sie nehmen. (p. 54)

b) *Work in groups of three.*

A: You're the shop assistant.
B: You're in a shop. You see a nice T-shirt.
C: You're with your friend in the shop.

Part 1

A: Grüße B und C und biete Hilfe an.
B: Sag, dass du das rote T-Shirt magst. Frage, ob du es anprobieren kannst.
A: Sag ja, natürlich.
B: Frag C, ob es gut aussieht.
C: Sag ja.
B: Frag C, ob er/sie die Farbe mag.
C: Sag nein.

Part 2

A: Biete ein anderes T-Shirt an.
B: Frag C, ob er/sie die Farbe mag.
C: Sag ja. Sage B, dass er/sie das T-Shirt anprobieren soll.
A: Frag, ob es passt.
B: Sag ja und dass du es nehmen wirst.
B und C: Sagt vielen Dank und Tschüs.
A: Sag auf Wiedersehen.

The SHoCK Team

Look at the pictures. What do you think?

- Is the man at the Pretty Polly B&B Mr Green/a spy/a bank robber/...?
- Who's in the SHoCK Team? The man? Jack and his friends?

It's 7.45 on Wednesday night. Mr and Mrs Hanson aren't at home. Mr Green is the only guest at the Pretty Polly B&B. And he isn't there. Jack is alone in his room. Suddenly there's a noise downstairs. He listens. Yes, there it is again. He goes to the stairs and looks. Downstairs, outside Mr Green's room, there's a man in black jeans and a black sweatshirt. Jack can't see his face, but he looks very scary.

Jack — Er, excuse me! Can I help you?
The man sees Jack and runs.
Polly — Hurry up! Hurry up!
Jack runs downstairs and out of the house. He looks, but the street is empty.
Jack — Where is the man in black? I have to call the police.

Jack runs back into the house. He goes to Mr Green's room.
Jack — It's locked! Maybe I don't have to call the police.

The next day Jack tells his friends about the scary visitor.
Ananda — You have to tell your parents.
Dan — You have to call the police.
Jo — You have to tell Mr Green.
Jack — But I think this is about Mr Green.
Sophie — About Mr Green?
Jack — I think maybe he's a spy ... or a bank robber ... or ... I know: This is what we have to do. We have to find out about Mr Green. We have to be detectives.
Sophie — Great idea, Jack.
Jo — Yes! 'Detective Jo Shaw' – I like it.

Sophie — I need a piece of paper.
Ananda — I've got a piece of paper.
Sophie — Good. And a pencil?
Jo — I've got a pencil. Why do you need it?
Sophie — Well, we need a name for our team of detectives.

Sophie writes and writes. The others watch. Suddenly ...

Sophie — I've got it. We're the SHoCK Team.
Jack — We're what?!
Sophie — Look: S for Shaw, H for Hanson, C for Carter-Brown and K for Kapoor. Add one little 'o' and you've got SHoCK: The SHoCK Team.
Jack — Great, Sophie! The SHoCK Team: I like it. Right, team, when we aren't at school, we watch Mr Green. We start today at five o'clock. Synchronize watches!

Working with the text

1 What's the story about?

Which statement matches the story?

a) Jack sees a bank robber at the Pretty Polly B&B. He and his friends watch him and then tell the police.

b) Jack and his friends think Mr Green is a spy or a bank robber. They start a team of detectives. They plan to watch him.

c) Jack and his friends start a team at school. They plan to play bank robbers in their free time.

2 Right or wrong?

Correct the wrong sentences.

1 On Wednesday night Mr and Mrs Hanson are alone in the house.
2 A scary man in black jeans and a black sweatshirt is outside Mr Green's room.
3 The next day Jack sees the scary visitor at school.
4 Jack and his friends start a team of bank robbers – 'the B&B Robbers'.
5 The children plan to watch Mr Green after school.

▸ *WB 17 (p. 44)*

3 Extra Jack's report

Complete Jack's report on the SHoCK Team.

Report on the SHoCK Team
The name of our new team of ... is the SHoCK Team: S for ..., H for ..., C for ... and K for ...
We watch Mr Green. Mr Green is a ... at the B&B.
Scary ... come to his room. I think Mr Green is a ... or a ...
Jack

4 Extra Join the SHoCK Team

Why not design a SHoCK Team T-shirt? You can print your design on a real T-shirt.

Checkpoint 3 ▸ *WB (p. 46)*

An English jumble sale

At a jumble sale people sell things – old, used things. They give the money to a charity like Oxfam, or a local hospital, or a youth group.

1 The money

▸ *WB Activity page 2*

Pounds and pence

	You say:
1p	one p [piː]
45p	forty-five p
£1	one pound
£1.25	one (pound) twenty-five (p)
£2	two pounds
£3.69	three (pounds) sixty-nine (p)

Euros and cents

	You say:
1c	one cent
20c/€0.20	twenty cents
€1	one euro
€50	fifty euros
€9.55	nine (euros) fifty-five (cents)

2 The jumble

a) *Work in a group. Bring jumble to school (old clothes, games, books, etc.). Or you can make a cake, biscuits, a model, ...*

b) *Listen. How much are these things?*

red T-shirt
CDs
Spiderman book

€1 | 50c | €1.20

c) *Discuss your prices. Write your price list on a piece of paper.*

A: What about ... for this?
B: Good idea!
C: No, that's too much/not enough.

3 Your jumble sale

When you are ready, start your jumble sale.

Excuse me, how much | is the T-shirt/...? / are the books/...?

▼

Let's see: | It's ... / They're ...

▼

Oh, no, that's too much. I've only got ...

▼

Well, I can take ten cents off.

▼

OK, I'll take it. Here's one euro/...

▼

Thank you. Here's your change.

▸ *WB 18 (p. 45)*

Party, party!

I can …

… talk to my partner about food and drink.

My favourite food/drink is … What about you?
I like/I don't like …
I always/sometimes have … for breakfast/lunch/dinner.
…

1 Food and drink

a) Write down the numbers 1–14. Match words from the box to the numbers in the photo.

birthday cake • cheese • chicken • chips • chocolate biscuits • cola • crisps • fruit salad • lemonade • orange juice • salad • sandwiches • sausages • sweets

b) GAME What is it?

Where are the things in the photo?

It's They're	in the on the	red green ...	bottle bowl glass jug plate

A: It's on the big yellow plate.
It's brown.
B: It's ...
A: That's right. Your turn./
That's wrong. Try again.

2 Extra Food for your dream party

a) Make a list of food and drink for your dream party. You can have seven things.

b) Agree on a new list of seven things.

A: Let's have chips/a chocolate cake/...
B: Yes, good idea. / No, I hate chips.

c) Work in groups of four. Agree on a list of the seven best things.

3 A food poster

Make a poster of your dream party buffet. Prepare dialogues to go with your poster.

A: What's on the big yellow plate?
B: That's chicken.
Would you like some?
A: Yes, please. / No, thank you.
B: What about a drink?
A: Yes, I'd like a glass of cola, please.
B: Here you are.
A: Thanks.

▸ P 1–2 (p. 75) • WB 1–3 (pp. 48–49)

7 The Carter-Browns are getting ready for the party

1

2

3

4

5

6

It's 12 o'clock on Saturday. Sophie's dad is cleaning the bathroom. Her mum is in the kitchen. She's making the birthday cake. Sophie is tidying her room.

Prunella — I'm helping too!
Sophie — No, Prunella! You aren't helping, you're making a mess. Please go away!

It's 2.30 now. Sophie's mum is making the sandwiches.

Mum — Where's baby Hannah?
Toby — She's with me, Mum! We're taking the hamster up to my room.
Emily — Mum, I'm going to Jenny's now, OK?
Mum — No, Emily, it isn't OK. The others are helping.
Emily — Dad is watching sport on TV. He isn't helping!
Mum — And you aren't going to Jenny's! You can go later. Now please put the sandwiches on the table. Dennis! Are you ...?
Dad — I'm not watching TV, dear! I'm ... cleaning the living room.

> *Find a sentence in **7** for each picture.* Picture 1: She's making ...

Looking at language

What are the Carter-Browns doing?
*Make a chart. Put sentences from **7** in the chart.*

	form of 'be'	*-ing form*
Sophie's dad	*is*	*cleaning ...*
Her mum	*is*	...
...	...	...
You	*aren't*	...
...	...	

▸ *GF 15a–b: Present progressive (p. 142–143) • P 9–11 (pp. 78–79) • WB 11–14 (pp. 53–54)*

8 Now you

What is your mother/father/brother/sister/grandma/pet doing now?

is dancing • is eating • is playing • is reading • is shopping • is singing • is sleeping • is working • is writing • ...

Tell the class.

I think my	mum grandpa ...	is sleeping is working is shopping ...	now.

9 What's he doing now?

Look at the pictures. Can you complete the sentences?

1 Maybe Ananda is ...
2 Maybe Jack is ...

at home • at the station • in the pet shop • at school • in front of the pet shop • ...

3 Maybe Jack is talking to ...
4 Maybe Ananda is watching ...

a man • a woman • Ananda • his mother • Mr Green • Sophie

Ananda Jack, is that you?
Jack Yes, Ananda. Are you still following Mr Green?
Ananda Yes, of course I am.
Jack I can hear trains. Are you calling from the station?
Ananda Yes, I am. Mr Green is waiting for the train from London ... here it is now ...
Jack And?
Ananda I think he's meeting somebody. A woman is getting off the train.
Jack Sorry, I can't hear you, Ananda ... Ananda?
Ananda A woman is getting off the train! Now he's talking to her ... she's giving Mr Green a little parcel. Now he's looking round ... oops ...
Jack Ananda! What's happening?
Ananda I'm hiding! Now they're running.
Jack Where are they running?
Ananda They're running to another train ... she's getting on the train back to London! But he isn't getting on.
Jack So what's he doing?
Ananda He's walking out of the station ... see you at the party, Jack.
Jack Ananda, about our present ... I've got this idea and Mrs Carter-Brown says it's OK. Sophie would like a ... Ananda? Ananda!

10 Which picture?

a) *Decide together: Which pictures are right for text 9 on p. 73 – a or b?*

b) *Put the pictures in the right order.*

1 a

b

2 a

b

3 a

b

4 a

b

5 a

b

6 a

b

11 Extra What's Mr Green doing?

a) *Write down the numbers 1–7.*
Mr Green is leaving the station. What can you hear next? Listen and take notes.

drinking • laughing • opening a … • playing • reading • running • writing

b) *Compare notes.*

A: What's Mr Green doing in **1**?
B: He's running.
A: I've got that too. / No, I think he's …

▸ GF 15c: Present progressive questions (p. 143) • P 12–15 (p. 79–80) • WB 15–17 (p. 55)

12 GAME Musical statues

Write an activity on a card.
Put the cards in a box.

Now make two groups.
Group 1: Take a card.
Group 2: Close your eyes.
The teacher starts the music.

Group 1: Mime to the music.
When the teacher stops the music, freeze.
Group 2: Open your eyes and guess the activity.
Swap after three mimes.

We're swimming.

We're singing.

We're riding a bike.

1 WORDS Food and drink

a) *Match the phrases and the words in the box.*

a basket of *apples*, …
a bottle of *cola*, …
a bowl of …
a glass of …
a jug of …
a packet of …
a piece of …
a plate of …

apples • bananas • biscuits • cake • carrots • cheese • chicken • chips • chocolate • cola • crisps • fish • juice • lemonade • meat • milk • mints • oranges • pizza • salad • sandwiches • sausages • sweets • toast • water

b) *Combine the words from the box.*

apple cake, cheese sandwich, …

DOSSIER ***My favourite party food***

Make a list of party food and drinks.

Food
Carrot salad
Chicken
Chocolate cake

2 REVISION A quiz about the Bristol people in your book (Subject pronouns + be)

a) *Answer these questions.*

1 Is Dilip Ananda's brother?
– Yes, he is.
2 Are Ananda's parents from Germany?
– No, they aren't. Mr Kapoor is from …, and Mrs …
3 Is Mr Kingsley's name John?
4 Is Polly a dog?
5 Is Mr Hanson in a wheelchair?
6 Are Bill and Ben Sophie's pets?
7 Is Emily Sophie's sister?
8 Is Jack Sophie's brother?
9 Are Dan and Jo twins?
10 Are Prunella and Sophie friends?

b) **Extra** *Make five quiz questions for your partner.*

// ○ 3 I can see him (Object pronouns) ▸ D p. 119

Complete what Sophie and Ananda say.

Sophie:

Look, I can see | Jack. / Dan and Jo. / my garden. / Emily. / two rabbits. / you and me. / our school. / you. / your mum. / me.

Ananda:

I can see | her/him / them/him / it/him / him/her / him/them / us/them / her/it / her/me / him/her / you/her | too.

Sophie: Look, I can see Jack.

Ananda: I can see him too.

4 Can you help me? (Object pronouns)

a) *Complete the sentences with:* ***me • it • them***

1 I need help. Can you help *me*?
2 Please take the juice and put ... on the table.
3 These glasses look bad. Please wash ...
4 The cake is very good. Try ...
5 These are the good plates. Don't drop ...!
6 There's the salad. Put ... on the table.
7 Emily, I can't open the window. Can you open it for ..., please?

● ***b)*** *Complete the sentences with:*
me • you • her • him • it • them

Kim Do you like parties?
Jim Yes, I really like ...
Kim Well, my party is on Friday.
Jim Invite ..., please!
Kim OK. You can help me to plan ...
Jim OK. What about Laura? Can I invite ...?
Kim Of course.
Jim Who are the others?
Kim Well, there's Tim –
Jim Oh, I don't like ...
Kim Do you like pizza?
Jim No, I hate ... – I only eat banana sandwiches. Please make lots of ...
Kim I don't know why I invite ... to my parties!

5 WORDS Fourth word

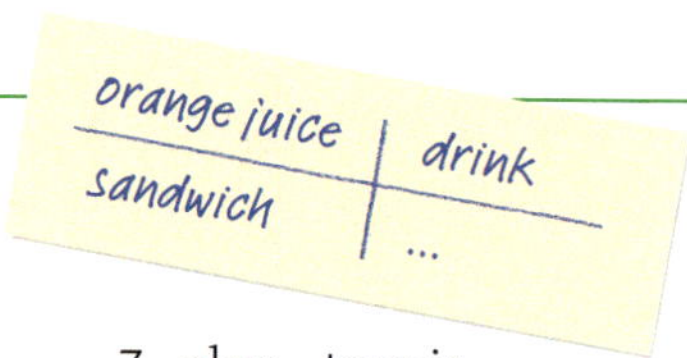

a) *Complete the word groups on pieces of paper like this:*

1 orange juice – drink
sandwich – ...
2 evening – dinner
morning – ...
3 push – pull
open – ...
4 black – white
big – ...
5 married – divorced
together – ...
6 collect – stamps
... – models
7 play – tennis
... – judo
8 sing – a song
... – a story

b) **Extra** *Cut the pieces of paper into four.*
Who can make the word groups again first? (Close your books!)

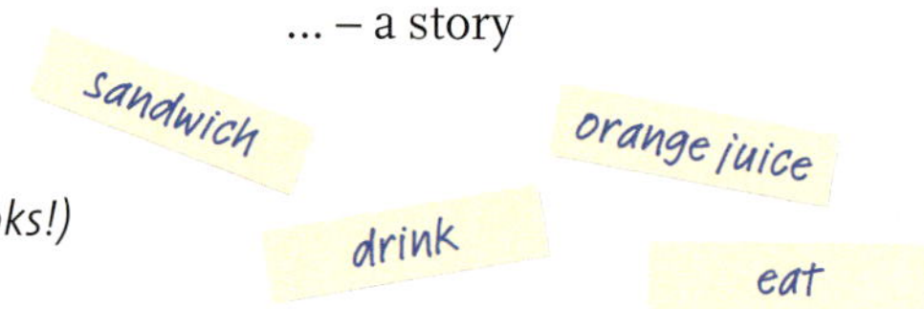

6 STUDY SKILLS Key words

a) *Partner B: Go to p. 115. Partner A: Read this story about Jack to your partner.*

Jack is alone and he isn't very happy. It's 11.30 and he still hasn't got a present for Sophie.
He goes to 'Computers & more'. That's his favourite shop. But then he thinks: The present isn't for me – it's for Sophie!
Jack meets his dad. They go and have a cola and a hamburger. Suddenly Jack is happy.
He has got a great idea for a present for Sophie.

b) *Listen to your partner's key words. Are they in the right order? Look at your story and check.*

c) *Listen to your partner's story about Ananda. Put the key words in the right order.*

A Mr Green – to shop
B 11.30 – Ananda follows Mr Green
C walk to Jack's house
D Mr Green gets up – Ananda follows
E sits in park – reads – eats – drinks
F buys newspaper – cola – sandwich

d) *Read your key words to your partner. He/She can check the order.*

7 Shopping day at the Carter-Brown house (some and any)

a) *Complete the dialogue.*

1 *A:* Is there any milk in the fridge, Sophie?
B: No, there isn't any milk, but there's some lemonade.

2 *A:* Is there ... apple juice in the fridge?
B: No, there isn't ... apple juice, but there's ... orange juice.

3 *A:* Are there ... sausages in the fridge?
B: No, there aren't ..., but there's ... cheese.

4 *A:* Are there ... apples in the basket?
B: No, there aren't ..., but there are ... oranges.

5 *A:* Are there ... cornflakes in the cupboard?
B: No, ..., but there's ... muesli.

6 *A:* Are there ... sweets in the cupboard?
B: No, ..., but there are ... biscuits.

b) **Extra** *Act out the dialogue.*

8 Happy birthday! (some and any)

Partner B: Go to p. 116.
Partner A: Tell your partner about your picture. Ask about his/her picture.

I've got I haven't got	some any	bananas • biscuits • books • cakes • CDs • chicken • crisps • fruit salad • lemonade • orange juice • presents • sausages • soap • socks • sweets	in my picture.

A: I've got some crisps in my picture. What about you?
B: Yes, I've got some crisps too. And I've got some books. What about you?
A: No, I haven't got any books. I've got some ...

9 It's 10 o'clock on Saturday (Present progressive)

a) *Complete the sentences with the correct form of 'be': **am • is • are***

1 It's 10 o'clock on Saturday and the twins *are buying* a present for Sophie.
2 Their dad is at home. He ... cleaning the house.
3 Now it's 1 o'clock. Mr Shaw ... making sandwiches and Jo ... putting food in the cats' bowls.
4 'Dan, lunch is ready!' calls Mr Shaw. – 'I ... coming, Dad! I ... talking to Ananda.'
5 Now the twins and their dad ... eating the sandwiches.
6 It's 3.20. Mr Shaw ... reading a book, the twins ... walking to Sophie's house.

● ***b)*** *Complete the sentences with the correct form of 'be' and the -ing form of the verb.*

1 It's 3.45. Mr Shaw ... (call) a friend.
2 'Hi, Indira. I ... (make) tea. Have you got time to come?'
3 'Thanks, Mike, but I ... (write) e-mails now.'
4 It's 3.55. Mr Shaw ... (call) again. 'I've got a nice cake. I ... (put) it on the table now.'
5 'Sorry, Mike, but now I... (get) things ready for our jumble sale.'
6 It's 4.15 and Mr Shaw is on the phone again. 'Indira? I ... (put) some nice music in the CD player.'
7 'OK, OK, Mike. I ... (come)!'

// ○ 10 Bill and Ben are playing (Present progressive) ▸ D p. 119

It's 11 o'clock on Saturday, 26th March. Look at the pictures. Say what everybody is and isn't doing.
Bill and Ben are playing in the park. They aren't eating fish. Jack is ...

1 play in the park/ eat fish

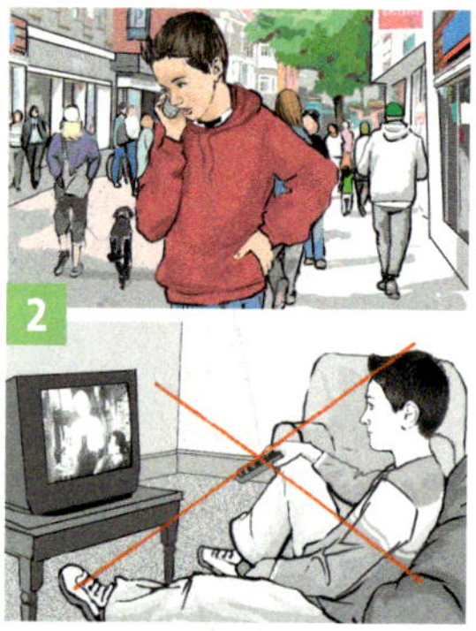

2 talk on his mobile/ watch TV

3 watch Mr Green/ play hockey

4 play football/ play the piano

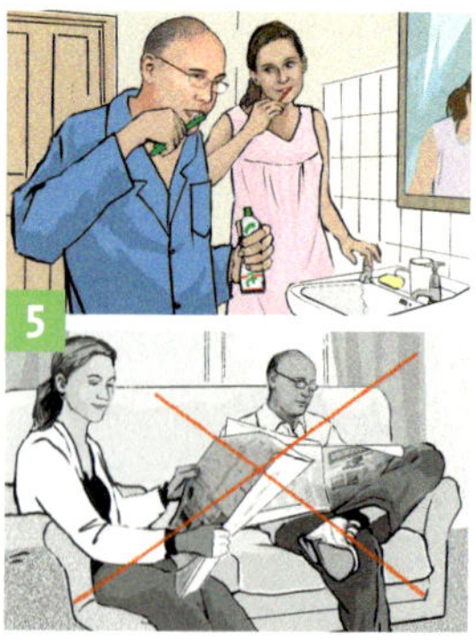

5 clean their teeth/ read the newspaper

6 feed the rabbits/ play tennis

7 work in the shop/ clean the kitchen

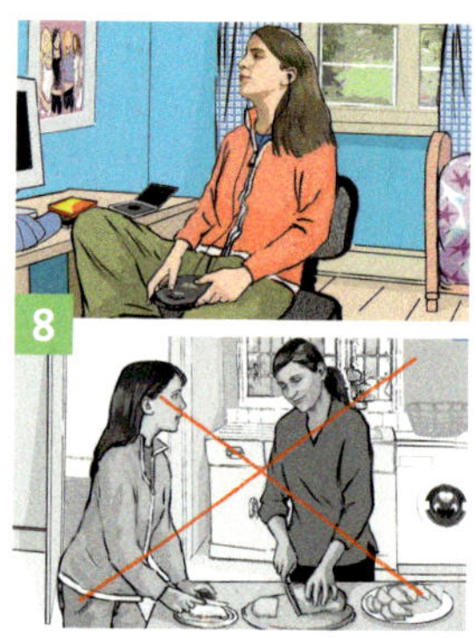

8 listen to music/ make sandwiches

11 I think Sophie is … (Present progressive)

Which group can find more right answers?
a) *Look at the pictures. Say what you think the people are doing. Then write it down.*

A: I think Sophie is eating.
B: No. She's isn't eating. I think she's …
C: I think that's right. Let's write 'Sophie is …'

b) *Tell to your class.*
Group A: We think Sophie is …
Group B: We think that's right. / No, we think she's …

c) *Who's right? Check on p. 117.*

1

2

3
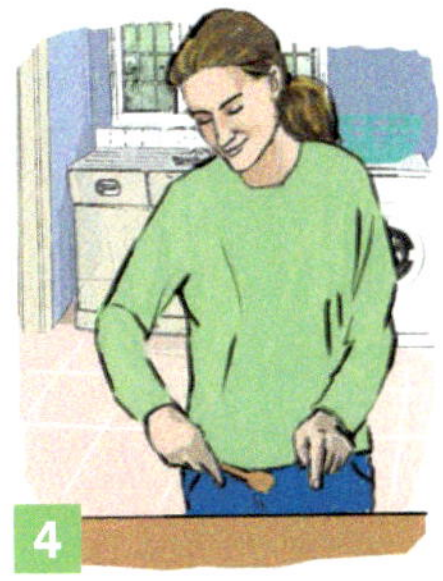
4

5

6

7

8

12 Questions and answers (Present progressive: questions)

a) *Jo is at a friend's house. He is talking to Dan on the phone. Complete their dialogue.*

1 *Jo* — Hi, Dan. *Are* you *doing* (do) your homework?
Dan — No, I'm not.
2 *Jo* — … Dad … (work)?
Dan — No, …
3 *Jo* — … you … (watch) our new DVD?
Dan — No, …
4 *Jo* — … you and Dad … (cook) dinner?
Dan — Yes, we …
5 *Jo* — … you … (make) my favourite pizza?
Dan — Yes, we …
Jo — OK, I'm coming home now. Bye, Dan!

● ***b)*** **Extra** *Dilip is listening to CDs. He can't hear what Ananda is saying. Complete his questions.*
Use: ***where • what***

1 *Ananda* — Hey, Dilip, Mum is ★ ing.
Dilip — Sorry, *what* is Mum doing?
2 *Ananda* — She's working in the ★.
Dilip — Sorry, … is she working?
3 *Ananda* — In the shop. And Dad is ★ ing.
Dilip — Sorry, … is Dad doing?
4 *Ananda* — He's cleaning the shop windows. And I'm trying to ★.
Dilip — Sorry, … are you trying to do?
5 *Ananda* — I'm trying to talk to you, Dilip. But you're ★ ing it difficult.
Dilip — Sorry, … am I doing?
6 *Ananda* — You're making it difficult with your music. I'm going out. BYE!

13 The Hokey Cokey

Children sometimes dance the Hokey Cokey at English parties.

a) *Listen. Do you know it?*

b) *Do you know these words?*

circle • arm • shake • leg • jump • turn around • hold hands • knee • bend • stretch

If not, look them up in the Dictionary on pp. 179–191.

c) *Now listen and dance. And sing the song!*

14 PRONUNCIATION [əʊ] or [ɒ]

a) *Say these words. Are they yellow words [əʊ] or orange words [ɒ]?*

dog • alone • poster • clock • orange • home • yellow • throw • hello • stop • don't

b) *Listen to the words. When you hear a yellow word, hold up a yellow pencil; when you hear an orange word, hold up an orange pencil.*

c) *Say the words. What is the odd word out?*

1 got – joke – lots
2 sock – most – close
3 shop – box – phone
4 bowl – drop – throw
5 not – toast – boat
6 photo – road – top

Listen and check.

d) *Listen to Sophie and Ananda. Learn the dialogue and practise it.*

15 GETTING BY IN ENGLISH Would you like ...?

John, a student from Bristol, is staying with Marcel Schmidt in Münster. Tonight he's having dinner with Marcel's grandmother.

a) *Match the words to the pictures.*

Frankfurter sausages • potato salad • roll

1

2

3

b) *Grandma can't speak English. Marcel has to help her and John. Complete his sentences. (Look at p. 69 for help.)*

Oma Frag John, ob er ein Brötchen oder etwas Kartoffelsalat essen möchte.
Marcel Would you like a ... or some ...?
John I'd like some potato salad, please.
Marcel Er möchte ...
Oma Mag er Würstchen zum Salat?
Marcel Would you like ... with your ...?
John Yes, please.
Marcel Ja bitte.
Oma Möchte John Orangensaft oder Wasser?
Marcel Would you like ... or ...?
John I'd like some orange juice, please.
Marcel Oma, er möchte ...

c) *Practise the dialogue.*

Sophie's party – a play

Look at the pictures. Who's at the party? What are they doing?

Scene 1:
Saturday, 26th March, 3.34 pm. Sophie and her mum are waiting for the party guests in the living room. Prunella is there too.

Sophie — They aren't coming, Mum.
Mum — Don't worry, Sophie. Good guests always come five minutes late!
Sophie — Really?
Mum — Really!
Prunella — To audience The doorbell!
Mum — See? There's somebody now.

At the front door

Sophie — Hello, Dan. Hello, Jo. Come in.
Dan — Hi, Sophie!
Jo — And happy birthday! We've got a present for you – here!
Sophie — Thank you. Thanks a lot.
Dan — You're welcome.
Prunella — What's the present? What is it? Oh, the doorbell again.
Sophie — Oh, sorry, there's the doorbell again.

Back at the front door

Sophie — Hello, Jack. Come in.
Jack — Hi, Sophie. Happy birthday! This present is from Ananda and me.
Sophie — Thank you. But where *is* Ananda?
Jack — She's following Mr Green.
Sophie — Wow! Tell me everything later.

Scene 2:
Now all the guests are there. Sophie is opening Dan and Jo's present.

Sophie — A necklace! Wow, it's great. Thanks, Dan, thanks, Jo.
Jo — Now open Jack and Ananda's present.
Dan — Look, there's a box inside.
Jo — With holes.
Dan — Maybe it's a pet. A hamster?
Jo — Or a snake?
Dan — Or a tortoise?

Sophie — It's a mouse! Fantastic!
Jack — And your mum says it's OK, you can have a mouse.
Sophie — Oh, it's so sweet! Thank you, Jack!
Prunella — To audience And Emily is afraid of mice, so that's great too! – Oh good, here's the birthday cake! Let's sing ...
All — Happy birthday to you, happy birthday to you, happy birthday, dear Sophie, happy birthday to you!

Scene 3:
After tea it's time for some party games.

Prunella — Look, they're playing 'Pass the parcel' now. The music is playing and they're passing a parcel round ... Oops! No more music. Jack has got the parcel.
Jo — Open it, Jack! Hurry up!
Jack — OK, OK. Ah, here's a piece of paper.
Ananda — What's on it?
Jack — 'Sing a song.'

Prunella Ouch: Jack can't sing! Ah, good, now the music is playing again … Oh, no more music! And who has got the parcel?

Dan Hurry up, Jo!

Jo I *am* hurrying! It's another note: 'Choose a partner and walk arm in arm.' … Sophie?

Prunella How sweet! Jo and Sophie are walking arm in arm. Oh, now the parcel is going round again … and … no more music!

Dan Is it another note, Ananda?

Jo Hurry up, Ananda. We're all waiting!

Ananda It's the prize! A really cool pen!

Scene 4:
The party games are over – but now Prunella is playing games.

Prunella Mmm, Dan's crisps are good!

Dan Hey, Jo, don't eat from my plate!

Jo What are you talking about?!

Prunella Hee, hee, hee! Now let's pull Ananda's hair.

Ananda Ouch! Who was that?

Jack Who was what?

Sophie Stop that, Prunella! Go away! This party is for real people.

Prunella Hee, hee, hee!

Dan Are you talking to me, Sophie?

Sophie To you? No, I'm talking to … oh, here's my sister.

Emily Hi, Baby Soph! How's the party? Any orange juice for me?

Jo Baby Soph! Is that your nickname, Sophie? I like it! Baby Soph, Baby Soph … uuurrrgghh …

Suddenly there's a piece of cake in Jo's mouth.

Emily Ha, ha, ha! That's a big piece of cake! Aaaah!

And now there's a mouse on Emily's head.

Emily Take it away! Take it away!

Ananda What's happening here? How can a little mouse get from a box to …?

Sophie Ananda, come and tell me all about Mr Green.

Working with the text

1 Titles for the scenes

Read the play. Give each scene a title. You can use these ideas.

- Prunella is happy
- Prunella is playing games
- Great presents!
- Time for some games
- Sophie is nervous
- Sophie's presents
- Pass the parcel
- Where are the guests?

2 Extra Act out the play

Which character would you like to play? Act out the play.

► *WB 18 (p. 56), Activity page 3*
Checkpoint 4 ► *WB (p. 57)*

Extra Party doorstoppers

**Make your own party doorstopper.
You need ...**

brown or white bread, butter, chutney

a board, knives, salt and pepper, cocktail sticks

lettuce, tomatoes, cucumber, avocados

ham, chicken, salami

cheese

How to do it

1 Put butter on three pieces of bread.

2 Put ingredients on one piece of bread. Put a second piece of bread on top. Add more ingredients and the third piece of bread.

3 Cut your doorstopper like this.

You can make ...

an Italian doorstopper – with tomato, mozzarella cheese and lettuce.

an Indian doorstopper – with cucumber, chicken and chutney.

ACTIVITY

Think of two new doorstoppers. Give them a name. Now you can make them.

School: not just lessons

I can ...

... talk about my school.

a) *Collect your ideas in a mind map.*

b) *What can you say about your school?*

Lessons start/finish at ...
We're in Class ...
My favourite subjects are ...
...

1 The notice board

Find Ananda, Jack, Sophie, Dan and Jo. What clubs are they in? What are they doing in the photos?

dance • make the programme • paint a ship • play the clarinet • sing

Dan is in the Art Club. He's painting ...

2 Activities at Cotham and at your school

a) *Make a chart.*

Cotham School	*My school*
Camera Club	...

b) *Compare Cotham School and your school.*

A: At Cotham School they've got a ... Club.
B: We've got a ... too. / We haven't got a ... Club.

3 Radio Cotham

a) *Look at the notice board and listen. Which photos and notices are they talking about? Point to them.*

b) *Would you like to be in a show? Why? Why not?*

It looks interesting/exciting/boring/...
I like/don't like music/dancing/drama.
I can/can't play the guitar/the clarinet/...

▸ P 1–2 (p. 90) • WB 1–2 (p. 58)

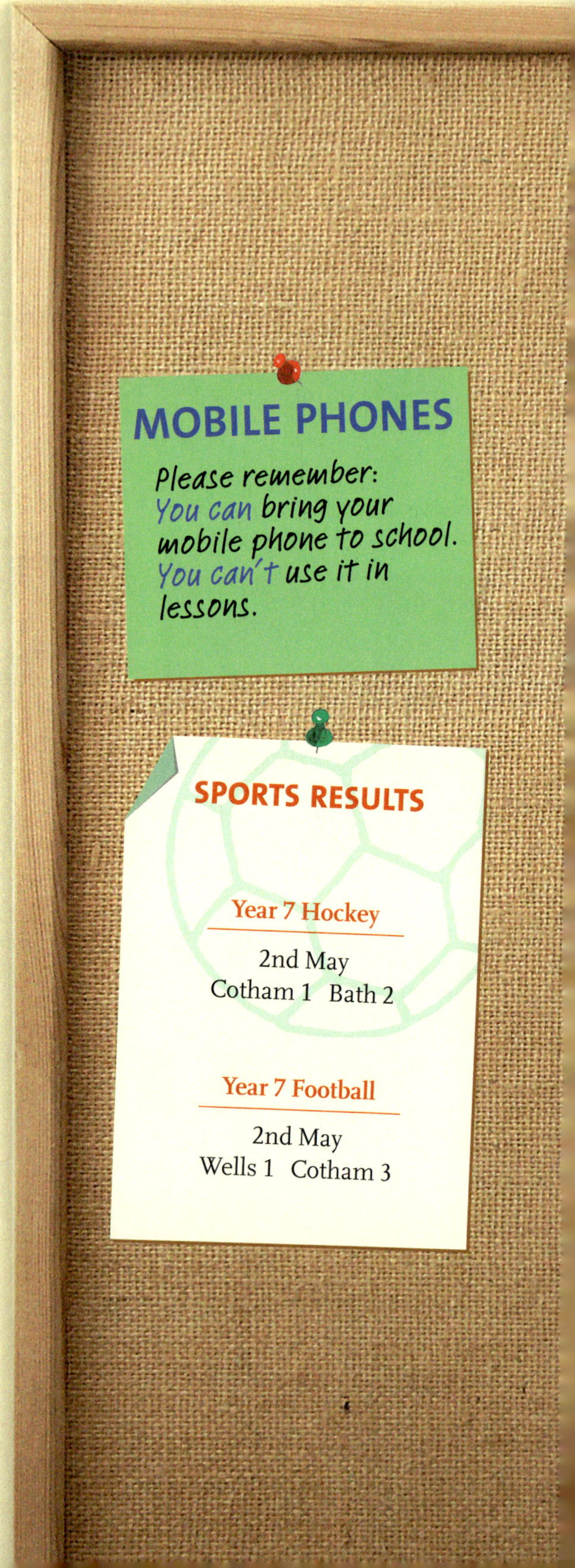

Rehearsals for the Spring Show

Photos by the Camera Club

Remember! Spring Show: 6th May

The Junior Choir is getting ready for the Spring Show.

The Dance Club is rehearsing with the Drama Club!

The Art Club is painting a pirate ship for Wednesday's show.

The Computer Club is making the programme. It has to be ready on 6th May!

The Junior Band is practising for the big day.

1 After the rehearsal: Sophie

Prunella You're late, Sophie. Where were you?
Sophie I was at the dress rehearsal.
Prunella How was it?
Sophie It was OK. We were all very nervous because the show is tomorrow.
Prunella And was the Music teacher happy?
Sophie Miss White? Yes, I think she was.
Prunella And were you good?
Sophie Well, I wasn't bad. My group was in the big pirate scene at the end.
Prunella Pirates? Wow! Oh, the show sounds so good, and I can't go.
Sophie I'm sorry. Poor Prunella.

> *How old are the kids in the show?*
(Remember: The kids in this book are in Year 7. How old are they?)
– *When does the show start?*
– *How much are tickets for a family with two parents and two children?*

> *Right or wrong?*
1 Sophie was home from school early.
2 The dress rehearsal was the day before the show.
3 The kids in the rehearsal weren't nervous.
4 Sophie's group wasn't in a pirate scene at the end.

Extra *Correct the wrong sentences.*

Looking at language

In ***1*** *Sophie and Prunella are talking about the past.*
When do they use ***was****?*
When do they use ***were****?*
– I was ...
– You ...

2 Now you

Partner A: Say a time.

A: At 4 o'clock	yesterday.
At 10 o'clock	last Saturday.
At 3 o'clock	on Tuesday morning.
...	on Monday afternoon.
	...

Partner B: Find out where your partner was.

B: Were you	at home? / in bed?
	at judo/music/... lessons?
	at the cinema?
	at the swimming pool?
	at the sports centre?
	...

A: Yes, I was. / No, I wasn't.

Take turns.

▸ *GF 16–17: Simple past: was/were (p. 144) • P 3–5 (pp. 90–91) • WB 3–5 (pp. 59–60)*

3 After the rehearsal: Jack

Jack was home at 6 o'clock. 'Hi, Mum. Hi, Dad – I'm home!' he shouted.
'I'm in here, Jack,' his dad answered from the kitchen. 'How was your rehearsal?'
'We were fantastic, Dad! Yesterday we were terrible! But today the band played two songs without a mistake.'
'That's great. Mum and I can't wait to see this show. We talked about it last night.'
'Where *is* Mum?' Jack asked.
'Upstairs, I think. She was here a minute ago. Dinner is ready. Can you tell her?'

On the way upstairs Jack stopped at Mr Green's door. Mr Green was on the phone. Jack listened.
'Great idea. Of course, I can use plastic explosives.'
Jack walked to the stairs. 'Plastic explosives? I have to tell the SHoCK Team. This is no joke!'

4 Who was it?

Complete the sentences.

Jack

Mr Green

Jack's dad

1 ... shouted.
2 ... talked to Jack.
3 ... asked about his mum.
4 ... listened at Mr Green's door.
5 ... was on the phone.
6 ... wanted to talk to the SHoCK Team.

Looking at language

a) *When was it? Find time words and phrases in the first part of **3**.*

at 6 o'clock
yesterday
...

b) *Make a chart with these verbs and their simple past forms from **3**.*
shout • answer • play • talk • ask
What letters do you add for the simple past?
*Find more simple past forms in **3**.*

► *GF 18a: Regular verbs (p. 145) • P 6–8 (pp. 91–92) • WB 6–9 (pp. 61–62)*

5 Now you

Tell a partner what you did.

I	phoned ... helped ... listened to ... played ... talked to ... watched ...	yesterday evening. at the weekend. last Wednesday. two weeks ago.

What about you?

6 Pirate King

a) *Listen. Put the jobs in the right order.*

b) *Listen again. Do the jobs.*
Sing the chorus with the Cotham students.

All — For I am a Pirate King!
And it is, it is a glorious thing
To be a Pirate King!
For I am a Pirate King!

Girls — You are!

Boys — Hurrah for the Pirate King!

1

2

3

4

7 A diary

Tuesday, 5th May
We had our dress rehearsal today after school. My pirate ship looked fantastic. Of course Jo said it was silly! I was cross.

When I saw Jo in his pirate costume, I laughed. Then he was cross!

Wednesday, 6th May
The show was this evening. We were all very good. We came home very late!

Thursday, 7th May
SHoCK Team news: Jack told us about Mr Green. What is he doing with plastic explosives?

Saturday, 9th May
Today was a nice, easy day. We all got up late.
Jo and I went swimming in the morning. In the evening we watched TV.
SHoCK Team: no news

Who's writing the diary?
Where can you add these sentences to the diary? On Tuesday, Wednesday, Thursday or Saturday?

In the afternoon we helped Dad.

The show is tomorrow.

Jo was good too. :-)

The SHoCK Team has to find out.

Looking at language

a) *Find these simple past forms in* **7**.
came • got up • had • said • saw • told • went

b) *Match the simple past forms with the infinitives:*
tell • see • go • have • come • get up • say

▸ GF 18b: Irregular verbs (p. 145) • P 9–12 (pp. 92–93) • WB 10–11 (pp. 62–63)

8 Extra After the Spring Show

Listen. What was the highlight of the Spring Show for Ananda? And for Mr Shaw?

9 In the school magazine

The Computer Club *by Ananda Kapoor* (7PK)
It was a good year for the Computer Club. We were part of the Spring Show. We didn't sing or dance, of course :-) We made the programmes. And we made a CD cover too. We were happy with it. Here it is:

The History Club Trip *by Rosie Scott* (7CR)
We wanted to find out more about pirates. But we didn't go to Penzance and we didn't go to the Caribbean. No, we stayed in Bristol! First we went to Bristol City Museum. We saw a film about Blackbeard and lots of other Bristol pirates. Then we went to the harbour and saw an old ship. We had a really great day.

>>> To all school clubs: How was your year? Did you go on a trip? Tell us about it. Write a report for the next school magazine!

10 Now you

a) *Make a list of five things you did at the weekend.*
On Saturday/Sunday
I went/made/watched/cleaned/helped/...

go to a museum • go swimming • go to bed early • make a cake • make breakfast • watch TV • clean my room • help my parents • ...

b) Extra *Say two things you **didn't** do.*
I didn't go/make/watch/clean/help ...

Extra

► *GF 19–20: Negative statements/questions (p. 146)* • *P 13–16 (pp. 93–94)* • *WB 12–15 (pp. 63–64)*

DOSSIER *A special day*

Write about a special day for your English diary or for your English school magazine.

My diary: 5th May | A trip to ... | My Saturday | My birthday

Today/Saturday/5th May/... | was a fantastic/exciting ... day.

In the morning/afternoon/evening | I went to the cinema/the sports centre/a party/...

with my friends/cousins/class ... | First I/we saw/watched/played ...

Then ... | I/We really had/It was | a great/an exciting/interesting day/trip.

► *P 17–18 (p. 95)*

1 REVISION Schools in England – schools in Germany

Compare your school to an English school.

Cotham School, Bristol	*Our school in Germany*
1 School starts at 8.45 am.	Our school starts at ...
2 Students wear school uniforms.	We don't ...
3 All lessons are 55 minutes.	Lessons here ...
4 Most students have lunch at school.	Most students ...
5 You can bring your mobile phone to school.	Here, you ...
6 Students do drama in school.	We ...
7 School finishes at 3.30 pm.	Our school ...
8 At Cotham there's a Camera Club.	At our school ...

2 WORDS The Cotham club-finder

a) *Students often ask: What club can I go to? Make a Cotham club-finder with these ideas.*

Can you act in plays? *Then go to the Drama Club.*

Can you ...?		Then go to the ...
act	with a computer	Art Club
paint	football	Junior Band
play	hockey	Junior Choir
sing	pictures	Computer Club
work	in plays	Drama Club
...	songs	football team
	the clarinet	hockey team
	...	...

b) **Extra** *Make a club-finder for your school.*

c) *GAME*

Write each activity from the club-finder on a card. Put the cards in a box.

sing songs

Take a card and mime the activity. Can the group guess which club you're in?

act in plays

A: You're shouting.
B: No, I'm not.
C: You're singing songs!
A: You're in the choir!
B: Right. Your turn.

...

3 Mr Kingsley's phone call (was/were, wasn't/weren't)

Fill in (+) was/were or (–) wasn't/weren't

Mr Kingsley Today is over. I'm so happy.

Friend Oh, why?

Mr Kingsley Well, it (+) ... a very exciting day! There (+) ... a lot of work at school. First there (+) ... seven lessons. Then there (+) ... the dress rehearsal for the Spring Show.

Friend How was the rehearsal?

Mr Kingsley We (+) ... all very nervous, but the rehearsal (+) ... OK. The students in my drama group (+) ... very good. The pirates (+) ... really scary.

Friend What about the music?

Mr Kingsley Poor Miss White, the new music teacher, (–) ... very happy. The kids in the choir (–) ... very good. First the songs (+) ... too quiet. But they (–) ... too bad at the end.

4 Were you at home yesterday? (was/were in questions and short answers)

Partner A: Ask questions. Partner B: Use short answers. Swap after four questions.

Were	you your parents your friends	at home/school/work in the garden/park/... at the shops/station/... at the football match with you ...	yesterday? at the weekend? on Saturday morning? on Monday evening? ...
Was	your mother your sister your pet your ...		

A: *Were you at school on Saturday?*
B: *Yes, I was. / No, I wasn't.*

A: *Were your parents at work on Monday evening?*
B: *Yes, they were. / No, they weren't. / I don't know.*

//○ 5 Mr Kingsley's old school (Wh-questions with was/were) ▸ D p. 120

Form 7PK is asking Mr Kingsley about his old school. Look at the answers on the right.
Then complete the questions with: What • When • Where • Who • How + was • were

1 ... *was* your old school? – It was in Bristol. I was here at Cotham too.
2 ... ... your favourite subject at school? – It was English, of course!
3 ... ... your best friends? – They were two boys – Mike and Winston.
4 ... old ... you on your first day at Cotham? – I was eleven.
5 ... ... you here at Cotham School? – I was there from ... Mmm, no, I don't want to tell you that!

6 School a hundred years ago (Simple past: regular verbs)

a) *Fill in the simple past forms of the verbs.*
A hundred years ago children usually (start) school early in the morning. They (walk) to school. After school they often (help) their parents in the house or garden. Lessons (look) very different. The teachers (talk) all the time and the children (listen) to them. They never (work) in groups, (talk) to their partners or (play) games in the lessons.

b) **Extra** *Write about your first year at school.*

My teacher I We My school ...	always usually often sometimes never	answer • ask • help • listen to • play • shout • start • talk • work	questions. in groups. stories. music. ...

I often answered questions. My teacher never ...

7 After school (Simple past: regular verbs in positive statements)

Partner B: Look at p. 116.
Partner A: Tell your partner what Jo did after school last week. Ask him/her about Dan.

A: On Monday Jo played football.
What about Dan?
B: He watched TV. On Tuesday Dan …
What about Jo?

On one day the twins did the same thing. When?

	Jo	Dan
Monday	play football	?
Tuesday	start his Maths project	?
Wednesday	work on his Maths project	?
Thursday	call his mum	?
Friday	listen to sport on the radio	?

8 PRONUNCIATION Past forms

blue verbs (*-ed* = no extra syllable)	red verbs (*-ed* = extra syllable)
Liz liked lists. Pat played the piano.	Harry hated homework. Sheila shouted at Shirley.

a) *Listen. Hold up a blue pen for the blue verbs and a red pen for the red verbs.*

b) **Extra** *How many words can you remember from a)? Make lists. Then compare your lists with a partner. Listen again and check.*

blue verbs	red verbs
watched	started
…	

c) *Listen to the poem. Read it to your partner.*

I climbed a tree and looked for Lee.
I wanted to play, I waited all day.
I lived in that tree till January.
I waited and waited for my good friend Lee.

//○ 9 Dan's report (Simple past in positive statements) ▸ D p. 120

Dan watched Mr Green yesterday.
Fill in the correct simple past forms in his report.

came • closed • looked • saw • started • stayed • waited • walked • was (2x) • went (2x) • were

19.35: We (be) all at Jack's house. Mr Green (go) out.
19.38: Outside the house he (look) round.
19.39: Then he (walk) to the end of the street.
19.42: Suddenly the man in black (be) in the street too.
19.46: Mr Green (see) him. He (start) to run.
19.52: Mr Green (come) back to the B&B. He (be) very nervous.
19.53: He (go) to his room and (close) his door.
20.00: We (wait) in Jack's kitchen, but Mr Green (stay) in his room.

19.35: We were all at Jack's house. Mr Green …

10 WORDS An e-mail to Ananda's cousin (Prepositions)

Complete Ananda's e-mail to her cousin Jay in New York.

Subject: Our Spring Show

Dear Jay
Our Spring Show was on (at/on) Wednesday. It was great. I wasn't (in/on) the show. I'm (at/in) the Computer Club – it was our job to make the programmes.
The week (before/for) the show, the kids practised every day (after/on) school. And (at/on) Tuesday, 5th May, we had our dress rehearsal (at/on) 4 o'clock. Then we were ready (at/for) the big day! The show was (at/in) the evening. Lots of people came. They all listened (from/to) the music and watched the scenes (of/from) different musicals. Jo was one (of/from) the pirates. Jack was very good (in/on) the band. (At/On) the end (for/of) the show we were all very happy.
What about your school? Are there shows there too? Tell me (from/about) them.
Love
Ananda

11 REVISION Our 'don't' alphabet (Simple present: negative statements)

a) *Make a 'don't' alphabet.*

We don't ...

A:	*... like*	*apple cake*
B:	*... read*	*books about spies*
C:	*... eat*	*chocolate*
D:	*...*	*d ...*

b) *Tell the class about your 'don't' alphabet.*

We don't listen to Anastacia CDs. We don't like bananas, we don't ...

For more ideas, look in the Dictionary!

12 WORDS Rhyme words

Find the rhyme words: late – wait, ...

late • never • tea • note • round • I • write • blue • well • take • wrong • fair • know

right • chair • break • clever • my • wait • boat • tree • song • no • pound • who • spell

13 Extra Mr Shaw's list (Simple past: negative statements)

a) *Mr Shaw has to do lots of things at weekends. So he always makes a list. Look at last weekend's list. Say what he* **didn't** *do.*

Last weekend Mr Shaw didn't clean his bike.
He didn't ...

b) *Make a list of your weekend activities. Tell a partner what you didn't do last weekend.*

I usually play basketball at weekends, but last weekend I didn't.

clean my bike
invite Indira to dinner ✓
check the boys' bikes ✓
call Grandma Thompson
help the neighbours
talk to the boys about the holidays
practise the piano
work in the garden
answer Catherine's e-mail
start my new book ✓
listen to my new CD

//○ 14 Extra 200 years ago they didn't watch TV (Simple past: mixed forms) ▸ D p. 120

*Say what's wrong in the sentences. Use **didn't**.*

1 200 years ago children watched TV in the evenings. (listened to stories)
200 years ago children <u>didn't watch</u> TV in the evenings. They listened to stories.
2 They went to school in cars. (walked to school)
3 They had hamburgers and chips for dinner. (had meat and potatoes)
4 After dinner people washed the plates in the dishwasher. (washed them in the sink)
5 Mums went to work. (worked at home)
6 Boys played computer games after school. (played in the street)
7 Girls liked football. (liked dancing)

● 15 Extra The Dance Club – An article for the school magazine (Simple past: mixed forms)

Complete Sophie's article with the correct simple past forms.

'The Dance Club' by Sophie Carter-Brown (7PK)

It (be) a very good year for us. Last month we (dance) in the Spring Show. Lots of parents (go) to the show and they all (like) it. It (~~be~~) just good, it (be) great!

And the Spring Show (~~be~~) the only highlight of the year. Three months ago, Cotham's dancers (be) at the Hippodrome Theatre. We (~~be~~) the only dancers, of course. There (be) dance clubs from eight schools in Bristol, and we (wait) for a long time before it (be) our turn. We (be) very nervous, but we (~~look~~) nervous and we (~~make~~) any mistakes. It (be) a fantastic day. Our parents and teachers (come) to see us. And there (be) lots of people from Bristol and other places too. They all (look) very happy after the show.

16 Extra Did Prunella go to the rehearsal? (Simple past: questions)

Match the questions and answers.

1 Did Prunella go to the rehearsal?
2 Did Dan listen at Mr Green's door?
3 Did Sophie sing in the show?
4 Did Dan and Jo play football on Thursday?
5 Did the kids in the band play in the show?
6 Did Ananda write an article?

a) No, they didn't. They went swimming.
b) Yes, she did. The article was for the school magazine.
c) Yes, they did. They were very good.
d) No, she didn't. She stayed at home.
e) No, he didn't. Jack listened at Mr Green's door.
f) No, she didn't. But she danced.

17 LISTENING The elephant sketch

Here's a sketch from the Spring Show. There are six people on a train: three kids, a man, a woman from the luggage van, and the ticket inspector*.*

a) *Read the sentences. Then listen and put the sentences in the right order.*

1 A woman comes in.
2 The ticket inspector comes in. He tells the man he has to stop.
3 The kids find a place to sit.
4 The kids ask the man why. He says he is scaring away* the elephants.
5 The woman says her elephant is very afraid.
6 A man starts to throw pieces of paper out of the window.

b) **Extra** *Act out the elephant sketch. Your teacher can give you the text.*

** Look up new words in the Dictionary (pp. 179–191)!*

18 GETTING BY IN ENGLISH Last weekend

a) *What is it in English?*
(The answers are on these pages.)

1 Wie war's? (p. 86)
2 Ich war nicht schlecht. (p. 86)
3 Gestern waren wir schrecklich. (p. 87)
4 Heute waren wir toll. (p. 87)
5 Mutti und ich können es kaum erwarten, die Show zu sehen. (p. 87)
6 Wir sind alle spät aufgestanden. (p. 88)
7 Am Abend haben wir ferngesehen. (p. 88)

b) *Prepare one dialogue. Then act it out.*

Dialogue 1

A: Frag B, wie sein/ihr Wochenende war.
B: Sag, dass es nicht schlecht war. Sag, dass du bei einer Show in der Schule warst und zwei Bands gesehen hast.
A: Frag, ob die Bands gut waren.
B: Sag, dass die erste Band schrecklich war.
A: Frag, wie die zweite Band war.
B: Sag, dass sie toll war. Du kannst es kaum erwarten, ihre nächste Show zu sehen.

Dialogue 2

B: Frag A, wie sein/ihr Wochenende war.
A: Sag, dass du am Samstag spät aufgestanden bist. Am Nachmittag bist du schwimmen gegangen.
B: Frag, wo A am Sonntag war.
A: Sag, dass du zu einem Basketballspiel gegangen bist.
A: Frag, ob es gut war.
B: Sag, dass es toll war.

STUDY SKILLS Unbekannte Wörter verstehen

Nachschlagen oder nicht?
Du kannst beim Lesen viel Zeit sparen, wenn du nicht jedes unbekannte Wort nachschlägst. Manchmal brauchst du das Wort zum Verständnis des Textes nicht. Und häufig kannst du die Bedeutung erschließen.

Wie?
Schau dir die Bilder an. Oft zeigen sie Dinge, die du im Text nicht verstehst. Manchmal kennst du ein ähnliches Wort – auf Deutsch oder auf Englisch. Und oft hilft der Zusammenhang, die Bedeutung zu erraten.

► *SF 6 (p. 128) • WB 16 (p. 65)*

A pirate story

Part 1

It was in the Caribbean in the year 1719. The night was dark and windy. The ships were in the harbour, the sailors were in the tavern. They sat with their drinks and talked and laughed.

'And what ship are you from, friend?' said one young man to a sailor at his table,
'The *Silver Swordfish*,' answered the sailor.
'A great ship. Do many men sail on her?' asked the young man.
'Yes, 40 men.'
'Ah! 39 poor sailors on the ship and you here in the tavern!'
'No, no, boy, only two sailors are still on the ship,' said the sailor. 'The others are all here.'
'That's good, that's good,' said the young man.
'It is! Tell me, boy, what's your name?' asked the sailor.
'Bonny.'
'Well then, cheers, Mr Bonny!'
'Cheers!' said the young man. 'And goodbye.'

Part 2

It was 2 o'clock in the morning. The harbour was dark. Two men ran to the *Silver Swordfish*: Mr Bonny and his captain, Jack Rackham. They had swords and pistols. In the shadows their men watched and waited.

Without a sound Captain Rackham and Mr Bonny climbed onto the ship.

'Who goes there?' called one of the sailors.
'A friend!' said Mr Bonny. 'But not *your* friend!' He took out his sword and killed the sailor.
'Who goes ... aaaaagh!' The second sailor was dead on the deck.
Captain Rackham called his men. They came out of the shadows and ran to the ship.
'We sail tonight, men!'

Part 3

Captain Rackham and his men sailed for three days and three nights. On the fourth day the look-out saw a ship.
'Ship ahoy!' he shouted.
The pirates saw that it was a Spanish galleon.
'There's gold on that galleon,' said one of the pirates. 'And we want it!'

The *Silver Swordfish* rammed the galleon.

Mr Bonny started to take the gold back to the *Silver Swordfish*. Suddenly he saw a cabin boy.
'You!' he shouted. 'Help me with this gold!'
'Yes, Sir,' said the boy. He was very scared.

At last all the gold was on the *Silver Swordfish*.
'You, boy!' said Mr Bonny to the cabin boy. 'What's your name?'
'Jonah,' said the boy.
'Jonah!' shouted Mr Bonny. 'Go and clean the captain's cabin. Now!'

Part 4

The cabin boy did his work. Then he sat down in a dark corner. 'Just for a minute,' he said. But he was very tired and soon he was asleep.
When the captain and Mr Bonny came into the cabin, they didn't see the boy in the corner.
Later Jonah opened his eyes. At the table sat Captain Rackham and ... a beautiful woman. But who was the woman?
'Ah, my pretty Ann Bonny!' the captain said.
'*Ann* Bonny!' shouted Jonah. Suddenly all was clear. 'But, but ... a woman on a ship is bad luck!'
Then the captain and Ann Bonny saw Jonah.
'Bad luck for you, boy!' Ann Bonny said. 'Our secret goes to the bottom of the sea ... with you!'

Part 5

Boom ... boom ... boom. The sound of a drum mixed with the sound of the sea and the wind. All the men were on deck. The boy was on the plank. The captain pushed him with his sword. 'Walk, boy, walk!'
'Yeah. Walk the plank!' shouted the pirates. The boy took a step. The captain pushed. He took another step, and another ... and then: down, down, down ...

THUD!

Jo opened his eyes. He was cold ... and on the floor of his room. Dan was asleep in the other bed.

Working with the text

1 New words

Find these words in the story.

windy • sailor • tavern • silver • captain • sword • sail • Spanish • galleon • gold • rammed • cabin • secret • plank

Did you
- *understand them from the pictures?*
- *understand them because they are like German words or other English words?*
- *understand them from the context?*
- *look them up in the Dictionary?*

2 The story

a) *The story has five parts. Match the headings to the parts.* Part 1 is ... **The ship** **The tavern** **The boy** **The end** **The gold**

b) *Put these ideas in the right order.*

1 *a)* There were a lot of sailors in the tavern.
b) In 1719, the *Silver Swordfish* was in a harbour in the Caribbean.
c) Only two sailors were on the *Silver Swordfish*.

2 *a)* They killed two sailors.
b) The captain and Mr Bonny climbed onto the *Silver Swordfish*.

3 *a)* Jonah helped Mr Bonny with the gold.
b) The *Silver Swordfish* rammed a Spanish galleon.

4 *a)* Jonah opened his eyes and saw a pretty woman.
b) The cabin boy cleaned the Captain's cabin.
c) After a few minutes the boy was asleep.

5 *a)* Jonah was on the plank.
b) Jo was on the floor of his bedroom.
c) The pirates shouted.

▸ *WB 17 (p. 66)*

c) **Extra** *Make a comic. Choose one part from* **2b**. *Draw a picture for each sentence. Write speech bubbles for your pictures.*

Checkpoint 5 ▸ *WB (p. 67)*

Extra Poems

1 Enjoy the poems

a) *Read the poems quietly. Then listen to them.*

b) *Choose one poem. Say it for the class.*

c) *Write down your favourite poem. Draw a picture to go with it.*

Ode to a Goldfish

O
Wet
Pet!

Gyles Brandreth

Orders of the Day

Get up!
Get washed!
Eat your breakfast!
That's my mum,
Going on and on and on ...

Sit down!
Shut up!
Get on with your work!
That's my teacher,
Going on and on and on ...

John Cunliffe

The Poetry United Chant

WHAT DO WE WANT clap clap clap
WHAT DO WE LIKE clap clap clap
WHAT DO WE LOVE clap clap clap

GIVE US A P clap clap clap
GIVE US AN O clap clap clap
GIVE US AN E clap clap clap
GIVE US A T clap clap clap
GIVE US AN R clap clap clap
GIVE US A Y clap clap clap

GIVE US THE RHYTHM ... POETRY
WHAT WE WANT IS POETRY

clap clap clap
clap clap clap
clap clap clap
YES!

Les Baynton

2 Write a new poem

a) *Write your own ode.*
Here are some ideas:
Ode to Jo
Ode to Mum
...

b) *Make a new chant.*
Swap the word POETRY for another word.
Try ENGLISH or FOOTBALL.
Act out your chant in class.

c) *Make a new verse for* **Orders of the Day**.

Come here!
_____ !
_____ !

Come here! • Go to bed! • Play with me! • Help me! • Don't fight! • Get ready! • Wait! • Wash the plates! • ...

That's _____ ,

my little sister • my brother • my dad • ...

Going on and on and on ...

Great places for kids

I can ...

... talk about where I live.

I live in ...
It's a city/town/village.

I live in a flat/house.
My bedroom/The garden/... is ...

There's
a park/church/... near my home.
It's nice/great/...

My favourite place is ...

...

Cabot Tower: climb it and see Bristol or have a picnic in the park – it's all free

Clifton Suspension Bridge: walk or ride your bike over it

Horse World: come and see the horses

4
The SS Great Britain: see a great old ship

5
Explore-at-Bristol: see tornados and lots more

6
Park Street: go shopping and meet friends

1 Great places?

Look at photos 1–6. Are they great places for kids? Why? Why not?

I think ... is — interesting • fun • cool • fantastic • boring • old • expensive • cheap • ...

Kids like / Kids don't like — parks • old things • sport • shopping • ...

You can — have a picnic • climb ... • play with ... • go shopping • walk or ride your bike • learn things • watch ... • ... — there.

2 Form 7PK's project

a) *Listen to Mr Kingsley.*
Which photo (1–6) is he talking about?

b) *Which three questions do the students have to ask? Listen again and check your answer.*

Is it easy to get there?

Is it in Bristol?

Is it old?

Is the price OK?

Is it nice to look at?

Is it interesting or fun for kids?

▸ P 1–2 (p. 106) • WB 1 (p. 68)

THE PROJECT Part 1

1 The project starts

Form 7PK project:

Great places for kids

Placemat activity

1 Make a placemat like this on a big piece of paper:

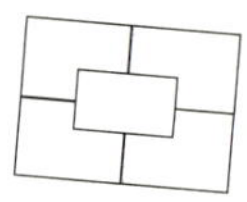

2 Each student must write three (or more) places in one corner of the placemat. (3 minutes)

3 Talk in your group. Agree on the best three places. Write them in the middle of the placemat. (5 minutes)

Ananda, Jack, Jo and Sophie are in a group together. This is their placemat.

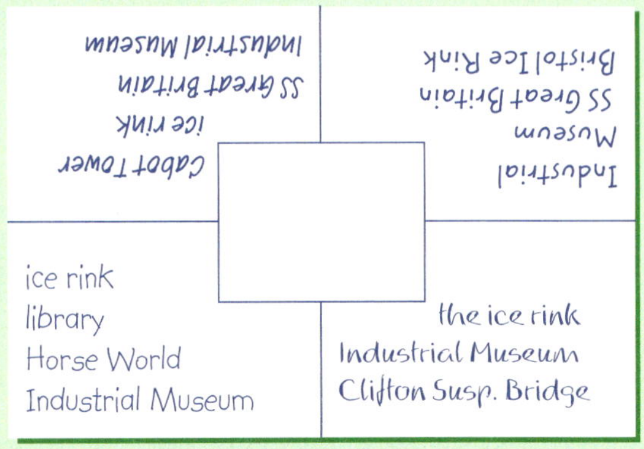

> *Which two ideas have all the kids got?*

2 Three places

Sophie — We've all got the Industrial Museum and the ice rink. That's two places.
Jo — So what's our third place?
Sophie — What about Horse World?
Jack — I don't like horses.
Ananda — And it's difficult to get there. You need a car.
Sophie — OK. Our other ideas are Cabot Tower, the *SS Great Britain* and the library.
Ananda — And the bridge.
Jo — The tower and the bridge are boring. My favourite is the *SS Great Britain*.
Ananda — I'm not for the Industrial Museum *and* the ship. That's too much history!
Sophie — You're right. So let's take the library.
Jack — Good idea. It's a great place.
Ananda — And it's free. OK, Jo?
Jo — OK.

> *Which three places do they agree on?*

Start your project: Great places for kids

Step 1 *Make a placemat. Agree on three great places near you. You can use these phrases.*

We've all got …
Our other ideas are …
What about …?
My favourite is …

Good idea.
I like … too.
I'm for …
That's boring.
I don't like …
I'm not for …

It's fun.
It's cheap/expensive/free.
It's easy/difficult to get there.

You're right.
OK.
Let's take …

Step 2 *Find out more about your places.*

3 At the library

'It's really quiet,' Ananda whispered.
'I like that,' Sophie whispered back. 'I come here because it's always so loud at home.'
'Hey, Jack,' Jo said. 'Isn't that Mr Green?'
'Yes,' said Jack. 'He's looking at plans of Clifton Suspension Bridge. What ...'
'Ssh, you two!' said Sophie.

▸ P 3 (p. 106) • WB 2–4 (p. 69)

4 Extra A library tongue-twister

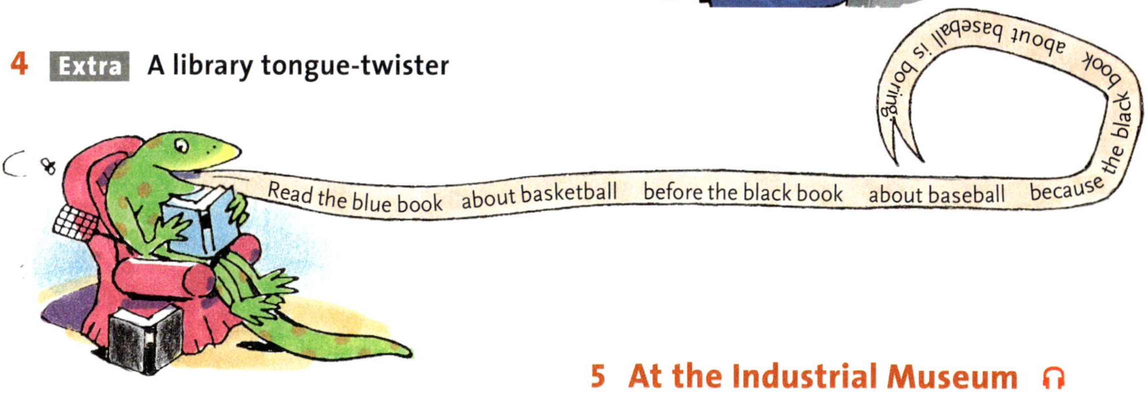

5 At the Industrial Museum

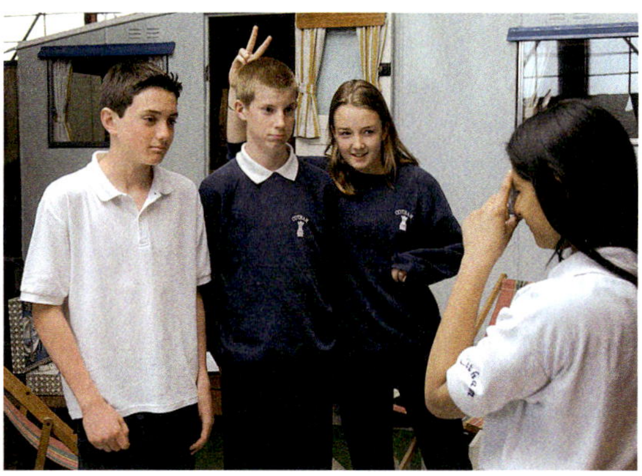

'Let's take a photo over there, in front of that old car,' Jo said.
'No, here,' Jack said. 'This car is better.'
'All these cars look the same,' Sophie said.
'Let's take a photo of those buses over there.'
'The cars don't look the same, Sophie,' Jo said.
'You always ...'
'I always what, Jo?' Sophie asked. 'I hate it when people don't finish their sentences.'
'And I hate it when people argue,' said Ananda.
'Let's take a photo in front of that caravan.
Ready? OK, smile please!'

6 Now you

a) *What do you like? What do you hate? Write down two things.*

I like it when I hate it when	my mum the bus my room my friend ...	is	cross • nice • funny • silly • hot • cold • clean • quiet • early • late • nervous • ...
			shouts • sings • takes my things • helps me • gives me presents • ...

b) *Make appointments for 1, 2 and 3 o'clock. Ask what your partners like or hate. Take notes.*

▸ GF 21: Word order (p. 147) • P 4–6 (p. 107) • WB 5–9 (pp. 70–71)

c) *Tell the class:*
Lennart likes/hates it when ...
I like/hate it when ...

7 You always make a mess!

Sophie — You always make a mess, Jo!
Jo — I'm not making a mess!
Sophie — Yes, you are. Look! Now you're using too much glue. I never use so much glue.
Jo — You know what, Sophie? You grumble all the time.
Sophie — I'm not grumbling.
Ananda — Hurry up, you two! Give me the glue, Jo. We still have to practise our presentation.

Looking at language

Copy and complete the sentence pairs from **7**.

You ... ... a mess, Jo!	I'm not ... a mess!
I ... ... so much glue.	Now you're ... too much glue.
You ... all the ...	... not grumbling.

Which verb form do you use with ***all the time***, ***always***, ***never***? *Which verb form do you use to talk about* ***now***?

▸ *GF 22: Simple present and present progressive (pp. 147–148)* • *P 7–9 (p. 108)* • *WB 10–15 (pp. 72–74)*

8 The poster

Great places for kids in Bristol

Sophie Carter-Brown, Jack Hanson, Ananda Kapoor, Jo Shaw

← Bristol Ice Rink

- ★ Lots of fun
  - Meet friends
  - Junior disco on Saturdays
- ★ In city centre: Frogmore Street
- ★ Not too expensive: £3.50 for students

Bristol Industrial Museum →

9 Presentation time

a) *Look at the phrases.*
Try and write them down in the right order.
1 Our three places are ...
2 Ananda is first ...
3 ...

b) *Listen and check.*

c) *Listen again. Who used the yellow phrases? Who used the pink phrases?*

That's the end of our presentation.

Ananda is first.

We like ... for lots of reasons.

Have you got any questions?

I'd like to talk about ...

First, ...

Second, ...

And third, ...

Jo is next.

Our three places are ...

STUDY SKILLS Präsentation

Vorbereitung *Notiert euch in Stichworten, was ihr sagen wollt. Spielt die Präsentation mindestens einmal ganz durch.*
Arbeitsteilung *Teilt euch beim Vortrag so auf, dass jede/r etwas sagt. Zum Beispiel so: Eine/r führt durch die Präsentation und die anderen präsentieren je einen der Orte.*

▸ SF 7 (p. 129)

Finish your project: Great places for kids

Step 3 *Make a poster for your presentation. Use pictures and key words like in* **8**.

Step 4 *Present your poster to the class. Use ideas from* **9**.

1 WORDS Are you a words champion?

a) *Put the words from the box in the right baskets. Who can finish first?*

b) *Add more words and phrases to the baskets.*

c) *How many words and phrases have you got?*

1–25: You aren't a words fan.
26–44: Good. You know lots of English words.
45–60: Great! You're a words champion!

badminton • basketball • birthday cake • bridge • church • clean your room • dance • do homework • do yoga • downstairs • drama lesson • flat • Geography • go swimming • go to bed • have a shower • have breakfast • hutch • invitation • kitchen • learn • lunch break • Maths • museum • open a present • party game • player • teacher • team • village • win • wardrobe

● 2 WORDS Word partners

a) *Which words go with these verbs?*

take have	away • breakfast • fun • lunch • notes • the train
get do make	dressed • judo • homework • home • a mess • ready • models • a mistake • up late

b) *Which nouns go with these verbs?*
watch – read – look at – play – write – ride – listen to *watch TV/a show/...*

//○ 3 REVISION Three great places (Simple past) ▸ D p. 121

Complete the text. Use verbs from the box.

had • liked • looked • saw • told • took • was • went (2x) • were

For their project Jack, Sophie, Ananda and Jo *went* to their three favourite places. First they ... to the ice rink. They ... a lot of fun. They all ... it very much.
In the library Jo ... Mr Green. He ... Jack. Sophie ... cross because they ... too loud.
At the Industrial Museum they ... at old cars and buses. Ananda ... some good photos.

4 Remember? (Word order in subordinate clauses)

Do you remember the stories in the book? Make sentences and write them in your exercise book.

1 In Unit 1: The twins were nervous because ... (it / the first day at school / was).
The twins were nervous because it was the first day at school.
2 In Unit 1: Dan and Jo's mum isn't in Bristol because ... (she / to New Zealand / went)
3 In Unit 1: Mr Kingsley wasn't happy when ... (Jo / about Sophie's name / made a joke)
4 In Unit 2: Prunella helped Sophie when ... (an essay for homework / she / had to write)
5 In Unit 3: The SHoCK Team started when ... (Jack / about the man in black / told his friends)
6 In Unit 4: Ananda followed Mr Green when ... (went / to the station / he)
7 In Unit 4: Sophie saw a mouse when ... (opened / Jack and Ananda's present / she)
8 In Unit 5: Dan was happy because ... (the Spring Show a lot / his dad / liked)

5 PRONUNCIATION th: [θ] and [ð]

The th in the word teeth [θ]:

The th in the word brother [ð]:

a) *th from teeth or the th from brother? Make lists. Then listen and check.*

that • mother • thing • thanks • think • they • both • together • then • Maths • those • teeth • father • other • bathroom • Thursday • three • this

b) **Extra** *Say one of the words in these pairs. Your partner then points to the word.*

1 ten – then
2 they – day
3 teeth – teas
4 things – sings
5 first day – Thursday
6 say – they
7 both – boat
8 three – free

c) **Extra** *Just for fun. Listen. Then try and learn this tongue-twister.*
My other brother thinks my mother's Maths is bad.

6 Ananda and Dilip (this, that, these, those)

a) *Write sentences with this is/these are.*

1 ... my room.
2 ... my wardrobe.
3 ... my stamps.
4 ... my new hockey shoes.
5 ... my sports T-shirts.
6 ... my school bag.
7 ... my new CD player.

b) *Write sentences with that is/those are.*

1 ... my brother Dilip's room.
2 ... his comics.
3 ... his mobile phone.
4 ... his skateboard.
5 ... his favourite CDs.
6 ... his MP3 player.
7 ... Dilip's books about India.

7 REVISION Prunella's project (Simple present)

Prunella is working on a project. Finish her sentences. Use the simple present.

I (~~know~~) lots of places because I'm a poltergeist. I (live) in the Carter-Browns' house. But my Uncle Henry (always/tell) me about fantastic places in different parts of the world. (you/know) Paris? Well, my Uncle Henry (often/go) there. He (say) it's beautiful. My favourite place (be) my room. I (share) it with my friend Sophie. She (always/say) it (be) her room, but it (be) really *our* room.

8 REVISION Ananda is reading a book (Present progressive)

Partner B: Look at p. 117.
Partner A: Look at the pictures. Tell your partner what the people are doing. Then ask your partner what they're doing in his/her pictures. Two pictures are the same – find out which.

A: In my picture 1, Ananda is reading a book. What's she doing in your picture 1?
B: In my picture 1, she's ...

1 read

2 make

3 listen to

4 write

5 work

6 follow

7 look at

8 go to

9 Extra Today is different (Simple present and present progressive)

Today Prunella is trying to be nice.
Say what she usually does and what she's doing today.

1 Prunella *often drops* (often/drop) cakes, but today she's *making* (make) a cake.
2 She (usually/hide) Sophie's T-shirts, but today she (wash) them.
3 She (sometimes/play) football in the living room, but today she (clean) the room.
4 She (often/make) a mess in Sophie's room, but today she (tidy) it.
5 She (usually/throw) plates, but today she (wash) them.
6 She (sometimes/hide) Emily's sandwiches, but today she (make) them.

The Mr Green mystery THE STORY SO FAR

a) *Put the pictures in the right order. If you're not sure, find the pictures in the book.*

b) *Match the pictures and the boxes. What word do the letters make?*

A Jack hears Mr Green on the phone. He talks about plastic explosives.

S Mr Green is a new guest at the Pretty Polly B&B. Jack thinks he's a spy or a bank robber.

C The Cotham friends start a team of detectives. Sophie thinks of a good name: the SHoCK Team.

E A woman gets off the London train and gives Mr Green a parcel.

K One Saturday Jack and Ananda see Mr Green in a shop. He's in a hurry.

M Jo sees Mr Green in the library. He's looking at plans of Clifton Suspension Bridge.

T Ananda follows Mr Green to the station.

O Jack tells his friends about Mr Green.

H One day Jack sees a man in black at Mr Green's door.

THE STORY GOES ON ...

Jack opened the front door.

'Oh, hi Sophie! You're early!' he said. 'The others aren't here yet.'

'Hi, Jack! I'm sorry, I know the SHoCK Team meets at 6 o'clock, but ...'

'Oh, that's OK. Come into the kitchen.'

'Hello, Polly,' said Sophie.

'Hello, hello, hello!' called Polly from her cage.

Just then they heard a noise in the hall. Jack opened the kitchen door a little bit.

'Look, Sophie. It's Mr Green,' he whispered. Sophie came and looked too. Then there was a voice in the hall. It wasn't Mr Green's voice.

'Hello, Michael!'

'How do you know my name? Who are you?' Mr Green sounded scared.

'I know everything about you, Michael ... We have to talk, you and me. Let's go into your room.'

The man pushed Mr Green into his room.

'Jack, we have to call the police,' Sophie whispered.

'You're right,' Jack whispered back.

Sophie called the police on her mobile. Jack went to Mr Green's door. It was a little bit open. He listened and watched.

'Do you work for Howard?' Mr Green asked.

'Yes. And you know what he wants.'

'When I worked for him, he took all my ideas,' Mr Green said. 'But he can't have this idea!'

'Can't? Howard hates it when people say *can't*,' the man said. 'I don't want to hurt you, but ...' He pulled Mr Green's arm. Mr Green looked very scared.

'No!' Jack shouted. He ran into the room.

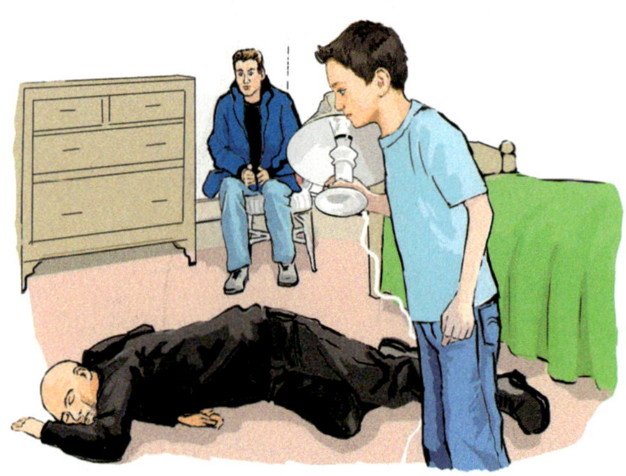

Working with the text

1 Right or wrong?

Correct the wrong sentences.

1. Jack is at Sophie's house for a SHoCK Team meeting.
2. The man in black's name is Howard.
3. Sophie calls the police.
4. Jack helps the man in black.

3 The end of the story

Listen to the CD. Look at the pictures. Which pictures go with the story?

1

2

3

▸ *WB 16 (p. 75)*

2 What happens next?

Talk to a partner about these questions.

1. Is the man dead?
2. Does the man hurt Jack?
3. Does the SHoCK Team come?

4

5

6

7

Checkpoint 6 ▸ *WB (p. 76)*

Extra Merry Christmas

1 Christmas in Britain

a) *What do you know about Christmas in Britain?*

– Christmas songs
– Christmas food
– …

b) *Look at the Christmas cards. Where can you see Father Christmas, presents, Christmas food, Christmas decorations, snow?*

3 Christmas songs

a) *Look at the songs. Match them to a Christmas card.*

b) *Learn the songs and sing them to the music. Which song is the class favourite?*

O Christmas Tree

O Christmas tree, O Christmas tree,
Your leaves are so unchanging.
O Christmas tree, O Christmas tree,
Your leaves are so unchanging.

only green in summer's heat,
t also winter's snow and sleet.
O Christmas tree, O Christmas tree,
Your leaves are so unchanging.

Deck the Halls

Deck the halls with boughs of holly,
Tra la la la la, fa la la la la.
'Tis the season to be jolly,
Tra la la la la, fa la la la la.

Fast away the old year passes,
Tra la la, tra la la, fa la la.
Hail the new year, lads and lasses.
Tra la la la la, fa la la la la.

2 Now you

Talk about your family:

We don't write Christmas cards.

We don't have Christmas, but we have … , and we eat … and we …

We have … for Christmas dinner.

4 ACTIVITY Make a Christmas cracker

1 Make a hat.

You need:

2 Write a joke.

3 Cut the paper.

4 Put the hat, the joke and a small toy inside, roll up the cracker. Tie it.

▸ *WB Activity page 4*

Unit 1

11 WORDS The new timetable

a) *Answer your partner's questions.*

b) *What lessons aren't in your timetable? Ask your partner.*

B: What's lesson 4 on Monday?
A: Drama.

	Monday	Tuesday	Wednesday	Thursday	Friday
1	Maths	...	German	Geography	RE
2	Science	Geography	...	Maths	Drama
3	Science	...	English	English	Science
4	...	English	PE	...	PE
5	Music	PE	...	PE	...
6	...	Music	Drama	German	Maths

Unit 2

2 Where are the pets?

b) *Copy the chart. Listen. Tick the right boxes.*

	Sophie	Jack	Ananda	Dan and Jo
Sheeba				
Hip and Hop				
Harry				
Polly				
Bill and Ben				

7 What they do every day (Simple present: positive statements)

a) *Look at the chart. What can you say about Jack and Ananda?*

A: Jack gets up at 7.15. What about Ananda?
B: Ananda gets up at ... She gets dressed at ... What about Jack?

b) *What about you? Complete a copy of the chart. Talk to your partner.*

A: I get up at ... What about you?
B: I get up at ... I get dressed at ... What about you?

	Ananda	Jack	You	Your partner
get up	at 7.30	...	...	...
get dressed	at 7.40	...	...	...
have breakfast	at 7.50	...	...	
go to school	at 8.05	...		
come home from school	at 4.10			
listen to CDs	at 7.30			
go to bed	at 8.45			

c) **Extra** *Write about your partner's day.*

Unit 3

9 Sport in different countries (Simple present: wh-questions)

Look at the chart.

Name	Sophie	Yoko	Sanjay	Britta and Lars	Your partner
Where ... come from?		Tokyo		Stockholm	
What sport ... do?	goes riding		plays table tennis		
When ... do sport?		at the weekend		on Mondays and Fridays	

a) *First answer your partner's questions. Then ask him/her questions. Write the missing information in your exercise book.*

A: What sport does Sophie do?
B: She goes riding.
A: Where does Yoko come from?
B: She ...

b) **Extra** *Write texts like this:*
Sophie comes from Bristol. She goes riding on Saturdays.
Yoko ...

Unit 4

6 STUDY SKILLS Key words

a) *Listen to your partner's story about Jack. Put the key words in the right order.*

- A goes – his favourite shop
- B 11.30 – Jack alone – not happy
- C meets his dad – have a cola/a hamburger
- D Jack – great idea
- E still no present for Sophie

b) *Read your key words to your partner. He/She can check the order.*

c) *Read this story about Ananda to your partner.*

It's 11.30. Ananda sees Mr Green and follows him.
First Mr Green goes to a little shop and buys a newspaper, a cola and a sandwich. Then he goes to a park and ... sits.
Mr Green sits in the park and reads his newspaper. He drinks his cola and eats his sandwich.
Suddenly Mr Green gets up. Ananda follows him again. They walk and walk ... back to Jack's house, the Pretty Polly Bed and Breakfast.

d) *Listen to your partner's key words. Are they in the right order? Look at the story and check.*

Unit 4

8 Happy Birthday! (some and any)

Tell your partner about your picture. Ask about his/her picture.

I've got I haven't got	some any	bananas • biscuits • books • cakes • CDs • chicken • crisps • fruit salad • lemonade • orange juice • presents • sausages • soap • socks • sweets	in my picture.

A: I've got some crisps in my picture. What about you?
B: Yes, I've got some crisps too. And I've got some books. What about you?
A: No, I haven't got any books. I've got some ...

Unit 5

7 After school (Simple past: regular verbs in positive statements)

Tell your partner what Dan did after school last week. Ask him/her about Jo.

A: On Monday Jo ...
What about Dan?
B: He watched TV. On Tuesday Dan ...
What about Jo?

On one day the twins did the same thing. When?

	Jo	Dan
Monday	?	watch TV
Tuesday	?	clean his dad's car
Wednesday	?	listen to music
Thursday	?	call his mum
Friday	?	play cards with Jack

Unit 6

8 REVISION Ananda is reading a book (Present progressive)

Look at the pictures. Tell your partner what the people are doing. Then ask your partner what they're doing in his/her pictures. Two pictures are the same – find out which.

A: In my picture 1, Ananda is reading a book. What's she doing in your picture 1?
B: In my picture 1, she's …

1 follow

2 sit

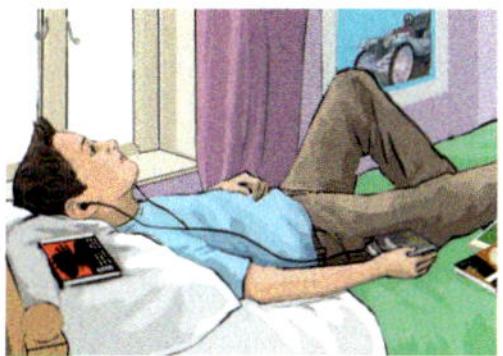
3 listen to

4 feed

5 work

6 take notes

7 ride

8 go to

Unit 4 (Lösung)

11 I think Sophie is …

Were you right? Here are the correct pictures.

1

2

3

4

5

6

7

8

Unit 3

//● 5 Does it fit? (Simple present: questions)

Ananda needs more things. Make Mrs Kapoor's questions.

1 *Ananda* The T-shirt fits.
Mrs K. *Does the sweatshirt fit too?*
2 *Ananda* We need white T-shirts for tennis.
Mrs K. ... you ... white shorts too?
3 *Ananda* I like the black shoes.
Mrs K. ... you ... red shoes too?
4 *Ananda* I like jeans.
Mrs K. ... your friends ... jeans too?
5 *Ananda* The green top looks nice.
Mrs K. ... the black top ... nice too?
6 *Ananda* The red shorts fit.
Mrs K. ... the white shorts ... too?

//● 10 An interview about hobbies (Simple present: questions)

a) *Look at the girl's answers. Then write the boy's questions. Sometimes you need a question word, sometimes you don't.*

1 *Do you like ...?*
Yes, I like sport a lot.
2 *What sports ...?*
Well, I like all sports, but I really like basketball.
3 ...?
Yes, I play for a team – the team at my school
4 ...?
We play at our school or at other schools.
5 ...?
We play after school or at weekends.
6 ...?
Yes, I do other things in my free time. I collect things.
7 ...?
Well, I collect football cards and stamps.
8 ...?
Yes, I like music a lot. I often listen to music in the evening.

b) *Think of five questions about hobbies for your partner. Interview him or her.*

Unit 4

//● 3 I can see him (Object pronouns)

Complete what Sophie and Ananda say.

Sophie:		*Ananda:*		
Look, I can see	Jack.	I can see	me	too.
	Dan and Jo.		you	
	my garden.		him	
	Emily.		her	
	two rabbits.		it	
	you and me.		us	
	our school.		them	
	you.			
	your mum.			
	me.			

Sophie: Look, I can see Jack. *Ananda:* I can see him too.

//● 10 Bill and Ben are playing (Present progressive)

It's 11 o'clock on Saturday, 26th March. Look at the pictures. Say what everybody is and isn't doing.
Bill and Ben are playing in the park. They aren't eating fish. Jack is ...

1

2
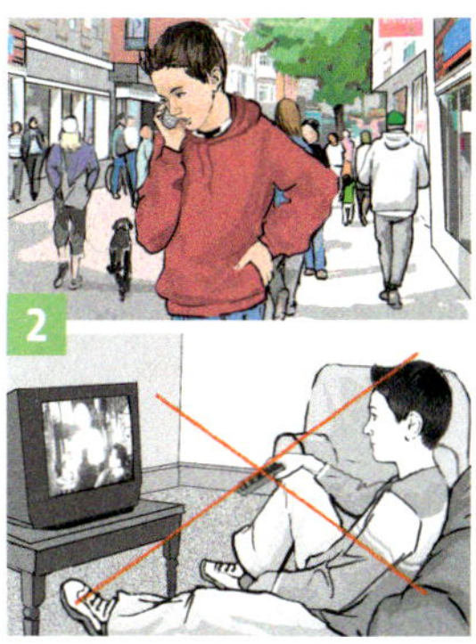

3

4

5
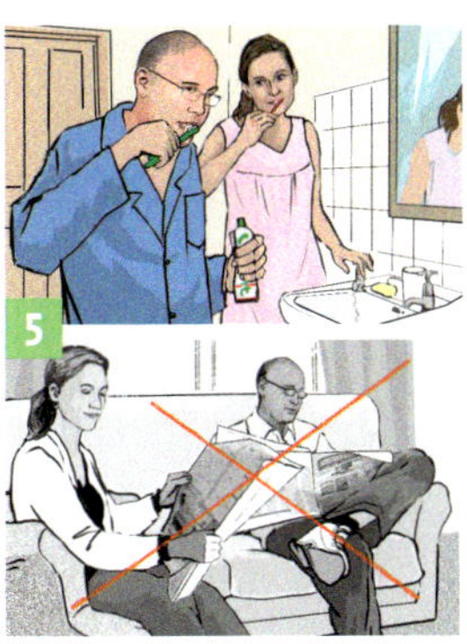

6

7

8
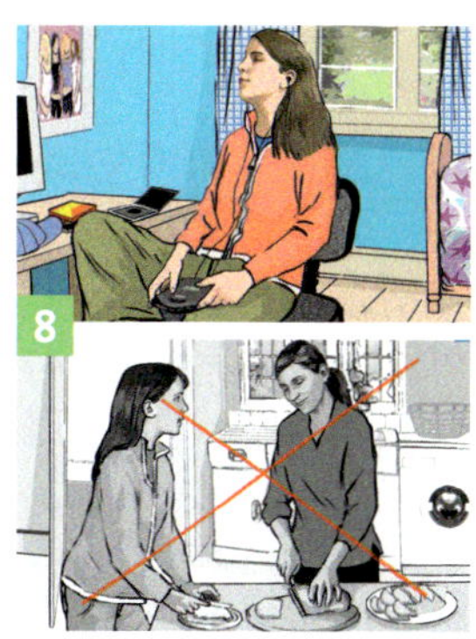

Unit 5

//● 5 Mr Kingsley's old school (Wh-questions with was and were)

a) *Form 7PK is asking Mr Kingsley about his old school.*
Write the questions with:

What • When • Where • Who • How + was • were

Then match them to the answers on the right.

1 ... your old school?
2 ... your favourite subject at school?
3 ... your best friends?
4 ... old ... you on your first day at Cotham?
5 ... you here at Cotham School?

a) It was English, of course!
b) I was eleven.
c) It was in Bristol. I was here at Cotham too.
d) They were two boys – Mike and Winston.
e) I was there from ... Mmm, no, I don't want to tell you that!

b) *Ask one or more of your teachers the questions. How many teachers were at schools in your town? Was English their favourite subject?*

//● 9 Dan's report (Simple past in positive statements)

Dan watched Mr Green yesterday. Fill in the simple past forms in his report. Be careful: The ***blue verbs*** *are irregular!*

19.35 We (be) all at Jack's house. Mr Green (go) out.
19.38 Outside the house he (look) round.
19.39 Then he (walk) to the end of the street.
19.42 Suddenly the man in black (be) in the street too.
19.46 Mr Green (see) him. He (start) to run.
19.52 Mr Green (come) back to the B&B.
He (be) very nervous.
19.53 He (go) to his room and (close) his door.
20.00 We (wait) in Jack's kitchen, but Mr Green (stay) in his room.

19.35: We were all ...

//● 14 Extra 200 years ago they didn't watch TV (Simple past: mixed forms)

Say what's wrong. Use ***didn't****.*

1 200 years ago children watched TV in the evenings. (listen to stories)
200 years ago children didn't watch TV in the evenings. They listened to stories.
2 They went to school in cars. (walk to school)
3 They had hamburgers and chips for supper. (have meat and potatoes)
4 After dinner mums put plates in the dishwasher. (wash them in the sink)
5 Mums went to work. (work at home)
6 Boys played computer games after school. (play in the street)
7 Girls liked football. (like dancing)

Unit 6

// ● 3 REVISION Three great places (Simple past)

Complete the text with verbs from the box.
Put the verbs in the simple past.

be (2x) • go (2x) • have • like •
look • see • take • tell

For their project Jack, Sophie, Ananda and Jo *went* to their three favourite places. First they ... to the ice rink. They ... a lot of fun. They all ... it very much.
In the library Jo ... Mr Green. He ... Jack. Sophie ... cross because they ... too loud.
At the Industrial Museum they ... at old cars and buses. Ananda ... some good photos.

SF 1 Wörter lernen (Units 1–6)

Hier sind ein paar Tipps, wie du Vokabeln lernen kannst. Probiere jede Möglichkeit in den nächsten Monaten einmal aus. Dann weißt du, welche für dich am besten ist.

Vokabeln lernen mit dem Vocabulary

Wörter lernen muss man von Anfang an. Im Vocabulary (S. 150–178) sind die neuen englischen Wörter und Wendungen aufgelistet sowie weitere Informationen. Auf S. 146 wird erklärt, wie das Vocabulary aufgebaut ist.

Schritt 1:

(to) **watch TV** [ti:'vi:]	fernsehen	TV = television ['telɪvɪʒn] ! <u>im</u> Fernsehen = <u>**on**</u> TV: a good film **on TV**
after that	danach	First I feed the pets. **After that** I have my breakfast.

- Lies das englische Wort laut.
- Lies dann die deutsche Übersetzung in der mittleren Spalte.
- Beachte auch die Hinweise oder Beispielsätze in der rechten Spalte.
- Mach dies zunächst mit etwa 7–10 Wörtern.

Schritt 2:

Teste dich, ob du die Wörter weißt. Geh Zeile für Zeile durch.

- Deck die mittlere Spalte ab und sag die deutsche Übersetzung.
- Nun deck die linke und die rechte Spalte ab. Sag die englischen Wörter und – wenn du kannst – auch den Beispielsatz

So kannst du dir eine Lernhilfe zum Abdecken der Spalten basteln:

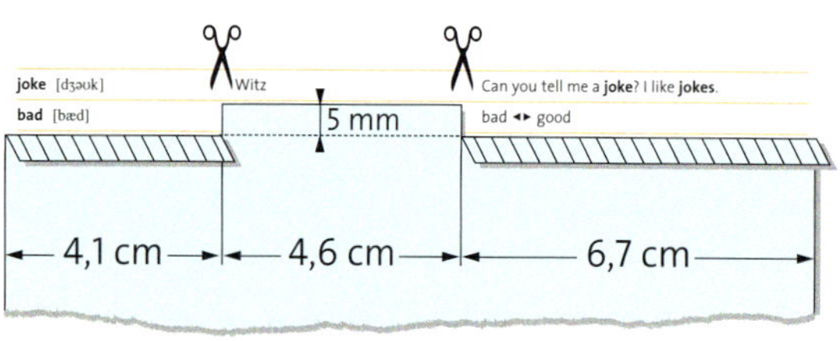

englisch – deutsch

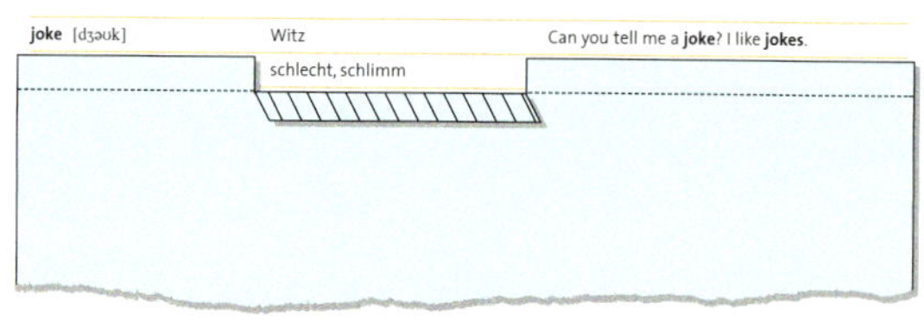

deutsch – englisch

Tipp

- Lerne immer 7–10 Wörter auf einmal.
- Lerne Vokabeln regelmäßig – lieber jeden Tag 5–10 Minuten als einmal zwei Stunden.
- Wiederhole „alte" Vokabeln einmal pro Woche.
- Es macht mehr Spaß, wenn du die Vokabeln mit jemandem zusammen lernst. Fragt euch z.B. gegenseitig ab.

Abschreiben erwünscht!

Besonders gut lernt man Vokabeln, wenn man sie aufschreibt.

■ **Dreispaltiges Vokabelverzeichnis**

Leg ein Vokabelheft (mindestens DIN A5) mit drei Spalten – wie im Vocabulary – an:

- Links das englische Wort,
- daneben die deutsche Übersetzung.
  Achte darauf, dass du die Wörter richtig abschreibst.
- In der dritten Spalte kannst du Beispielsätze aus dem Vocabulary bzw. der Unit aufschreiben oder ein Bild malen.
- Lies die geschriebenen Wörter noch einmal laut.

■ **Elektronisches Wörterverzeichnis**

Es gibt Computerprogramme, die dich beim Üben und Wiederholen wie ein „Vokabeltrainer“ unterstützen. Du kannst dazu dein *e-Workbook* und den *English Coach* benutzen.

■ **Networks**

Ordne neue Wörter in Gruppen – zum Beispiel mithilfe eines *network*.

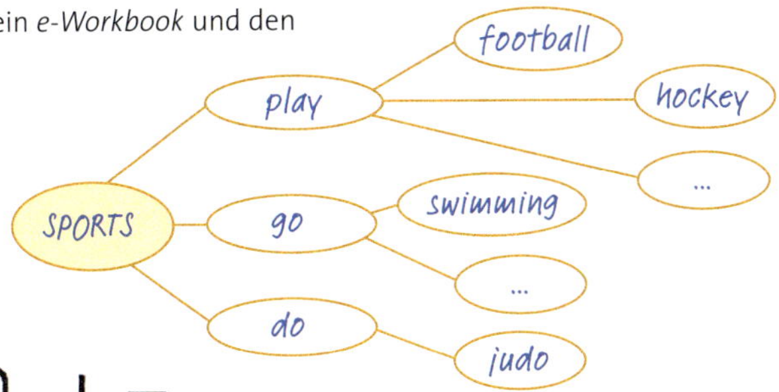

■ **Persönliches „Bilderbuch“**

Zeichne eine kleine Skizze für ein neues Wort.

■ **Karteikarten**

Auf die Vorderseite schreibst du das englische Wort mit einem Beispielsatz, auf die Rückseite die deutsche Übersetzung. Diese Karteikarten kannst du in einem Kasten sammeln (siehe unten).

Vorderseite Rückseite

Alles im Kasten – Vokabeln lernen mit einem Karteikasten

In einer Pappschachtel, die du in fünf unterschiedlich große Fächer unterteilst, kannst du deine Karteikarten aufbewahren.

Schritt 1: Die beschrifteten Karteikarten kommen in das erste Fach. Ist das Fach voll, dann nimm den Packen heraus und prüfe, ob du die Vokabeln kannst.

Schritt 2: Vokabeln, die „sitzen“, kommen in das nächste Fach. Vokabeln, die du nicht kannst, steckst du immer zum Wiederholen ins erste Fach zurück.

Schritt 3: Immer wenn ein Fach zu voll ist, überprüfe, wie gut du die Vokabeln dort beherrschst. Steck die Karten ein Fach weiter oder zurück in Fach 1. (s. Schritt 2)

Schritt 4: Wenn du Vokabeln, die im 5. Fach angekommen sind, nach einiger Zeit immer noch beherrschst, kannst du sie herausnehmen, denn **fünfmal gekonnt ist wirklich gekonnt!**

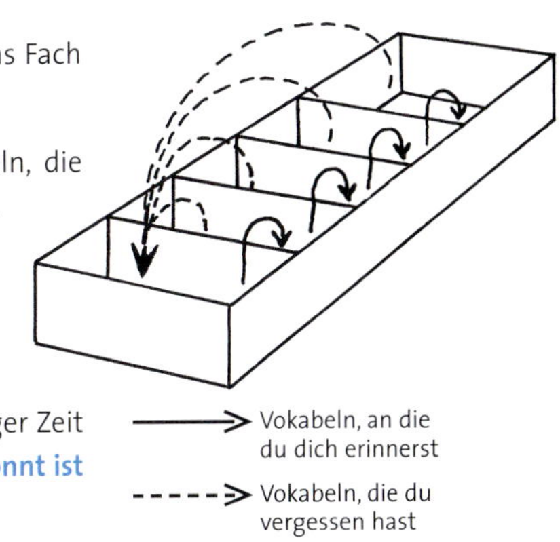

SF 2 Stop – Check – Go (Unit 1)

Viele Fehler bei den Hausaufgaben? Falsche oder keine Antworten im Unterricht? Die nächste Englischarbeit steht bevor? Dann solltest du STOP – CHECK – GO anwenden.

Stop
Mindestens einmal pro Unit, besser häufiger.

Check
Überprüfe, ob du den Stoff einer Unit verstanden hast. Was zum Stoff einer Unit gehört, kannst du z.B. im Inhaltsverzeichnis nachschauen – oder frag deine/n Lehrer/in.
Für Unit 1 könntest du dich z.B. fragen:

Kenne ich die Formen von *'be'* und die Personalpronomen?

Kann ich alle neuen Wörter schreiben und aussprechen? Weiß ich, was sie bedeuten?

Kann ich sagen, was ich und andere (nicht) tun können?

Kann ich Namen buchstabieren?

Kann ich sagen, wie ich heiße und wo ich herkomme?

Kann ich mich über Schulfächer unterhalten?

Der Checkpoint im Workbook hilft dir am Ende jeder Unit bei der Überprüfung. Dort findest du Testaufgaben.

Go
Was kannst du besser machen? Frag deine/n Lehrer/in um Rat oder probier die Vorschläge unten aus.

Tipp

Probleme mit den Vokabeln?
- Wenn du dir manche Wörter nicht merken kannst, schreib sie auf Karteikarten (siehe SF 1, S. 123) oder mal ein Bild dazu.
- Lass dich von jemandem abhören.
- Mach z. B. die WORDS-Übungen noch einmal.

Probleme mit der Grammatik?
- Vielleicht kann dir dein Partner/ deine Partnerin helfen, wenn du etwas nicht verstanden hast.
- Suche z. B. über das Inhaltsverzeichnis das passende Kapitel im Grammar File (ab S. 130).
- Mach die Übungen dazu in der Unit noch einmal.

Probleme mit dem Inhalt?
- Übe kurze Dialoge zu den A-Sections der Unit mit einem Partner/einer Partnerin.
- Mach die *Getting by in English*-Übung im Practice-Teil mit einem Partner/einer Partnerin.
- Benutze Hilfsmittel, z. B. die Listening-CD zum Schülerbuch oder das Workbook.

SF 3 Mindmaps (Unit 2)

Wozu sind Mindmaps gut?

Mithilfe von Mindmaps kannst du deine Ideen sammeln und ordnen, wenn du etwas vortragen sollst oder einen Text vorbereiten willst.

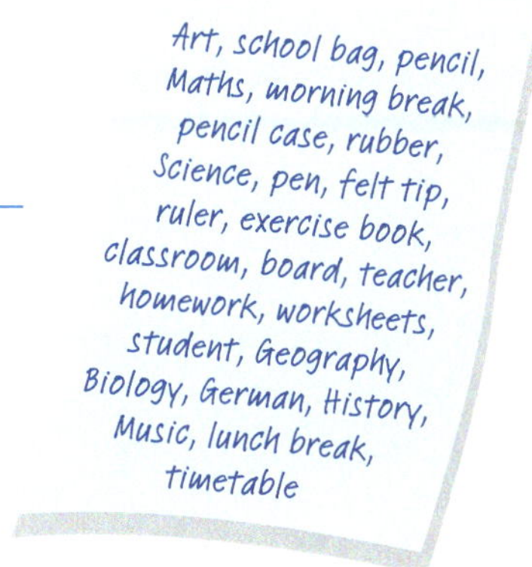

Wie mache ich eine Mindmap?

Wie in diesem Beispiel zum Thema „Schule“ kannst du als Erstes alles in einer Liste sammeln, was dir einfällt.

Was brauche ich?

- ein leeres, unliniertes Blatt Papier im Querformat
- Stifte in verschiedenen Farben

Wie gehe ich am besten vor?

1. Schreib das Thema in die Mitte des Blattes. Male einen Kreis oder eine Wolke drumherum.

2. Überleg dir, welche Oberbegriffe zu deiner Sammlung von Ideen passen. Verwende unterschiedliche Farben.

3. Ergänze jede Idee, die zu einem Oberbegriff passt, auf einem Nebenast. Nimm dafür nur einzelne Schlüsselwörter.

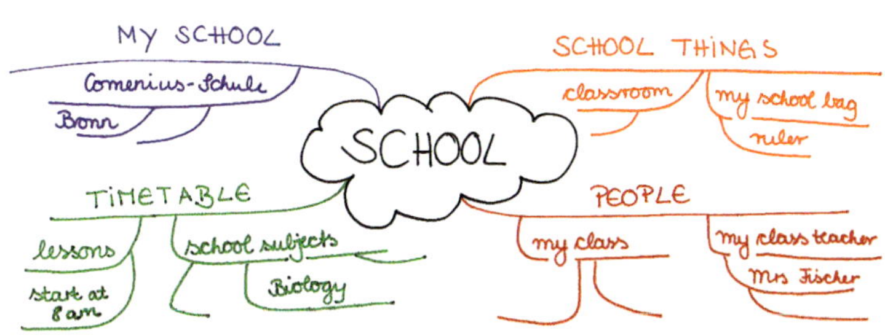

Du kannst statt Wörtern auch Symbole verwenden und Bilder ergänzen.

Es gibt auch Computerprogramme, mit denen man Mindmaps erstellen kann.

- Alles verstanden? Dann probier doch mal Aufgabe 4 auf S. 42.

SF 4 Wörter nachschlagen (Unit 3)

Wozu ist das Dictionary gut?

Wenn du beim Lesen über ein Wort stolperst, das du noch nicht kennst oder vergessen hast, dann hilft dir das English-German Dictionary (S. 179–191) weiter.
Es enthält alle Wörter und Wendungen, die im Buch vorkommen.

Wie benutze ich das Dictionary?

1. Die blau gedruckten Stichwörter (z.B. family, fan) sind alphabetisch angeordnet (also f vor g, fa vor fe und fla vor flo).
2. Beachte auch die Wörter, die schwarz hervorgehoben sind. Es sind:
   - zusammengesetzte Wörter (z.B. **family tree**)
   - abgeleitete Wörter (z.B. **finder** von find) oder
   - längere Ausdrücke (z.B. **the first day**).
3. Zusammengesetzte Wörter und längere Ausdrücke findest du oft unter mehr als einem Stichwort, z.B. **so far** unter so und unter far.
4. Aussprache und Betonung stehen in den eckigen Klammern. Du bist bei den Lautschriftzeichen unsicher? Dann schau dir S. 149 an.
5. Es ist wichtig, den ganzen Eintrag nach dem Stichwort zu lesen. Oft findest du zusätzliche Hinweise, z.B. auf
   - besondere Pluralformen
   - Änderungen der Schreibweise, z.B. Doppel-t bei fit – fitting.
6. Die Ziffern **1.**, **2.** usw. zeigen, dass das englische Stichwort mehrere Bedeutungen hat.

Was bedeuten die Abkürzungen und Symbole im Dictionary?
– Schau nach auf S. 179.

- Alles verstanden?
  Dann probier doch mal Aufgabe 11 auf S. 61.

family ['fæməli] Familie Welc (12/153)
family tree (Familien-)Stammbaum 2 (41)
fan [fæn] Fan 6 (106)
°fancy-dress party [ˌfænsi'dres] Kostümfest
fantastic [fæn'tæstɪk] fantastisch, toll 4 (81))
°far [fɑː]: **so far** bis jetzt, bis hierher
father ['fɑːðə] Vater Welc (12/153)

find [faɪnd] finden Welc (10) • **find out (about)** herausfinden (über) 3 (65) • **finder** Finder 5 (90)
finger ['fɪŋgə] Finger 4 (80/173)
finish ['fɪnɪʃ] beenden, zu Ende machen; enden 5 (84/85)
first [fɜːst] **1.** erste(r, s) Welc (14)
the first day der erste Tag Welc (14)
be first der/die Erste sein 6 (105)
2. zuerst, als Erstes 1 (20)
fish, *pl* **fish** [fɪʃ] Fisch 2 (37/161)
fit **(-tt-)** [fɪt] *(in der Größe)* passen 3 (54)
flat [flæt] Wohnung Welc (14)
floor [flɔː] Fußboden 5 (98)
follow ['fɒləʊ] folgen; verfolgen 4 (71)
food [fuːd] **1.** Essen; Lebensmittel 1 (24); **2.** Futter 2 (39)

SF 5 Notizen machen (Unit 4)

Worum geht es beim Notizen machen?

Wenn du beim Lesen oder Zuhören Notizen machst, kannst du dich später besser daran erinnern – z.B. wenn du etwas vortragen sollst.

Wie mache ich Notizen?

In diesem Beispiel soll eine Schülerin herausfinden, wie Anne Halloween feiert. Sie markiert das Wichtige und macht sich in Stichworten (*key words*) Notizen.

Dear Maria

Do I have a Halloween party? Yes, I do – every year. I invite some girls from the hockey team and from my class, but I don't invite any boys. It's a girls' party. This year I'm a vampire – that's me in the photo. Mum is a poltergeist. The party usually starts at seven o'clock. We play games like Poltergeist Party or Dance of the Vampires. Then we eat pizza and chocolate cake. My mum always tells a scary story at the end of the party. I like scary stories like 'Dracula'. Mum tells the best scary stories in the world!

Your friend
Anne

Anne: ✔ Halloween party – every year
invites some girls, ~~boys~~
Anne: vampire
party starts: at 7
play games, eat pizza + choc. cake
end of party: Mum tells scary story ☺

Tipp

- Verwende Ziffern (z.B. „7" statt „seven").
- Verwende Symbole und Abkürzungen, z.B. ✔ (für Ja) und + (für und). Du kannst auch eigene Symbole erfinden.
- Verwende „not" oder ✗ statt „doesn't" oder „don't".

- Alles verstanden? Dann sieh dir noch einmal Aufgabe 6 auf S. 76 an und probier Aufgabe 7 im Workbook auf S. 51.

SF 6 Unbekannte Wörter verstehen (Unit 5)

Worum geht es beim Verstehen unbekannter Wörter?

Das Nachschlagen unbekannter Wörter im Wörterbuch kostet viel Zeit und nimmt den Spaß am Lesen. Dabei kannst du oft die Bedeutung von Wörtern selbst herausfinden.

Was hilft mir, unbekannte Wörter zu verstehen?

1. Bilder sind eine große Hilfe. Sie zeigen oft die Dinge, die du in einem Text nicht verstehst. Was kann mit 'look-out' im folgenden Textauszug gemeint sein?

On the fourth day the look-out saw a ship.

2. Viele englische Wörter werden ähnlich wie im Deutschen geschrieben oder klingen ähnlich. Was bedeuten wohl diese Wörter?

cabin • captain • deck • gold • kill • pistol • silver • Spanish • young

3. Manchmal stecken in unbekannten Wörtern bekannte Teile.

singer • **friend**ly • un**happy** • **end**less

4. Oft helfen dir auch die Wörter, die vor oder nach dem unbekannten Wort stehen. Was kann mit 'sail' in diesem Textauszug gemeint sein?

'A great ship. Do many men sail on her?' asked the young man.

- Alles klar? Dann probier mal selbst herauszufinden, was **was asleep** in **He was very tired and soon he was asleep** bedeutet.

SF 7 Präsentation (Unit 6)

Worum geht es in einer Präsentation?

Die Ergebnisse einer Einzel- oder Gruppenarbeit sollen der ganzen Klasse vorgestellt werden. Wie erreichst du, dass alle gern und aufmerksam zuhören? Die folgenden Hinweise helfen dir dabei.

Wie mache ich eine gute Präsentation?

Vorbereitung

Schreib die wichtigsten Gedanken für dich als Notizen auf (vgl. SF 5), z.B. auf nummerierte Karteikarten oder als Mindmap (vgl. SF 2).

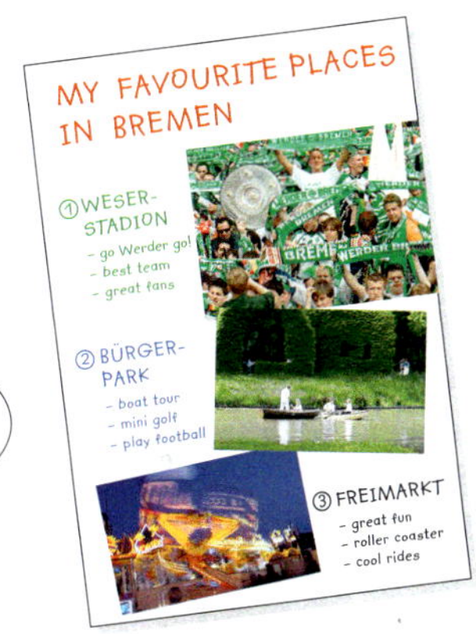

Bereite ein Poster oder eine Folie vor. Schreib groß und für alle gut lesbar.

Übe deine Präsentation laut zu Hause vor einem Spiegel oder übe mit deinem Partner/deiner Partnerin in der Schule. Das gibt Sicherheit.
Sprich deutlich und langsam.

Durchführung

Bevor du beginnst, hänge das Poster auf bzw. lege deine Folie auf den ausgeschalteten Projektor und sortiere deine Vortragskarten. Unbekannte Wörter hast du auf der Folie oder schreibst sie an die Tafel. Warte, bis es ruhig ist. Schau die Zuhörer an.

My presentation is about ...
First, I'd like to talk about ...
Second, ...

Erkläre zu Anfang, worüber du sprechen wirst.
Weise auf die unbekannten Wörter und ihre Bedeutung hin.

Here's a new word. /
Here are some new words.
... is ... in German.

Lies nicht von deinen Karten ab, sondern sprich frei.

Wenn du ein Poster benutzt, zeige während des Vortrags auch darauf.

This picture/photo/... shows ...

Schluss

Beende deine Präsentation deutlich. Frag die Zuhörenden, ob sie noch Fragen haben. Bedanke dich fürs Zuhören.

That's the end of my presentation.
Have you got any questions?

Thank you.

Die Regeln einer Sprache nennt man „Grammatik" (englisch: *grammar*). Im **Grammar File** (S. 130–148) findest du wichtige Regeln der englischen Sprache. Du kannst hier nachsehen, wenn
– du selbstständig etwas lernen oder wiederholen möchtest,
– du die Übungen aus dem Practice-Teil deines Englischbuchs oder aus dem *Workbook* machst,
– du dich auf einen Test oder eine Klassenarbeit vorbereiten willst.

Die **Abschnitte** 1–22 fassen zusammen, was du in den sechs Units über die englische Sprache gelernt hast.
In der **linken Spalte** findest du **Beispiele**, die dir zeigen, was richtig ist, und **Kästen mit Übersichten**, in denen das Wichtigste zusammengefasst ist.
In der **rechten Spalte** stehen **Erklärungen** und nützliche **Hinweise**.
Besonders wichtig sind die roten **Ausrufezeichen** (**!**). Sie zeigen, was im Deutschen anders ist, und machen auf Fehlerquellen aufmerksam.

Hinweise wie ▸ *Unit 1 (p. 21)* • *P 5–7 (pp. 26–27)* zeigen dir, zu welcher Unit und welcher Seite ein **Grammar File**-Abschnitt gehört und welche Übungen du dazu im Practice-Teil findest.

Am Ende eines Abschnitts stellt dir Polly oft eine kleine Aufgabe. Damit kannst du überprüfen, ob du alles richtig verstanden hast. Schreib die Lösungen in dein *exercise book*. **Auf S. 148 kannst du deine Antworten überprüfen.**

Grammatical terms (Grammatische Fachbegriffe)

adverb of frequency [ˌædvɜːb_əv 'friːkwənsi]	Häufigkeitsadverb
imperative [ɪm'perətɪv]	Imperativ (Befehlsform)
infinitive [ɪn'fɪnətɪv]	Infinitiv (Grundform des Verbs)
irregular verb [ɪˌregjələ 'vɜːb]	unregelmäßiges Verb
negative statement [ˌnegətɪv 'steɪtmənt]	verneinter Aussagesatz
noun [naʊn]	Nomen, Substantiv
object ['ɒbdʒɪkt]	Objekt
object form ['ɒbdʒɪkt fɔːm]	Objektform (der Personalpronomen)
past [pɑːst]	Vergangenheit
person ['pɜːsn]	Person
personal pronoun [ˌpɜːsənl 'prəʊnaʊn]	Personalpronomen (persönliches Fürwort)
plural ['plʊərəl]	Plural, Mehrzahl
positive statement [ˌpɒzətɪv 'steɪtmənt]	bejahter Aussagesatz
possessive determiner [pəˌzesɪv dɪ'tɜːmɪnə]	Possessivbegleiter (besitzanzeigender Begleiter)
possessive form [pəˌzesɪv fɔːm]	*s*-Genitiv
present ['preznt]	Gegenwart
present progressive [ˌpreznt prə'gresɪv]	Verlaufsform der Gegenwart
pronoun ['prəʊnaʊn]	Pronomen, Fürwort
pronunciation [prəˌnʌnsi'eɪʃn]	Aussprache
question ['kwestʃən]	Frage(satz)
question word ['kwestʃən wɜːd]	Fragewort
regular verb [ˌregjələ 'vɜːb]	regelmäßiges Verb
short answer [ˌʃɔːt_'ɑːnsə]	Kurzantwort
simple past [ˌsɪmpl 'pɑːst]	einfache Form der Vergangenheit
simple present [ˌsɪmpl 'preznt]	einfache Form der Gegenwart
singular ['sɪŋgjələ]	Singular, Einzahl
spelling ['spelɪŋ]	Schreibweise, Rechtschreibung
subject ['sʌbdʒɪkt]	Subjekt
subject form ['sʌbdʒɪkt fɔːm]	Subjektform (der Personalpronomen)
subordinate clause [səˌbɔːdɪnət 'klɔːz]	Nebensatz
verb [vɜːb]	Verb
word order ['wɜːd_ɔːdə]	Wortstellung
yes/no question	Entscheidungsfrage

Unit 1

GF 1 Personal pronouns Personalpronomen

Nomen:	boy	girl	pencil

Pronomen:	he	she	it

Nomen stehen für Personen *(boy, girl)*, für Dinge *(pencil)* und für alles, was man nicht sehen und anfassen kann, also für Begriffe wie *name* oder *love*.

Auch **Pronomen (Fürwörter)** können für Personen, Dinge und Begriffe stehen.
Personalpronomen sind:
I, you, he, she, it, we, you, they.

Jack is eleven.
Jack is nice.
▼
He's nice.

Where's my pencil?
My pencil is red.
▼
It's red.

◀ Statt *Jack* und *my pencil* stehen hier die Personalpronomen *he* und *it*.

You are nice. = Du bist nett.
Ihr seid nett.
Sie sind nett.

! Die deutschen Personalpronomen **du**, **ihr** und **Sie** heißen im Englischen alle ***you***.

Personalpronomen

Bei einer männlichen Person	– he
Bei einer weiblichen Person	– she
Bei einem Ding oder Begriff	– it
Bei einem Haustier	– he oder she
Bei einem Tier ohne Namen	– it
Bei mehreren Personen, Dingen, Tieren	– they

What colour is ...

... **the pencil**? **der** Bleistift
– It's green. = Er ist grün.

... **the school bag**? **die** Schultasche
– It's red. = Sie ist rot.

... **the ruler**? **das** Lineal
– It's brown. = Es ist braun.

! Das Pronomen ***it*** steht für **alle** Dinge.
(Deutsch: „er", „sie", „es")

▸ *Unit 1 (p. 20) • P 3–4 (p. 26)*

Hast du alles verstanden? Dann kannst du jetzt die folgende Aufgabe lösen:
Suche die Personalpronomen. Wie viele sind es?

the • pencil • he • are • they • nice • you • your • I • we

Deine Antworten kannst du auf S. 148 überprüfen.

GF 2 The verb *(to) be* Das Verb *(to) be* („sein“)

a) Statements with *be*

Aussagen mit *be*

Wie du siehst, hat das Verb *be* in der Gegenwart *(present)* drei Formen: ***am***, ***are*** und ***is***.

Polly zeigt dir einige Lang- und Kurzformen von *be*.

***be* (present)**

Langformen: +	–	Kurzformen: +	–
I am	I am not	I'm	I'm not
you are	you are not	you're	you aren't
he/she/it is	he/she/it is not	he's/she's/it's	he/she/it isn't
we are	we are not	we're	we aren't
you are	you are not	you're	you aren't
they are	they are not	they're	they aren't

Beim Sprechen und in persönlichen Briefen werden meist die Kurzformen von *be* verwendet.

b) Questions with *be*

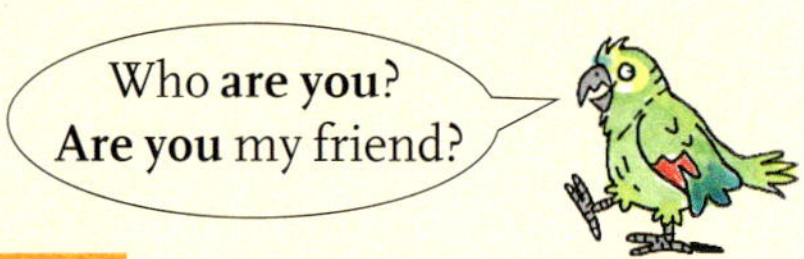

Fragen mit *be*

Fragen kannst du **mit Fragewort** *(Who …?)* oder **ohne Fragewort** *(Are you …?)* stellen.

Nach einem Fragewort wird *is* oft verkürzt:
Who's that?
Where's my book?
What's your name?

***be* (present)**

Fragen:

Am I …?	Are we …?
Are you …?	Are you …?
Is he/she/it …?	Are they …?

c) Short answers with *be*

Well, are you my friend?
– No, I'm not. Uhhh … Yes, I am.

Kurzantworten mit *be*

Fragen ohne Fragewort werden nicht nur mit *Yes* oder *No* beantwortet, das wäre unhöflich. Du solltest eine **Kurzantwort** benutzen, z.B. *Yes, I am* oder *No, I'm not*.

***be* (present)**

Kurzantworten:	+	–
	Yes, I am.	No, I'm not.
	Yes, you are.	No, you aren't.
	Yes, he/she/it is.	No, he/she/it isn't.
	Yes, we/you/they are.	No, we/you/they aren't.

! Nach *Yes* darfst du keine Kurzform verwenden.
Also nur
Yes, I am. / ***Yes, we are.***
usw.

▸ *Unit 1 (p. 21) • P 5–7 (pp. 26–27)*

Alles klar? Dann löse jetzt diese Aufgabe:
Wie könntest du auf die folgende Frage antworten? Welche Antworten sind üblich?

Are you eleven? – 1 Yes. • 2 Yes, I'm. • 3 Yes, I am. • 4 No. • 5 No, I'm not.

GF 3 *can*

a) Statements with *can* ('können')

Aussagen mit *can* („können")

Mit *can* und *can't* drückst du aus, was jemand tun kann oder nicht tun kann.
Es heißt immer *can* bzw. *can't*, egal, ob es um *I, you, he* oder *we* usw. geht.

Polly can talk, but she can't (cannot) sing.

Die Langform von *can't* heißt *cannot*.

Jo can play football.
Jo kann Fußball spielen.
Ananda can't play football.
Ananda kann nicht Fußball spielen.

! Anders als im Deutschen stehen *can/can't* und das Verb direkt hintereinander.

b) Questions with *can*

Fragen mit *can*

Fragen mit *can* bildest du so wie im Deutschen.

c) Short answers with *can*

Can you do tricks? – **Yes, I can. / No, I can't.**
Can Polly sing? – **No, she can't.**

Kurzantworten mit *can*

◄ So bildest du Kurzantworten mit *can* und *can't*.

> ***can* und *can't***
>
> Bei *can* und *can't* gibt es nur eine Form für alle Personen:
> I, you, he/she/it, we, you, they can
> I, you, he/she/it, we, you, they can't

► *Unit 1 (p. 22) • P 8 (p. 27)*

d) *can* ('dürfen')

Room 14 is empty. Can we go in?
Raum 14 ist leer. Dürfen wir hineingehen?
We can go in, but we can't write on the board.
Wir dürfen hineingehen, aber wir dürfen nicht an die Tafel schreiben.

can („dürfen")

Mit *can* und *can't* kannst du auch ausdrücken, was jemand tun darf oder nicht tun darf.

Extra

May we go in?
Dürfen wir hineingehen?
May I write on the board?
Darf ich an die Tafel schreiben?

Wenn du besonders höflich um Erlaubnis bitten möchtest, kannst du statt *can* auch *may* benutzen.

GF 4 **Imperatives** Befehle, Aufforderungen

Come in, please.
Komm/Kommt/Kommen Sie bitte herein.

Write the words on the board, please.
Schreib die Wörter an die Tafel, bitte.

Polly, don't sing. And don't talk, please.
Polly, sing nicht. Und rede bitte nicht.

Befehlsformen

+ Sing.
– Don't sing.

▸ *Unit 1 (p. 23) • P 10 (p. 28)*

Im Englischen gibt es nur eine Befehlsform, egal mit wem du sprichst.

Bei einem Verbot (= einem verneinten Befehl) steht *don't* davor: *Don't walk.* (Langform: *Do not walk.*)

◂ Aus Höflichkeit solltest du *please* verwenden, wenn du jemanden aufforderst, etwas zu tun oder nicht zu tun.

GF 5 **The verb *have got*** Das Verb *have got* („haben, besitzen")

a) Statements with *have got*

Jack has got a parrot.
Jack hat einen Papagei.

Sophie hasn't got a parrot. She's got a dog.
Sophie hat keinen Papagei. Sie hat einen Hund.

Jo and Dan have got pets too.
Jo und Dan haben auch Haustiere.

Aussagen mit *have got*

Die Form *have got* steht bei *I, you, we* und *they*.

Bei *he/she/it* heißt die Form *has got*.

! – *She's got a dog.* = *She has got a dog.*
(nicht: *She ~~is got~~ a dog.*)
– *She's very nice.* = *She is very nice.*

have got

Langformen: +	–	**Kurzformen:** +	–
I have got	I have not got	I've got	I haven't got
you have got	you have not got	you've got	you haven't got
he/she/it has got	he/she/it has not got	he's/she's/it's got	he/she/it hasn't got
we have got	we have not got	we've got	we haven't got
you have got	you have not got	you've got	you haven't got
they have got	they have not got	they've got	they haven't got

b) Questions with *have got*

Fragen mit *have got*

Have you got a pet? Has Jack got a pet?

What have you got next?
When have we got Maths today?

! In Fragen steht *got* nach dem Subjekt (*you, Jack, we*).

have got

Fragen:

Have I/you got ...?	Have we/you got ...?
Has he/she/it got ...?	Have they got ...?

c) Short answers with *have got*

Kurzantworten mit *have got*

Have you got a pet? – **Yes, I have. /**
No, I haven't.
Has Jack got a pet? – **Yes, he has.**
Has Sophie got a parrot? – **No, she hasn't.**

▸ *Unit 1 (p. 24)* • *P 13–14 (pp. 29–30)*

! **1** Bei der Kurzantwort fällt das *got* weg.
2 Nach *Yes* musst du immer die Langform verwenden.

Jetzt kannst du wieder eine Aufgabe lösen. Welche Sätze sind richtig?

1 Have you got a dog? – Yes, we have.
2 Has he got a pet? – Yes, he has got.
3 Have you got Maths now? – Yes, we've.
4 Has Jack got PE today? – No, he hasn't.

Unit 2

GF 6 The plural of nouns Der Plural der Nomen

a parrot (Singular)  two parrots [s] (Plural) 

Du bildest den Plural (die Mehrzahl) eines Nomens, indem du ***s*** an das Nomen anhängst.

Vorsicht bei der **Aussprache der Pluralendung**:

1 beds [bedz] • bags [bægz]
boys [bɔɪz] • trees [triːz]
sisters ['sɪstəz]

◂ **1** Nach **stimmhaften Konsonanten** (Mitlauten), z.B. [d], [g], [n], und nach **Vokalen** (Selbstlauten) klingt das Plural-*s* wie das Summen einer Biene: [z].

2 boxes ['bɒksɪz] • houses ['haʊzɪz]
hutches ['hʌtʃɪz] • cages ['keɪdʒɪz]

◂ **2** Nach **Zischlauten** wie [s], [z], [tʃ], [dʒ] ist die Aussprache [ɪz]. (Je nach Schreibung des Singulars wird ***es*** oder ***s*** angehängt: *box – box**es**, cage – cage**s**.*)

baby ▸ babies family ▸ families
activity ▸ activities hobby ▸ hobbies

! – ***y*** nach einem **Konsonanten** wird zu ***ies***.
(Aber ***y*** nach einem **Vokal** bleibt: ***boy*** → ***boys***.)

one mouse ▸ two mice one tooth ▸ two teeth
one fish ▸ two fish

– Einige Nomen haben **unregelmäßige Pluralformen**.

▸ *Unit 2 (p. 38)* • *P 2 (p. 42)*

GF 7 The simple present Die einfache Form der Gegenwart

a) Positive statements

Bejahte Aussagesätze

◀ Jo und Dan reden hier über das, was sie regelmäßig tun (*every morning*, „jeden Morgen"). Ihre Sätze stehen im *simple present* (einfache Form der Gegenwart).

Dan and Jo **go** to school together.
Hamsters and rabbits **eat** carrots.

Bei *I, you, we* und *they* haben Verben im *simple present* keine Endung.

Toby **helps** Sophie with Harry, the hamster.
He **cleans** his cage.
Sophie **gives** Sheeba meat and water.
Sheeba **eats** in the kitchen.

Aber bei *he/she/it* (3. Person Singular) wird ein ***s*** angefügt.

> *He, she, it* – das „s" muss mit!

! *can* und *can't* immer ohne ***s***:
Toby/He ***can help*** *Sophie.*

Simple present

Bejahte Aussagesätze:

I/You	like	
He/She/It	likes	apples and bananas.
We/You/They	like	

Simple present?
He, she, it?
YES, YES! An 's'!

▸ *Unit 2 (p. 39) • P 3, 6–7 (pp. 42–44)*

Versuche jetzt diese Aufgabe zu lösen:
Wo musst du ein **s** *hinzufügen?*

1 I like_ Maths.
2 Jo play_ football.
3 Ananda can_ play_ hockey.
4 Rabbits eat_ carrots.
5 Ben can_ climb_ trees.
6 Sophie feed_ the pets.

b) 3rd person singular: pronunciation and spelling

3. Person Singular: Aussprache und Schreibweise

Wie beim Plural der Nomen (S. 135, GF 6) gibt es ein paar Besonderheiten:

1 Toby **cleans** the cage. [-nz]
Jack **tells** his friends about Polly. [-lz]
Mrs Shaw **lives** in New Zealand. [-vz]
Ananda **plays** hockey. [-eɪz]

◀ 1 [z] wie das Summen der Biene nach **stimmhaften Konsonanten**, z.B. [n], [l], [v], und nach **Vokalen**,

2 Prunella **pushes** Sophie's bed. [-ʃɪz]
After his homework Jack **watches** TV. [-tʃɪz]
Dan **uses** a blue pencil. [-zɪz]

◀ 2 [ɪz] nach **Zischlauten**, z.B. [ʃ], [tʃ], [z].
(Je nach Schreibung des Infinitivs wird ***es*** oder ***s*** angehängt: *push – pushes, use – uses.*)

Toby **tries** to help Sophie.
Ananda **copies** sentences from the board.

! – ***y*** nach einem **Konsonanten** wird zu ***ies***:
try → tries, copy → copies.
(Aber ***y*** nach einem **Vokal** bleibt: *play → plays.*)

– Die Verben ***do***, ***go*** und ***say*** sind unregelmäßig:
go + es → goes
do + es → does (*I do* [duː] – *she does* [dʌz])
say + s → says (*I say* [seɪ] – *she says* [sez]).

Sophie **goes** to Cotham School in Bristol.

She **does** her homework in her room. [dʌz]

Prunella **says**, 'Sophie, get up!' [sez]

▸ *Unit 2 (p. 39) • P 5 (p. 43)*

c) Negative statements

Verneinte Aussagesätze

I don't need your help with the essay, Prunella.
You don't like me, Sophie.
We don't write essays every day.
Our teachers don't give homework every day.

Bei *I, you, we* und *they* verneinst du eine Aussage im *simple present* mit ***don't*** **+ Infinitiv** (Grundform).
Die Langform von *don't* heißt *do not*.

Prunella doesn't sleep.
Ananda doesn't like the Drama teacher.
Toby doesn't do judo on Saturdays.
Dan doesn't make his bed every morning.

Bei *he/she/it* benutzt du jedoch ***doesn't*** **+ Infinitiv**.
Die Langform von *doesn't* heißt *does not*.

! Das ***s*** der 3. Person Singular steckt schon im *doesn't*.
Also nicht: *She doesn't sleeps.*

Simple present

Verneinte Aussagesätze:

I	don't	like	apples and bananas.
You	don't	like	
He/She/It	doesn't	like	
We/You/They	don't	like	

Polly says,
In *doesn't* + verb
there's just one 's'!

▸ *Unit 2 (p. 40) • P 10–11 (p. 45)*

Jetzt kannst du diese Aufgabe lösen: Wie heißen die verneinten Formen?

1 We play hockey.
2 Toby does judo.
3 Parrots eat meat.
4 Sophie cleans the cage.

GF 8 Possessive determiners Possessivbegleiter

Sophie This is my room.
Prunella Your room, Sophie? No, it's our room.

Wörter wie „mein", „dein", „unser" zeigen an, wem etwas gehört: ***my** room, **your** room, **our** room.*

Im Kasten findest du alle besitzanzeigenden Begleiter.

Possessivbegleiter (Besitzanzeigende Begleiter)

my	room	*mein Zimmer*	our	room	*unser Zimmer*
your	room	*dein/Ihr Zimmer*	your	room	*euer/Ihr Zimmer*
his	room	*sein Zimmer*	their	room	*ihr Zimmer*
her	room	*ihr Zimmer*			
its	room	*sein/ihr Zimmer*			

Your sister isn't nice. But you're nice.
Deine Schwester ... Aber du bist ...

Their name is Carter-Brown. They're new here.
Ihr Name ... Sie sind ...

► *Unit 2 (p. 41) • P 15 (p. 46)*

! Einige Possessivbegleiter kann man leicht mit Kurzformen von *be* verwechseln.
Beachte auch:
- *his* sein/e — *he's* er ist
- *its* sein/e, ihr/e — *it's* er/sie/es ist

GF 9 The possessive form Der *s*-Genitiv

Wenn du sagen willst, dass jemandem etwas gehört, benutzt du den ***s*-Genitiv**.

Englisch: **Jack**'s room
Deutsch: **Jack**s Zimmer

! Anders als im Deutschen wird im Englischen das ***s*** mit einem Apostroph (**'**) angehängt.

Singular: The **dog**'s basket is in the kitchen.
Der Korb des Hundes ...
Our **teacher**'s name is Mr Kingsley.

◄ Im Singular wird ***'s*** an das Nomen angehängt. Für die Aussprache gelten dieselben Regeln wie für das Plural-***s*** (siehe Seite 135, GF 6).

Plural: The **Kapoors**' flat is over the shop.
The **twins**' mum is in New Zealand.

◄ Wenn die Pluralform auf ***s*** endet, hängst du nur einen Apostroph an das Nomen.

This is **Jo and Dan**'s family tree.
Dies ist **Jo**s und **Dan**s Familienstammbaum.

◄ Bei zwei Personen hängst du nur einmal ***'s*** an, und zwar an das zweite Nomen.

Der *s*-Genitiv

Singular: Nomen + 's (the **dog**'s basket)
Plural: Pluralform des Nomens + ' (the **rabbits**' hutch)

► *Unit 2 (p. 41) • P 16 (p. 47)*

Alles klar? Dann löse jetzt diese Aufgabe:
*Wie viele Personen oder Tiere sind es? Sind es **ein** oder **mehrere** Brüder, Kaninchen, Papageien, ...?*

1 **my brother**'s room
2 **my brothers**' room
3 **the rabbits**' hutch
4 **the parrot**'s cage
5 **the twins**' teacher
6 **Jo**'s CDs

Unit 3

GF 10 The simple present Die einfache Form der Gegenwart

a) Yes/No questions

Entscheidungsfragen

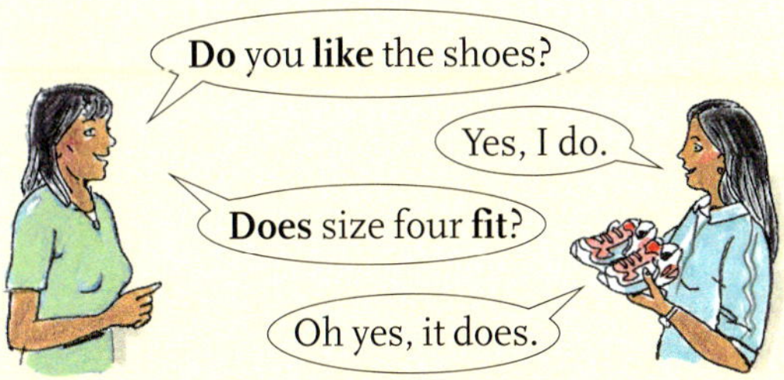

Entscheidungsfragen sind Fragen, auf die man mit „Ja" oder „Nein" antworten kann.

◄ Fragen im *simple present* bildet man mit ***do*** oder ***does***:
- ***do*** bei *I, you, we* und *they*,
- ***does*** bei *he/she/it* (3. Person Singular).

Do you **like** the colour, Ananda?
Do the shoes **look** OK, Mum?
Do we **need** help?

Die Wortstellung ist wie beim Aussagesatz:
*We **need** help.* (Aussagesatz)
*Do we **need** help?* (Fragesatz)

Does Ananda **want** the hockey shoes?
Does she **like** the T-shirt too?
Does it **fit**?

! Das ***s*** der 3. Person Singular steckt jetzt im *Does*.
Das Verb steht ohne Endung:

*Size four **fits**.* (Aussagesatz)
Aber: ***Does** size four **fit**?* (Fragesatz)

Simple present

Entscheidungsfragen:

Do	I	like ...?	Do	we	like ...?
Do	you	like ...?	Do	you	like ...?
Does	he/she/it	like ...?	Do	they	like ...?

Polly says,
In questions with *Does*
there's just one 's'!

▸ *Unit 3 (p. 54) • P 4–6 (p. 59)*

Stelle Fragen. Frage nach den Personen in Klammern.

1 Jack makes models. (Sophie?)
2 Dan and Jo go swimming. (Ananda and Dilip?)
3 Jack and Sophie like music. (Emily?)

b) Short answers

Kurzantworten

Do you **get up** early? – **Yes, I** do. / **No, I** don't.
Does Jack **like** computer games? – **Yes, he** does.
Does Ananda **play** football? – **No, she** doesn't.
Do we **need** a pen? – **Yes, we** do. / **No, we** don't.
Do the shoes **fit**? – **Yes, they** do.

Entscheidungsfragen werden nicht nur mit *Yes* oder *No* beantwortet, sondern mit einer Kurzantwort:
- bei der Antwort *Yes* mit *do* oder *does*,
- bei der Antwort *No* mit *don't* oder *doesn't*.

▸ *Unit 3 (p. 54) • P 7–8 (pp. 59–60)*

Welche Kurzantwort ist richtig?

Does Jack like football? – 1 No, he don't. • 2 No, she doesn't. • 3 No, he doesn't.

c) Questions with question words

When do you **play** tennis, Prunella?
And **where do** you **play**?

How does Uncle Henry **play** without a head?
And **why does** he **take** my racket?

▸ *Unit 3 (p. 55) • P 9–10 (pp. 60–61)*

Fragen mit Fragewörtern

Fragen, die mit einem Fragewort *(When, Where, What, How, Why)* beginnen, bildest du wie Entscheidungsfragen (siehe Seite 139, GF 10 a):

Do *you* ***play*** *tennis?*	(Entscheidungsfrage)
When ***do*** *you* ***play*** *tennis?* *How* ***does*** *he* ***play*** *tennis?*	(Fragen mit Fragewort)

Wie heißen die Sätze richtig? Bringe die Wörter in die richtige Reihenfolge.

1 does – When – come – Uncle Henry?
2 Prunella – play – Where – tennis – does?
3 you – do – do – What – in your free time?

GF 11 Adverbs of frequency: word order Häufigkeitsadverbien: Wortstellung

I never **sleep**.
I usually **go** in all the rooms at night.
I sometimes **play** tennis.

Die Häufigkeitsadverbien *always, usually, often, sometimes, never* drücken aus, wie regelmäßig etwas geschieht oder nicht geschieht.

◂ Sie stehen gewöhnlich direkt **vor dem Vollverb** (z.B. *sleep, go, play*).

Jack always **writes** great stories.
Jack schreibt immer tolle Geschichten.

Prunella **can** often **help** Sophie.
Prunella kann Sophie oft helfen.

But Sophie **doesn't** always **need** her help.
Aber Sophie braucht ihre Hilfe nicht immer.

! Anders als im Deutschen stehen Häufigkeitsadverbien nie zwischen Verb und Objekt:

	Verb	Objekt			Verb		Objekt
Jo often	***plays***	***football***	.	*Jo*	***spielt***	*oft*	***Fußball*** .

I'**m** usually nice to Sophie.
Emily **is** never nice to her.

◂ Häufigkeitsadverbien stehen **hinter** *am/are/is*.

▸ *Unit 3 (p. 56) • P 15 (p. 63)*

Und wieder eine kleine Aufgabe: Welches **always** *steht an der richtigen Stelle,* **1** *oder* **2***?*

Jay **always** (1) goes **always** (2) to basketball games.

GF 12 The verb *(to) have to* Das Verb *(to) have to* („müssen“)

I **have to** get up early every day.
I **have to** help in the kitchen.

Wenn du ausdrücken willst, was du oder andere tun müssen, benutzt du *have to*.

Yes, Jack **has to** get up very early.
He **has to** help. Me too! Me too!

Bei *he/she/it* (3. Person Singular) heißt es *has to*.

! Das ***to* nach *have*** und ***has*** muss immer dabeistehen.

Jack's parents have to **make** breakfast for the guests. But they don't have to **make** lunch.
Jacks Eltern müssen das Frühstück ... machen. Aber sie müssen nicht das Mittagessen machen.

Every evening Jack has to **lay** the table.
But he doesn't have to **go** to yoga.

Do you have to **help** a lot, Jack? – **Yes, I** do.
And does Polly have to **work**? – **No, she** doesn't!

◄ Verneinte Sätze, Fragen und Kurzantworten werden mit *do/does* gebildet – wie bei anderen Verben auch.

(to) have to

+		–		?	
I/you	have to	I/you	don't have to	Do I/you	have to ...?
he/she/it	has to	he/she/it	doesn't have to	Does he/she/it	have to ...?
we/you/they	have to	we/you/they	don't have to	Do we/you/they	have to ...?

▶ *Unit 3 (p. 57) • P 17–18 (pp. 63–64)*

Bringe die Wörter in die richtige Reihenfolge:

1 help – Jack – his mum – has to.
2 doesn't – He – have to – clean – the rooms.
3 he – make – Does – breakfast – have to?

Unit 4

GF 13 Personal pronouns: object forms Personalpronomen: Objektformen

I can't do this homework. You can help me.
You don't know me, but I know you.
There's Jack. **He**'s nice. Can you see him?
Ananda? **She**'s nice. We all like her.
It's my birthday cake. Do you like it?
We go swimming on Fridays. Come with us.
Dan and Jo, **you** like fruit. So this is for you.
The twins? **They** aren't here. I can't see them.

I like her.	Ich mag **sie**. *(Sophie, meine Lehrerin, ...)*
I like it.	Ich mag **sie**. *(meine Schule, die Stadt, ...)*
I like them.	Ich mag **sie**. *(meine Eltern, die Stiefel, ...)*

▶ *Unit 4 (p. 70) • P 3–4 (pp. 75–76)*

◄ Bei den Personalpronomen unterscheiden wir die **Subjektformen** *(I, he, ...)* und die **Objektformen** *(me, him, ...)*.

Anders als im Deutschen gibt es für jede Person nur eine Objektform:
– *You can help me.* *Du kannst **mir** helfen.*
– *You can ask me.* *Du kannst **mich** fragen.*

! Das deutsche „sie“ (Objektform) kann auf Englisch *her, it* oder *them* heißen.

GF 14 *some* and *any* *some* und *any*

We've got **some** crisps and **some** cheese.

Wir haben einige Kartoffelchips und etwas Käse.

◀ *some* steht vor allem in bejahten Aussagesätzen. Es kann „einige“ oder „etwas“ heißen.

But we haven't got **any** orange juice. Have we got **any** biscuits?

Aber wir haben keinen Orangensaft. Haben wir Kekse?

◀ In verneinten Aussagesätzen und in Fragen steht meist *any*.

! Im Deutschen kann man fragen „Haben wir Kekse?“, aber im Englischen wird meist *any* eingefügt: *Have we got any biscuits?*

Yes, of course we've got **some** – with chocolate on.

Ja, natürlich haben wir welche – mit Schokolade.

Angebot: Would you like **some** biscuits? Möchtest du ein paar Kekse?

Bitte: Can I have **some** juice, please? Kann ich (etwas) Saft haben, bitte?

! Wenn du mit einer Frage etwas anbietest oder um etwas bittest, verwendest du *some*.

▸ *Unit 4 (p. 71) • P 7–8 (p. 77)*

Sieh dir die Zeichnungen an: Wo brauchst du some, *wo brauchst du* any?

Toby has got ..., but he hasn't got ...

GF 15 The present progressive Die Verlaufsform der Gegenwart

a) The simple present and the present progressive

Die einfache Form der Gegenwart und die Verlaufsform der Gegenwart

simple present I **help** in the kitchen **every day**.

present progressive **I'm helping** in the kitchen **now**.

Mit dem ***simple present*** (einfache Form der Gegenwart) kannst du über die Gegenwart sprechen, z.B. über das, was jemand jeden Tag tut. (Siehe Seite 136/137, GF 7.)

Wenn du allerdings sagen möchtest, dass jemand **gerade in diesem Moment** etwas tut, musst du das ***present progressive*** (Verlaufsform der Gegenwart) verwenden.
Eine Verlaufsform gibt es im Deutschen nicht.
Wir sagen aber manchmal „Ich bin gerade dabei, fernzusehen“ (= *I'm watching TV*).

b) The present progressive: positive and negative statements

Sophie is helping in the kitchen.
Sophie hilft (gerade) in der Küche.
Emily isn't helping.
Emily hilft (gerade) nicht.
Mr Carter-Brown and Toby are watching TV.
Mr Carter-Brown und Toby schauen (gerade) fern.

Sophie You're making a mess, Prunella.
Prunella I'm not making a mess, Sophie. I'm getting things ready for the party.
Sophie But you're dropping mum's plates ...

Die Verlaufsform der Gegenwart: bejahte und verneinte Aussagesätze

Du bildest das *present progressive* mit *am/are/is* + *-ing*-Form des Verbs:
*Sophie **is helping**. Emily **isn't helping**.*

Die *-ing*-Form ist der Infinitiv + *-ing*:
***help** + **ing** = **helping**.*

! Merke aber:
1 Ein stummes ***e*** fällt weg:
make → making, give → giving.
2 Nach einem einzelnen, betonten Vokal (a, e, i, o, u) wird der Konsonant (p, t, g, m, n, ...) verdoppelt:
drop → dropping, get → getting, run → running.

Present progressive

+		–	
I'm	working	I'm not	working
you're		you aren't	
he's/she's/it's		he isn't/she isn't/it isn't	
we're		we aren't	
you're		you aren't	
they're		they aren't	

▸ *Unit 4 (p. 72) • P 9–11 (pp. 78–79)*

Jetzt kannst du wieder eine Aufgabe lösen:
Wie bildest du die -ing-Formen dieser Verben?
*Ordne die Verben den Buchstaben **A** bis **C** zu, z.B. **1 A**.*

1 clean • 2 come • 3 eat • 4 run • 5 make • 6 sit

A: help → helping
B: ride → riding
C: swim → swimming

c) The present progressive: questions and short answers

Are you working, Dad?
– Yes, I am. / No, I'm not.
Is Sophie's mum making a salad?
– Yes, she is. / No, she isn't.
Are Dan and Jo running in the park?
– Yes, they are./ No, they aren't.
What are you doing? – I'm reading.
Where's Jack going? – To the park.

▸ *Unit 4 (p. 74) • P 12 (p. 79)*

Die Verlaufsform der Gegenwart: Fragen und Kurzantworten

In Fragen sind Subjekt *(you, Sophie's mum)* und *am/are/is* vertauscht.

Die Kurzantworten sind genauso wie beim Verb *be* (siehe S. 132, GF 2 c).

Ein Fragewort *(What, Where)* steht wie im Deutschen am Anfang der Frage.

Bringe die Wörter in die richtige Reihenfolge:

1 Sophie's dad – What's – watching on TV?
2 What's – doing – Mr Green?

Unit 5

GF 16 The simple past Die einfache Form der Vergangenheit

Before the rehearsal the students were nervous.

Mit dem *simple past* kannst du über Vergangenes berichten – z.B. wenn du eine Geschichte erzählst.

Last week Ananda followed Mr Green to the station.
Letzte Woche ist Ananda Mr Green zum Bahnhof gefolgt. /
Letzte Woche folgte Ananda Mr Green zum Bahnhof.

Mit Zeitangaben wie *last week, yesterday, three days ago* sagst du, **wann** etwas geschehen ist oder **wann** jemand etwas getan hat.

GF 17 The simple past of the verb *(to) be*

Die einfache Form der Vergangenheit des Verbs *(to) be*

Beim *simple past* von *be* gibt es nur zwei Formen:
I, he/she/it *was*
you, we, they *were*

◄ Die verneinten Formen heißen ***wasn't*** und ***weren't***.

◄ Die Frage bildest du mit ***Was I ... / Were you ...?*** usw.

◄ Die Kurzantworten heißen ***Yes, I was. / No, you weren't.*** usw.

Where were you after the dress rehearsal?

Fragewörter stehen wie immer am Satzanfang.

► *Unit 5 (p. 86)* • *P 3–5 (pp. 90–91)*

Welche Kurzantwort ist richtig?

Was Sophie in the big pirate scene at the end? –
1 No, she was. 2 Yes, she were.
3 Yes, she was. 4 Yes, she wasn't.

GF 18 The simple past: positive statements
Die einfache Form der Vergangenheit: bejahte Aussagesätze

a) Regular verbs

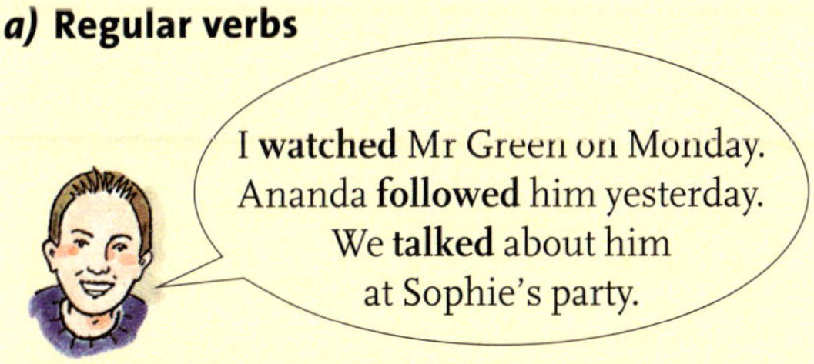

1 Jack phoned Ananda on her mobile.

2 Jack stopped at Mr Green's door.

3 He tried to be very quiet.

4 He wanted to listen to Mr Green.
Mr Green sounded happy.

▸ *Unit 5 (p. 87) • P 6–8 (pp. 91–92)*

Regelmäßige Verben

Bei regelmäßigen Verben bildest du das *simple past* durch Anhängen von ***ed*** an den Infinitiv:
watch → watched, follow → followed, talk → talked.

Es gibt für **alle** Personen nur eine Form.

! Merke aber:

1 Ein stummes ***e*** fällt weg: *phone → phoned.*

2 Einige Konsonanten werden verdoppelt:
stop → stopped, plan → planned
(vergleiche Seite 143, GF 15 b).

3 ***y*** nach einem Konsonanten wird zu ***ied***:
***try** → tried, **hurry** → hurried.*
(Aber ***y*** nach einem **Vokal** bleibt: *pla**y** → pla**yed**.*)

4 Nach ***t*** und ***d*** wird die ***ed***-Endung [ɪd] ausgesprochen: *wanted, sounded.*

b) Irregular verbs

Lots of people went to the Spring Show.
(Infinitiv: **go**)

The Hansons came home late after the show.
(Infinitiv: **come**)

Mr Hanson said, 'The show was great!'
(Infinitiv: **say**)

After the show they had dinner very late.
(Infinitiv: **have**)
One of the pirates had a parrot.
(Infinitiv: **have got**)

▸ *Unit 5 (p. 88) • P 9 (p. 92)*

Unregelmäßige Verben

Wie im Deutschen gibt es auch im Englischen eine Reihe unregelmäßiger Verben, deren *simple past*-Formen du einzeln lernen musst.

▸ *Unregelmäßige Verben (p. 178)*

! *had* ist die *simple past*-Form von *have* und von *have got*.
Also nie: *One of the pirates ~~had got~~ a parrot,*
sondern: *... had a parrot.*

Welche dieser Formen sind simple past-*Formen?*

1 talked • 2 go • 3 had • 4 went • 5 say
6 were • 7 came • 8 tell • 9 looked • 10 told

GF 19 Extra The simple past: negative statements

Die einfache Form der Vergangenheit: verneinte Aussagesätze

◄ Eine Aussage im *simple past* verneinst du immer mit ***didn't*** + **Infinitiv**.

Verneinte Aussagesätze

Merke:

Simple present	I don't **play** the clarinet.	Jo doesn't **play** the clarinet.
Simple past	I didn't **play** the clarinet.	Jo didn't **play** the clarinet.

► *Unit 5 (p. 89)* • *P 13–15 (pp. 93–94)*

GF 20 Extra The simple past: questions and short answers

Die einfache Form der Vergangenheit: Fragen und Kurzantworten

Did your dad **go** to the Spring Show, Jo?
– **Yes, he** did. / **No, he** didn't.

Did your parents **like** the show, Jack?
– **Yes, they** did. / **No, they** didn't.

What did all the teachers **say**?
When did the show **finish**?

◄ Fragen im *simple past* bildest du immer mit ***did***:
Did he go?
(Nicht: *Did he ~~went~~?*)

Das Fragewort steht wie immer am Anfang.

Fragen

Merke:

Simple present	Do you **play** the clarinet?	Does Jo **play** the clarinet?
Simple past	Did you **play** the clarinet?	Did Jo **play** the clarinet?

► *Unit 5 (p. 89)* • *P 16 (p. 94)*

Kannst du jetzt die Fragen vervollständigen?

1 Jack's parents went to the show. Did Mr Shaw ... to the show too?
2 The Carter-Browns liked the show. ... the Hansons ... the show too?

Unit 6

GF 21 Word order in subordinate clauses Die Wortstellung in Nebensätzen

▸ *Unit 6 (p. 103) • P 4 (p. 107)*

Anders als im Deutschen ist die Wortstellung im Nebensatz genauso wie im Hauptsatz, nämlich **Subjekt – Verb (– Objekt)**:

Hauptsatz			Nebensatz			
S	V	O		S	V	O
I	*like*	*the library*	*because*	*I*	*like*	*books*.
		…,	*weil*	*ich*	*Bücher*	*mag*.

Wieder eine kleine Aufgabe: Welches ist der Nebensatz, **A** *oder* **B**?

1 Jack doesn't go to football matches (A) because he hates sport. (B)

2 When it's hot (A) the Bristol kids often go swimming. (B)

GF 22 The simple present and the present progressive in contrast
Die einfache Form und die Verlaufsform der Gegenwart im Vergleich

◂ Dan redet über das, was die Zwillinge und ihr Vater **regelmäßig** tun. Er verwendet die einfache Form der Gegenwart *(simple present)*.

Wörter wie ***often, usually, on Saturdays, every day*** zeigen dir, dass du die einfache Form verwenden musst.

◂ Jo redet über das, was sie **im Moment** tun oder nicht tun. Er verwendet die Verlaufsform der Gegenwart *(present progressive)*.

Das Wort ***now*** zeigt dir, dass du die Verlaufsform verwenden musst.

! Verben wie *know, want, need, like, hate, hear, see* werden normalerweise nicht im *present progressive* verwendet.

Simple present and present progressive

Simple present:

- Die **einfache Form** der Gegenwart *(simple present)* drückt aus, dass jemand etwas **wiederholt** tut:
  Polly usually cleans her cage on Saturdays.
- Die **einfache Form** wird auch verwendet, um **aufeinanderfolgende Handlungen** zu beschreiben, z.B. wenn man eine Geschichte erzählt (oft mit *First ..., then ..., after that ...*):
  First Ananda follows Mr Green to the station, then she watches him. After that she calls Jack on her mobile.

Present progressive:

Die **Verlaufsform** der Gegenwart *(present progressive)* drückt aus, dass jemand **gerade im Moment** etwas tut. Die Handlung ist **noch nicht abgeschlossen**:

Look, Polly is cleaning her cage now.

▶ *Unit 6 (p. 104) • P 7–9 (p. 108)*

Polly is cleaning her cage.

Und jetzt noch eine Aufgabe: Welche Sätze drücken aus, dass jemand gerade etwas tut?

1 Jo sometimes goes to bed late.
2 I'm doing my homework now.
3 Look, you're making a mess with the glue.
4 Mum usually does yoga on Mondays.
5 Ananda is helping her mum and dad in the shop.

Lösungen der Grammar-File-Aufgaben

p.131 he, they, you, I, we (5)
p.132 **3, 5**
p.135 **1, 4**
p.136 **2, 6**
p.137 1 We **don't play** hockey.
2 Toby **doesn't do** judo.
3 Parrots **don't eat** meat.
4 Sophie **doesn't clean** the cage.
p.138 1 Singular (eine Person)
2 Plural (mehrere Personen)
3 Plural (mehrere Tiere)
4 Singular (ein Tier)
5 Plural (mehrere Personen)
6 Singular (eine Person)
p.139/1 1 **Does** Sophie **make** models?
2 **Do** Ananda and Dilip **go** swimming?
3 **Does** Emily **like** music?
p.139/2 3
p.140/1 1 When does Uncle Henry come?
2 Where does Prunella play tennis?
3 What do you do in your free time?
p.140/2 1 (Jay always goes to basketball games.)
p.141 1 Jack has to help his mum.
2 He doesn't have to clean the rooms.
3 Does he have to make breakfast?
p.142 Toby has got **some** biscuits, but he hasn't got **any** orange juice.
p.143/1 **1A, 2B, 3A, 4C, 5B, 6C**
p.143/2 1 What's Sophie's dad watching on TV?
2 What's Mr Green doing?
p.144 3
p.145 **1, 3, 4, 6, 7, 9, 10**
p.146 1 Did Mr Shaw **go** to the show too?
2 **Did** the Hansons **like** the show too?
p.147 **1B, 2A**
p.148 **2, 3, 5**

English sounds (Englische Laute)

Die Lautschrift in den eckigen Klammern zeigt dir, wie ein Wort ausgesprochen und betont wird.
In der folgenden Übersicht findest du alle Lautzeichen.

Vokale (Selbstlaute)

[iː]	green	[eɪ]	skate
[i]	happy	[aɪ]	time
[ɪ]	in	[ɔɪ]	boy
[e]	yes	[əʊ]	old
[æ]	black	[aʊ]	now
[ɑː]	park	[ɪə]	here
[ɒ]	song	[eə]	where
[ɔː]	morning	[ʊə]	tour
[uː]	blue		
[ʊ]	book		
[ʌ]	mum		
[ɜː]	T-shirt		
[ə]	a partner		

Konsonanten (Mitlaute)

[b]	box	[f]	full
[p]	play	[v]	very
[d]	dad	[s]	sister
[t]	ten	[z]	please
[g]	good	[ʃ]	shop
[k]	cat	[ʒ]	television
[m]	mum	[tʃ]	teacher
[n]	no	[dʒ]	Germany
[ŋ]	sing	[θ]	thanks
[l]	hello	[ð]	this
[r]	red	[h]	he
[w]	we		
[j]	you		

Tipp

Am besten kannst du dir die Aussprache der einzelnen Lautzeichen einprägen, wenn du dir zu jedem Zeichen ein einfaches Wort merkst – das [iː] ist der **green**-Laut, das [eɪ] ist der **skate**-Laut usw.

Betonung

['] und [ˌ] sind **Betonungszeichen**.
Sie stehen immer vor der betonten Silbe.

['] zeigt die Hauptbetonung,
[ˌ] zeigt die Nebenbetonung.

Beispiel:
mobile phone [ˌməʊbaɪl 'fəʊn]
Hauptbetonung auf **phone**,
Nebenbetonung auf der ersten Silbe: **mobile**

Der „Bindebogen"

Der **Bindebogen** [‿] zeigt an, dass zwei Wörter beim Sprechen aneinandergebunden und wie ein Wort gesprochen werden.

Beispiele:
What colour is ...? [ˌwɒt 'kʌlər‿ɪz]
Mum and Dad [ˌmʌm‿ən 'dæd]
This is ... ['ðɪs‿ɪz]

The English alphabet (Das englische Alphabet)

a	[eɪ]	**h**	[eɪtʃ]	**o**	[əʊ]	**v**	[viː]
b	[biː]	**i**	[aɪ]	**p**	[piː]	**w**	['dʌbljuː]
c	[siː]	**j**	[dʒeɪ]	**q**	[kjuː]	**x**	[eks]
d	[diː]	**k**	[keɪ]	**r**	[ɑː]	**y**	[waɪ]
e	[iː]	**l**	[el]	**s**	[es]	**z**	[zed]
f	[ef]	**m**	[em]	**t**	[tiː]		
g	[dʒiː]	**n**	[en]	**u**	[juː]		

Diese Wörterverzeichnisse findest du in deinem Englischbuch:

- Das **Vocabulary** (Vokabelverzeichnis – S. 150–178) enthält alle Wörter und Wendungen, die du lernen musst. Sie stehen in der Reihenfolge, in der sie in den Units vorkommen.
- Das **Dictionary** besteht aus zwei alphabetischen Wörterlisten zum Nachschlagen:
  Englisch – Deutsch: S. 179–191
  Deutsch – Englisch: S. 192–200.

So ist das Vocabulary aufgebaut:

- Hier siehst du, wo die Wörter vorkommen.
  p. 21/A 3 = Seite 21, Abschnitt 3
  p. 27/P 7 = Seite 27, Übung 7

  p. 21/A 3 **mobile phone** [ˌməʊbaɪl ˈfəʊn]
  p. 27/P 7 **our** [ˈaʊə]

- Die Lautschrift zeigt dir, wie ein Wort ausgesprochen und betont wird. (→ Englische Laute: S. 149)

  p. 10 **empty** [ˈempti]
  full [fʊl]

- Eingerückte Wörter lernst du am besten zusammen mit dem vorausgehenden Wort, weil die beiden zusammengehören.
- Diese Kästen solltest du dir besonders gut ansehen.

  you – I / me
  you
  1. du **You** can sing.
  2. dich I can see yo...

- In diesen Kästen findest du Wörter und Wendungen, die du sicher schon aus deinem bisherigen Englischunterricht kennst.

  Remember?
  Du kennst bestimmt auch schon
  At school (In ...

Abkürzungen / Symbole

p.	=	page (Seite)
pp.	=	pages (Seiten)
pl	=	*plural* (Mehrzahl)
no pl	=	*no plural*
jn.	=	jemanden
jm.	=	jemandem
◂▸		ist das „Gegenteil"-Zeichen. Beispiel: **full ◂▸ empty** (**full** ist das Gegenteil von **empty**)
!		Hier stehen Hinweise auf Besonderheiten, bei denen man leicht Fehler machen kann.

Tipps zum Wörterlernen findest du im Skills File auf den Seiten 122 und 123.

'Hello' and 'Welcome'

Remember? (Erinnerst du dich?)

pp. 6–8 Du kennst bestimmt schon viele englische Wörter und Sätze. Hier sind einige, die dir sicher schon begegnet sind:

Hi, I'm Tatjana.	Hallo, ich bin Tatjana.	**I've got a brother and a sister.**	Ich habe einen Bruder und eine Schwester.
What's your name?	Wie heißt du?	**We live in Frankfurt, in ... Street.**	Wir wohnen in Frankfurt, in der ...straße.
– Hello. My name is ...	– Hallo. Ich heiße ... / Mein Name ist ...	**My favourite colour is ...**	Meine Lieblingsfarbe ist ...
Where are you from?	Wo kommst du her?	**I like apples.**	Ich mag Äpfel.
– I'm from ...	– Ich komme aus ... / Ich bin aus ...	**I don't like bananas.**	Ich mag keine Bananen. / Ich mag Bananen nicht.
My mum and dad are from ...	Meine Mutter und mein Vater kommen aus ...	**Can you sing a song in English?**	Kannst du ein Lied auf Englisch singen?
How old are you?	Wie alt bist du?	**– Yes, I can. / No, I can't.**	– Ja, kann ich. / Nein, kann ich nicht.
– I'm ... years old.	– Ich bin ... Jahre alt.		

p. 6	**pretty** [ˈprɪti]	hübsch	
	What about you? [ˌwɒt‿əˌbaʊt ˈjuː]	Und du? / Was ist mit dir?	I'm from Bristol in England. **What about you?**
p. 8	**Welcome (to Bristol).** [ˈwelkəm]	Willkommen (in Bristol).	
	I can talk to ... [tɔːk]	ich kann mit ... reden / ich kann mich mit ... unterhalten	
	my partner [ˈpɑːtnə]	mein Partner / meine Partnerin	

Aussprache

Wie ein englisches Wort ausgesprochen wird, zeigt dir die **Lautschrift**. Sie steht in eckigen Klammern:

- **welcome** ['welkəm]
- **talk** [tɔːk]
- **partner** ['pɑːtnə]

Zwei Dinge kannst du an diesen Beispielen sehen:
Erstens werden englische Wörter oft anders ausgesprochen, als man denkt.
Zweitens enthält die Lautschrift auch ein paar „komische" Zeichen wie [ə], [ɔː] oder [ɑː]:
[ə] ist ein schwaches „e" wie am Ende von „bitt**e**".
[ɔː] kennst du aus dem Wort „baseb**a**ll".
[ɑː] ist ein langes „a" wie in „Kr**a**m".

→ Übersicht über die englischen Laute und Lautschriftzeichen: S. 149

now [naʊ]	nun, jetzt	[aʊ] klingt wie das „au" in „bl**au**".
Meet Jack. [miːt]	Lerne Jack kennen. / Triff Jack.	
this is ['ðɪs‿ɪz]	dies ist	[ð] gibt es im Deutschen nicht. Der Laut klingt etwa so, als ob jemand die weichen „s"-Laute in „**S**en**s**e" lispelt.
he's [hiːz]	er ist	= he is [z] ist ein weiches „s" wie in „le**s**en".
she's [ʃiːz]	sie ist	= she is [ʃ] klingt wie das „sch" in „**sch**ön".
from Bristol **too** [tuː]	auch aus Bristol	❗ **too** steht am Ende des Satzes.
new [njuː]	neu	new ◂▸ old
with [wɪð]	mit	
his [hɪz]	sein, seine	
twin brother ['twɪn brʌðə]	Zwillingsbruder	Dan is Jo's **twin brother**. Dan and Jo are **twins**. [ʌ] klingt ähnlich wie das kurze „a" in „K**a**mm".
they're [ðeə] = **they are** [ðeɪ‿ɑː]	sie sind	This is Jo.  This is Dan. **They're** twins.
I can talk about ... [ə'baʊt]	ich kann über ... reden	
page [peɪdʒ]	(Buch-, Heft-)Seite	Abkürzung: **p.** 5 = **page** 5 • **pp.** 5–7 = **pages** 5–7

Remember?

p. 9 Erinnerst du dich an diese Wörter aus deinem bisherigen Englischunterricht?

boys

girls

trees

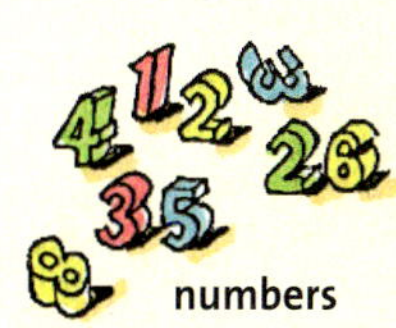
numbers

He is happy.

She is not happy.

Listen to the band!

We can play football.

a boat
water

a skateboard

rooms
a big house

	it's [ɪts]	er/sie/es ist	= it is
	a great place [ə greɪt 'pleɪs]	ein großartiger Ort/Platz, ein toller Ort/Platz	
	I can see a ... [siː]	ich kann ein/eine ... sehen	[s] ist ein hartes, scharfes „s" wie in „lassen".
	photo ['fəʊtəʊ]	Foto	**!** **auf** dem Foto = **in** the photo [əʊ] kennst du aus dem Wort „Show".
	kite [kaɪt]	Drachen	[aɪ] klingt wie das „ei" in „Kleid".
p. 10	**Park Road** [ˌpɑːk 'rəʊd]	Parkstraße	

a **kite**

Betonung

['] und [ˌ] sind Betonungszeichen.
Sie stehen immer vor der betonten Silbe.

['] zeigt die Hauptbetonung,
[ˌ] zeigt die Nebenbetonung.

Betonungszeichen helfen, die Wörter richtig zu betonen:
– Im Deutschen heißt es ***Park**straße*.
– Im Englischen sagt man *Park **Road*** [ˌpɑːk 'rəʊd]
(Hauptbetonung auf dem Wort „road").

when [wen]	wenn	Are you happy **when** the house is empty?
empty ['empti]	leer	
full [fʊl]	voll	full ◂▸ empty
I close ... [kləʊz]	ich schließe ... / ich mache ... zu	
thing [θɪŋ]	Ding, Sache	
I open ... ['əʊpən]	ich öffne ... / ich mache ... auf	open ◂▸ close
I push ... [pʊʃ]	ich drücke ... / ich schiebe ... / ich stoße ...	
I pull ... [pʊl]	ich ziehe ...	push ◂▸ pull
I drop ... [drɒp]	ich lasse ... fallen	[ɒ] klingt wie das „o" in „Bock" oder „doch".
then [ðen]	dann, danach	
I laugh [lɑːf]	ich lache	

you – I / me

you

1. **du**	**You** can sing.	=	**Du** kannst singen.
2. **dich**	I can see **you**.	=	Ich kann **dich** sehen.
3. **dir**	I can play with **you**.	=	Ich kann mit **dir** spielen.

I / me

1. **ich**	**I** can sing.	=	**Ich** kann singen.
2. **mich**	Can you see **me**?	=	Kannst du **mich** sehen?
3. **mir**	Play with **me**.	=	Spiel mit **mir**.

	you look [lʊk]	du schaust / du guckst	
	but [bət, bʌt]	aber	Sophie is a girl, **but** Jack is a boy.
	You can't find me. [faɪnd]	Du kannst mich nicht finden.	
	That's me. [ˌðæts 'miː]	Das bin ich.	
p. 11	**picture** ['pɪktʃə]	Bild	**!** **auf** dem Bild = **in** the picture [tʃ] klingt wie „tsch" in „**tsch**üs".
	I think [θɪŋk]	ich glaube / ich meine / ich denke	[θ] gibt es im Deutschen nicht. Der Laut klingt etwa so, als ob jemand den harten „s"-Laut in „be**ss**er" lispelt. [ŋ] ist wie „ng" in „Di**ng**" oder das „n" in „pi**n**k".
	That's right. [ˌðæts 'raɪt]	Das ist richtig. / Das stimmt.	

very nice [ˌveri 'naɪs]	sehr schön, sehr nett	**!** Das englische „v" wird wie in „Vampir" und „Vase" gesprochen – nicht wie in „Vater"!
You can take the baby. [teɪk]	Du kannst das Baby nehmen.	
You can help me. [help]	Du kannst mir helfen.	
in here [ɪn 'hɪə]	hier drinnen	
Who are you? [huː]	Wer bist du?	
there [ðeə]	da, dort	

Remember?

p. 12 Du kennst bestimmt auch schon viele englische Wörter zu den Themen „Schule" und „Familie":

At school (In der Schule)

a classroom

A family [1]

Mr[2] Scott, the father (dad)
Mrs[3] Scott, the mother (mum)
Sally Scott, Philip's sister
Philip Scott, Sally's brother
Their pets: Bob, the dog
Bella, the cat
Their friends: Jennifer Ray
Robbie Carter

The Scotts live in Bristol.
Die Scotts leben/wohnen in Bristol.

[1] a family – two families • [2] Mr ['mɪstə] • [3] Mrs ['mɪsɪz]

at 7 Hamilton Street [striːt]	in der Hamiltonstraße 7	
their father / their mother [ðeə]	ihr Vater / ihre Mutter	Dan and Jo and **their** father 
today [tə'deɪ]	heute	
the last day [ˌlɑːst 'deɪ]	der letzte Tag	
of the summer holidays [əv ðə ˌsʌmə 'hɒlədeɪz]	der Sommerferien	
Sorry, I'm late. ['sɒri], [leɪt]	Entschuldigung, dass ich zu spät bin/komme.	
shopping list ['ʃɒpɪŋ lɪst]	Einkaufsliste	
Let's look at the list. [lets]	Sehen wir uns die Liste an. / Lasst uns die Liste ansehen.	
you need ... [niːd]	du brauchst ... / du benötigst ...	
Me too. [tuː]	Ich auch.	I need a new school bag. – **Me too.**
pencil sharpener ['pensl ʃɑːpnə]	Bleistiftanspitzer	a **pencil sharpener** 

exercise book ['eksəsaɪz bʊk]	Schulheft, Übungsheft	
exercise ['eksəsaɪz]	Übung, Aufgabe	
for school [fə, fɔː]	für die Schule	I need a glue stick **for school**, Dad.
Let's go. [ˌlets 'gəʊ]	Auf geht's! (*wörtlich:* Lass uns gehen.)	
you two	ihr zwei	
I can say ... [seɪ]	ich kann ... sagen	

Remember?

p. 13

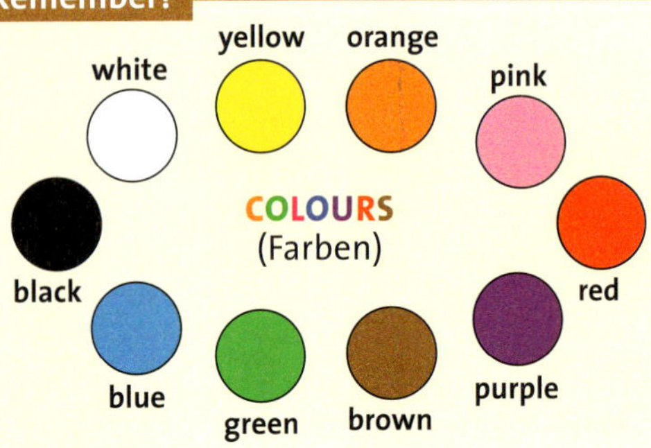

What colour is ...? [ˌwɒt 'kʌlər‿ɪz]	Welche Farbe hat ...?	**What colour is** your pencil? – It's green. And **what colour is** your school bag? – It's red.

Aussprache

Der **Bindebogen** [‿] zeigt an, dass zwei Wörter beim Sprechen aneinandergebunden und wie ein Wort gesprochen werden.

What colour is ...? [ˌwɒt 'kʌlər‿ɪz]
Mum and Dad [ˌmʌm‿ən 'dæd]
This is ... ['ðɪs‿ɪz]

plate [pleɪt]	Teller	a **plate** 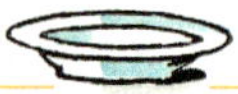
Oh well ... [əʊ 'wel]	Na ja ... / Na gut ...	

Remember?

p. 14

The days of the week

It's Monday morning ...

flat [flæt]	Wohnung	
over the shop [ˌəʊvə ðə 'ʃɒp]	über dem Laden / über dem Geschäft	
Well, ... [wel]	Nun, ... / Also, ...	**Well,** is your new school nice?
uniform ['juːnɪfɔːm]	Uniform	
tomorrow [tə'mɒrəʊ]	morgen	

	the first day [fɜ:st]	der erste Tag	[ɜ:] kennst du aus dem Wort „T-Sh**ir**t". (Nicht das „r" mitsprechen!)
	at the new school	an/auf der neuen Schule	
	Stop that! ['stɒp ðæt]	Hör auf damit! / Lass das!	
	You can go to the shop. [gəʊ]	Du kannst zum Laden gehen.	
	Why me? [waɪ]	Warum ich?	You can help your father now. – **Why me?**
	poem ['pəʊɪm]	Gedicht	
	week [wi:k]	Woche	
p. 15	**newspaper** ['nju:speɪpə]	Zeitung	
	I can have breakfast. [həv 'brekfəst]	Ich kann frühstücken.	
	What's your telephone number? ['telɪfəʊn]	Was ist deine Telefonnummer?	
	o [əʊ], **zero** ['zɪərəʊ]	null	! Wenn man seine Telefonnummer sagt, benutzt man **o** [əʊ]: 5 0 7 9 ... = five **o** seven nine ...
	double ['dʌbl]	zweimal, doppelt, Doppel-	My phone number is 5 0 7 9 3 3 2. (five o seven nine **double** three two)
	I can do tricks. [du: 'trɪks]	Ich kann (Zauber-)Kunststücke (machen).	
p. 16	**Bed and Breakfast (B&B)** [ˌbed‿ən 'brekfəst]	Frühstückspension (*wörtlich:* Bett und Frühstück)	
	parrot ['pærət]	Papagei	
	They welcome you to ...	Sie heißen dich in ... willkommen	
	wheelchair ['wi:ltʃeə]	Rollstuhl	[eə] kennst du aus dem Wort „f**air**". (Nicht das „r" mitsprechen!)
	at work [wɜ:k]	bei der Arbeit / am Arbeitsplatz	

Remember?

What's the time? (Wie spät ist es?)

It's eleven o'clock. | **It's quarter past 11.** (*oder:* **11.15**) | **It's half past 11.** (*oder:* **11.30**) | **It's quarter to 12.** (*oder:* **11.45**)

to  **past**

!  Englisch: **half past 11**
Deutsch: **halb zwölf**

p. 17	**Excuse me, ...** [ɪk'skju:z mi:]	Entschuldigung, ... / Entschuldigen Sie, ...	

„Entschuldigung"

Excuse me, ...
sagt man, wenn man jemanden anspricht, z.B. wenn man um etwas bittet:
Excuse me, what's the time, please?

Sorry, ...
sagt man, wenn man sich für etwas entschuldigen möchte:
Sorry, I'm late.

You're welcome.	Gern geschehen. / Nichts zu danken.	

welcome

• Wenn du jemanden willkommen heißen willst:	**Welcome to** Germany!	**Willkommen in** Deutschland!
• Wenn sich jemand bei dir bedankt hat:	*A:* What's the time, please? *B:* Half past seven. *A:* Thank you. *B:* **You're welcome.**	*A:* Wie spät ist es, bitte? *B:* Halb acht. *A:* Danke. *B:* **Bitte, gern geschehen. / Nichts zu danken.**

! Nie: **Thank you. – ~~Please~~.** Sondern: **Thank you. – You're welcome.**

Good luck (with ...)! [ˌgʊd 'lʌk]	Viel Glück (bei/mit ...)!	
trip [trɪp]	Reise; Ausflug	
back to Germany [ˌbæk tə 'dʒɜːməni]	zurück nach Deutschland	[dʒ] kennst du aus „Job" und „Jeans".

Unit 1: New school, new friends

Remember?

p. 18 Hier sind wieder einige Wörter, die du wahrscheinlich schon kennst.

lots of ['lɒts_əv]	eine Menge, viele, viel	
comic ['kɒmɪk]	Comic-Heft	I've got **lots of comics**.
there's [ðəz, ðeəz]	es ist (vorhanden); es gibt	= there is
there are ['ðər_ə, 'ðeər_ɑː]	es sind (vorhanden); es gibt	

There's ... / There are ...

Du kennst bereits **there** (= „da, dort"): **That's your room there.**

Mit **There's ...** und **There are ...** kannst du ausdrücken, ob etwas vorhanden ist oder nicht.
Im Deutschen sagt man meist „Es gibt ..." oder „Es ist/sind ...".

There's a football in my photo. But **there isn't a** skateboard in my photo.	Auf meinem Foto **ist ein** Fußball. Aber **es ist kein** Skateboard auf meinem Foto.
Are there skateboards in your photo? – Yes, **there are**. / No, **there aren't**.	**Gibt es** Skateboards auf deinem Foto? – Ja (, **gibt es**). / Nein (, **gibt es nicht**).
There are three books on the table.	**Es sind/Es liegen** drei Bücher auf dem Tisch.

! Nie: ~~**It gives**~~ ..., sondern immer: **There's ... / There are ...**

marmalade ['mɑːməleɪd]	(Orangen-)Marmelade	**!** Deutsch: Marmelade – Englisch: marmalade

p. 19	**in the morning**	am Morgen, morgens	
	word [wɜːd]	Wort	
	clock [klɒk]	(Wand-, Stand-, Turm-)Uhr	**clocks** 
	lamp [læmp]	Lampe	
	milk [mɪlk]	Milch	
	mobile phone ['məʊbaɪl]	Mobiltelefon, Handy	! Deutsch: **Handy** – Englisch: **mobile (phone)**
	money ['mʌni]	Geld	
	sandwich box ['sænwɪtʃ]	Brotdose	 **box** = Kasten, Kästchen, Kiste
p. 20/A 1	**before** [bɪ'fɔː]	vor *(zeitlich)*	
	lessons ['lesnz]	Unterricht	
	lesson ['lesn]	(Unterrichts-)Stunde	
	student ['stjuːdənt]	Schüler/in; Student/in	
	nervous ['nɜːvəs]	nervös, aufgeregt	
	first [fɜːst]	zuerst, als Erstes	
	clever ['klevə]	klug, schlau	
	mad [mæd]	verrückt	
	Don't listen to Dan. [dəʊnt]	Hör nicht / Hört nicht auf Dan.	
	Come. [kʌm]	Komm. / Kommt.	
	Sit with me. [sɪt]	Setz dich / Setzt euch zu mir.	
p. 20/A 2	**wrong** [rɒŋ]	falsch, verkehrt	That's wrong. ◂▸ That's right.
p. 21/A 3	**our** ['aʊə]	unser, unsere	We're twins. **Our** names are Dan and Jo.
	her [hə, hɜː]	ihr, ihre	Ananda is from Bristol. **Her** dad is from Uganda.
	together [tə'geðə]	zusammen	
	I'm sorry.	Entschuldigung. / Tut mir leid.	

sorry

Mit **sorry** kannst du …

• dich entschuldigen:	**Sorry**, I'm late.	**Entschuldigung**, dass ich zu spät komme.
• sagen, dass dir etwas leidtut:	My mum and dad aren't together. – Oh, **I'm sorry.**	Meine Mutter und mein Vater sind nicht zusammen. – Oh, **das tut mir leid**.
• nachfragen, wenn du etwas nicht richtig verstanden hast:	It's eleven o'clock. – **Sorry?**	Es ist elf Uhr. – **Wie bitte?**

teacher ['tiːtʃə]	Lehrer/Lehrerin	Mr Keller is my English **teacher**.

Remember?

p. 22

p. 22/A 6	**form** [fɔːm]	(Schul-)Klasse	Ananda is in **Form** 7PK.
	Tell me your names. [tel]	Sagt mir eure Namen.	**Tell** your teacher **about** your pets. (= Erzähle ... von ... / Berichte ... über ...)
	PE [ˌpiː‿ˈiː]	Sportunterricht, Turnen	
	enough [ɪˈnʌf]	genug	
	quiet [ˈkwaɪət]	leise, still, ruhig	
	joke [dʒəʊk]	Witz	Can you tell me a **joke**? I like **jokes**.
	bad [bæd]	schlecht, schlimm	bad ◂▸ good
	Can you remember that? [rɪˈmembə]	Kannst du dir das merken?	
p. 22/A 7	**or** [ɔː]	oder	Is Sophie in Form 7PK **or** in Form 7BW?
p. 22/A 8	**alphabet** [ˈælfəbet]	Alphabet	
	Throw a ball. [θrəʊ]	Wirf einen Ball.	
	Climb a tree. [klaɪm]	Klettere auf einen Baum.	Can cats **climb** trees? – Yes, they can.
	Write ... [raɪt]	Schreibe ...	
	Do what I do. [duː]	Tue, was ich tue.	
p. 22/A 9	**Spell ...** [spel]	Buchstabiere ...	
p. 23/A 10	**timetable** [ˈtaɪmteɪbl]	Stundenplan	
	Take out ... [ˌteɪk‿ˈaʊt]	Nehmt ... heraus	**Take out** your English books, please.
	Write down ... [ˌraɪt ˈdaʊn]	Schreibt ... auf	
	at 8.45 [ət, æt]	um 8.45	
	on Tuesday	am Dienstag	

on

The first lesson **on Tuesday** is English.	Die erste Stunde **am** Dienstag ist Englisch.
Write the words **on the board**, please.	Schreib die Wörter **an** die Tafel, bitte.
Write your names **on your exercise books**, please.	Schreibt eure Namen **auf** eure Hefte, bitte.
Your ruler is **on your chair**.	Dein Lineal liegt **auf** deinem Stuhl.
Look at the pictures **on page 24**.	Seht euch die Bilder **auf** Seite 24 an.

with [wɪð]	bei	**!** **with** = **1.** mit – Look, there's Jo **with** his brother. **2.** bei – It's English **with** Mr Kingsley.

School subjects [1]

Art [ɑːt]	Kunst	**Maths** [mæθs]	Mathematik
Biology [baɪˈɒlədʒi]	Biologie	**Music** [ˈmjuːzɪk]	Musik
Drama [ˈdrɑːmə]	Schauspiel, darstellende Kunst	**PE** [2] [ˌpiː‿ˈiː]	Turnen, Sportunterricht
French [frentʃ]	Französisch	**RE** [3] [ˌɑːr‿ˈiː]	Religion, Religionsunterricht
Geography [dʒiˈɒɡrəfi]	Geografie, Erdkunde	**Science** [ˈsaɪəns]	Naturwissenschaft
German [ˈdʒɜːmən]	Deutsch		
History [ˈhɪstri]	Geschichte		

[1] [ˈsʌbdʒɪkts] Schulfächer [2] Physical Education [ˌfɪzɪkəl‿edʒuˈkeɪʃn] [3] Religious Education [rɪˌlɪdʒəs‿edʒuˈkeɪʃn]

	after [ˈɑːftə]	nach *(zeitlich)*	after lessons ◂▸ before lessons
	break [breɪk]	Pause	Morning **break** is at 10.45 at Cotham School.
p. 23/A 11	**lunch** [lʌntʃ]	Mittagessen	**Lunch** is at 1.05.

p. 24/A 13	**food** [fu:d]	Essen; Lebensmittel	
	really ['rɪəli]	wirklich	
	I haven't got a chair. ['hævnt gɒt]	Ich habe keinen Stuhl.	I've got a sister, but **I haven't got a** brother.

at

Let's sit **at that table** there.	Setzen wir uns **an** den Tisch dort.
Look **at the board**, please.	Seht **an** die Tafel, bitte.
Let's look **at the list** now.	Sehen wir uns jetzt mal die Liste **an**.
The Shaws live **at 7 Hamilton Street**.	... **in** der Hamiltonstraße 7
Jo and Dan are **at school**, and Mrs Hanson is **at work**.	... **in** der Schule, ... **bei** der Arbeit
At 8.45 it's English with Mr Kingsley.	**Um** 8.45 ...

	bank robber ['bæŋk ˌrɒbə]	Bankräuber/in	
	all [ɔ:l]	alle; alles	Sophie, Ananda, Jack – they're **all** in Form 7PK. We need pens, felt tips and pencils. That's **all**.
	like [laɪk]	wie	My pencil case is **like** your pencil case.
	him [hɪm]	ihn; ihm	! **him** = **1.** ihn – There's Jack. Can you see **him**? **2.** ihm – Let's help **him**.
	idea [aɪ'dɪə]	Idee, Einfall	[ɪə] klingt wie das „ier" in „**hier**".
	What have we got next? [nekst]	Was haben wir als Nächstes?	
p. 24/A 14	**boring** ['bɔ:rɪŋ]	langweilig	
	class [klɑ:s]	(Schul-)Klasse	I'm in **Class** 5 now, and my sister is in **Class** 8.
p. 25/P 1	**different (from)** ['dɪfrənt]	verschieden, unterschiedlich; anders (als)	Cats and dogs are **different** – cats can climb, but dogs can't. Cats are **different from** dogs. ! anders **als** = different **from**

Classroom English

p. 28/P 9

Can we +work with a partner?	Können wir mit einem Partner/einer Partnerin arbeiten?
+What page are we on, please?	Auf welcher Seite sind wir, bitte?
+What's for homework? ['həʊmwɜ:k]	Was haben wir als Hausaufgabe auf?
Sorry, +I haven't got my exercise book.	Entschuldigung, ich habe mein Heft nicht dabei.
Can I help you with the +worksheets? ['wɜ:kʃi:ts]	Kann ich dir bei den Arbeitsblättern helfen?
+It's your turn. [tɜ:n]	Du bist dran. / Du bist an der Reihe.
Can I open/close the +window, please? ['wɪndəʊ]	Kann ich bitte das Fenster öffnen/schließen?
Can I go to the +toilet, please? ['tɔɪlət]	Darf ich zur Toilette gehen, bitte?

+ = new words

DOs and DON'Ts („Was man tun und nicht tun soll")

p. 28/P 10

DOs
Be quiet.
Look at the board.
Open your books.
Listen to your partner.
Help your partner.

DON'Ts

Don't +shout in the classroom.	Schreit/Ruft nicht im Klassenzimmer.
Don't look +out of the window.	Seht nicht aus dem Fenster.
Don't talk to your partner now.	Redet jetzt nicht mit eurem Partner.
Don't +forget your felt tips.	Vergesst eure Filzstifte nicht.
Don't write on your +desks.	Schreibt nicht auf eure Schreibtische.

+ = new words

How's the new school?

p. 31	**end** [end]	Ende	
	Hurry up. [ˌhʌri‿ˈʌp]	Beeil dich.	
	poor Sophie [pɔː, pʊə]	(die) arme Sophie	[ʊə] klingt wie das „ur" in „**Kur**". (Nicht das „r" sprechen!)
	Come in. [ˌkʌm‿ˈɪn]	Komm rein/herein.	
	everything [ˈevriθɪŋ]	alles	
	tea [tiː]	Tee; *(auch:) leichte Nachmittags- oder Abendmahlzeit*	
	classmate [ˈklɑːsmeɪt]	Klassenkamerad/in, Mitschüler/in	
p. 32	How **was …?** [wəz, wɒz]	Wie war …?	How **was** the first day at your new school?
	world [wɜːld]	Welt	
	See you.	Bis bald. / Tschüs.	
	Go on. [ˌgəʊ‿ˈɒn]	Mach weiter. / Erzähl weiter.	
	a packet of mints [ˌpækɪt‿əv ˈmɪnts]	ein Päckchen/eine Packung Pfefferminzbonbons	
	little [ˈlɪtl]	klein	
	Bye. [baɪ]	Tschüs!	Bye./Goodbye. ◄► Hi./Hello.
	more [mɔː]	mehr	
	Dilip likes …	Dilip mag …	I like tennis, and my brother **likes** football.
	her [hə, hɜː]	sie; ihr	**!** **her** = **1.** sie – There's Sophie. I can see **her**. **2.** ihr – Let's help **her**. **3.** ihr, ihre – There's Ananda and **her** dad. Where's **her** mum?
	He likes her **a lot.** [ə ˈlɒt]	Er mag sie sehr.	

Topic 1: Make a birthday calendar

Remember?

p. 34

The months[1] **of the year**

[1] [mʌnθs]

1 January [ˈdʒænjuəri]
2 February [ˈfebruəri]
3 March [mɑːtʃ]
4 April [ˈeɪprəl]
5 May [meɪ]
6 June [dʒuːn]
7 July [dʒuˈlaɪ]
8 August [ˈɔːgəst]
9 September [sepˈtembə]
10 October [ɒkˈtəʊbə]
11 November [nəʊˈvembə]
12 December [dɪˈsembə]

Make a calendar. [ˌmeɪk‿ə ˈkælɪndə]	Mache/Baue einen Kalender.	Let's **make a calendar** for our classroom. **!** Deutsch: Kalender – Englisch: calendar
birthday [ˈbɜːθdeɪ]	Geburtstag	**!** Deutsch: Ich **habe** im Mai Geburtstag. Englisch: My birthday **is** in May.

when?	wann?	❗ **when** = **1.** wann; **2.** wenn

birthdays

My birthday **is** in May. **When's** your birthday?	Ich **habe** im Mai Geburtstag. **Wann hast** du Geburtstag?
– My birthday is in June. **On** 13th June.	– Ich habe im Juni Geburtstag. **Am** 13. Juni.

❗ Du schreibst: **on 13th June** – Du sagst: **on the thirteenth of June**

Christmas ['krɪsməs]	Weihnachten
date [deɪt]	Datum

Unit 2: A weekend at home

p. 36	**weekend** [ˌwiːk'end]	Wochenende
	at home [ət 'həʊm]	daheim, zu Hause

home

Dan is **at home**.	Dan ist **zu Hause**.
Jo, **come home**!	Jo, komm **nach Hause**!
Go home now.	Geh jetzt **nach Hause**.

Remember?

[1][ʃelf] • [2][ʃelvz]

garden ['gɑːdn]	Garten	❗ Deutsch: Gar**t**en – Englisch: gar**d**en
small [smɔːl]	klein	
I **share** a room **with ...** [ʃeə]	Ich teile mir ein Zimmer mit ...	
people ['piːpl]	Menschen, Leute	The **people** in Bristol are very nice.

p. 37

Remember?

[1][maɪs] • [2][maʊs] • [3]['gɪni pɪg]

hutch [hʌtʃ]	(Kaninchen-)Stall

	cage [keɪdʒ]	Käfig	
	basket ['bɑ:skɪt]	Korb	
	budgie ['bʌdʒi]	Wellensittich	a **budgie** 
	tortoise ['tɔ:təs]	Schildkröte	a **tortoise** 
p. 38	**I can act** the song. [ækt]	Ich kann das Lied aufführen.	
	I **clean my teeth.** [kli:n], [ti:θ]	Ich putze mir die Zähne.	**Clean your teeth**, Jack. Dan, can you **clean** the bathroom, please?
	tooth [tu:θ], *pl* **teeth** [ti:θ]	Zahn	**!** one **tooth**  lots of **teeth** 
	I **wash my face**. [wɒʃ]	Ich wasche mir das Gesicht.	**Wash your face**, Jack. Dan, can you **wash** the car, please?
	early ['ɜ:li]	früh	early ◂▸ late
p. 38/A 1	**afternoon** [ˌɑ:ftə'nu:n]	Nachmittag	

The day: morning – afternoon – evening

morning ['mɔ:nɪŋ] Morgen, Vormittag **afternoon** [ˌɑ:ftə'nu:n] Nachmittag **evening** ['i:vnɪŋ] Abend

in the morning	morgens, am Morgen	**on Friday morning**	freitagmorgens, am Freitagmorgen
in the afternoon	nachmittags, am Nachmittag	**on Friday afternoon**	freitagnachmittags, am Freitagnachmittag
in the evening	abends, am Abend	**on Friday evening**	freitagabends, am Freitagabend
! **at the weekend**	am Wochenende		

	plan [plæn]	Plan	
	essay (about, on) ['eseɪ]	Aufsatz (über)	Write an **essay about** Bristol.
	life [laɪf], *pl* **lives** [laɪvz]	Leben	**!** **life** in Bristol [laɪf] – **das Leben** in Bristol We **live** in ... [lɪv] – Wir **leben/wohnen** in ...
	easy ['i:zi]	leicht, einfach	
	I **get up** at ... [ˌget‿'ʌp]	ich stehe um ... auf	
	(to)[1] **get up**	aufstehen	
	every ['evri]	jeder, jede, jedes	I get up at 6.45 **every** morning.
	(to) **sleep** [sli:p]	schlafen	
	hand [hænd]	Hand	
	bus [bʌs]	Bus	a **bus** 
	(to) **read** [ri:d]	lesen	
p. 39/A 2	(to) **get dressed** [ˌget 'drest]	sich anziehen	First I clean my teeth, then I **get dressed**.
	(to) **give** [gɪv]	geben	
	(to) **feed** [fi:d]	füttern	
	meat [mi:t]	Fleisch	Dogs eat **meat**.
	carrot ['kærət]	Möhre, Karotte	
	(to) **watch** [wɒtʃ]	beobachten, sich etwas ansehen; zusehen	

[1] Mit dem vorangestellten **(to)** kennzeichnen wir den Infinitiv (die Grundform) des Verbs.

	(to) **watch TV** [tiː'viː]	fernsehen	TV = television ['telɪvɪʒn] ❗ <u>**im**</u> Fernsehen = <u>**on**</u> TV: a good film **on TV**

(to) look – (to) see – (to) watch

Look. Can you **see** Sheeba? – Yes, I can **see** her.	**Schau./Guck mal**. Kannst du Sheeba **sehen**? – ...
Toby **watches** Sophie.	Toby **schaut** Sophie **zu**. / Toby **beobachtet** Sophie.
Don't **watch TV** now, Dan. You've got homework.	**Sieh** jetzt nicht **fern**, Dan. ...

	(to) **try to help/to play/...** [traɪ]	versuchen, zu helfen/zu spielen/...	Let's **try to play** my new game. (*or:* Let's **try and play** my new game.)
	(to) **put** [pʊt]	legen, stellen, *(etwas wohin)* tun	**Put** all the photos in the box. 
	after that	danach	First I feed the pets. **After that** I have my breakfast.
	food [fuːd]	Futter	❗ **food** = **1.** Essen, Lebensmittel; **2.** Futter
	(to) **drink** [drɪŋk]	trinken	
p. 39/A 3	**bowl** [bəʊl]	Schüssel; *hier:* Goldfischglas	a **bowl**   a goldfish **bowl**
	all day / all the time	den ganzen Tag (lang) / die ganze Zeit	
p. 40/A 5	**Thanks.** [θæŋks]	Danke.	= Thank you.
	help	Hilfe	❗ **help** = **1.** helfen; **2.** Hilfe
	of course [əv 'kɔːs]	natürlich, selbstverständlich	Is Prunella a Poltergeist? – Yes, **of course** she is.
	Here you are. [ˌhɪə juː‿'ɑː]	Bitte sehr. / Hier bitte.	

„bitte"

– in Bitten und Aufforderungen:	**please**	→ What's the time, **please**? / Open the window, **please**.
– wenn du jemandem etwas gibst:	**Here you are.**	→ Can you give me that pen, please? – **Here you are.**
– wenn sich jemand bei dir bedankt:	**You're welcome.**	→ Thank you. – **You're welcome.**
– wenn du etwas nicht richtig verstanden hast (**„Wie bitte?"**):	**Sorry?**	→ Where are the twins? – **Sorry?**

	This is **all wrong.**	Das ist ganz falsch.	Can I see your homework? – Oh no, it's **all wrong**.
	sometimes ['sʌmtaɪmz]	manchmal	
	(to) **argue** ['ɑːgjuː]	sich streiten, sich zanken	Sophie sometimes **argues** with her sister.
	(to) **do judo** ['dʒuːdəʊ]	Judo machen	
	till [tɪl]	bis *(zeitlich)*	On Sundays I sleep **till** 11 o'clock.
	night [naɪt]	Nacht	❗ **in** der Nacht, nachts = **at** night freitagnachts = **on** Friday night
p. 40/A 6	**letter** ['letə]	Buchstabe	lots of **letters** 

Orts- und Personennamen → S. 201 • Classroom English → S. 202 • Arbeitsanweisungen → S. 203

p. 41/A 7	**grandma** ['grænmɑː]	Oma	= grandmother
	grandpa ['grænpɑː]	Opa	= grandfather
	grandparents ['grænpeərənts]	Großeltern	Your grandmother and grandfather are your **grandparents**.
	parents ['peərənts]	Eltern	Your mother and father are your **parents**.
	at the top (of) [tɒp]	oben, am oberen Ende, an der Spitze (von)	
	because [bɪ'kɒz]	weil	Why are you late for school, Emily? – I'm late **because** the bus was late.
	dead [ded]	tot	
	child [tʃaɪld], *pl* **children** ['tʃɪldrən]	Kind	one **child** ! [tʃaɪld]  three **children** ! ['tʃɪldrən] 
	son [sʌn]	Sohn	
	daughter ['dɔːtə]	Tochter	
	uncle ['ʌŋkl]	Onkel	
	aunt [ɑːnt]	Tante	
	married (to) ['mærɪd]	verheiratet (mit)	! verheiratet **mit** = married **to**
	cousin ['kʌzn]	Cousin, Cousine	
	so [səʊ]	also; deshalb, daher	Polly is a parrot, **so** she lives in a cage.
	grandchild ['grænttʃaɪld], *pl* **grandchildren** ['-tʃɪldrən]	Enkel/in	
	single ['sɪŋgl]	ledig, alleinstehend	not married
	divorced [dɪ'vɔːst]	geschieden	divorced ◄► married
	without [wɪ'ðaʊt]	ohne	without ◄► with
	just [dʒʌst]	(einfach) nur, bloß	Don't **just** sit there. Come and help me.

here – there – where

p. 42/P 1

	Ort		**Richtung**	
here	**Here**'s Dan.	**hier**	Come **here**, Jo.	**hierher**
there	**There**'s the ball.	**da, dort**	Paul Road is nice. Let's go **there**.	**dahin, dorthin**
where	**Where**'s Sheeba?	**wo?**	**Where** can we put the basket?	**wohin?**

p. 45/P 11	(to) **remember** [rɪ'membə]	sich erinnern (an)	! Kannst du dich **an ihren Namen erinnern**? = Can you **remember her name**?
	quiz [kwɪz], *pl* **quizzes** ['kwɪzɪz]	Quiz, Ratespiel	
p. 47/P 17	**guest** [gest]	Gast	

A day in the life of ...

p. 48	**by** [baɪ]	von	'A day in my life' – an essay **by** Jack Hanson.
	(to) **have a shower** ['ʃaʊə]	(sich) duschen	I get up at 7.15, then I **have a shower**.
	shower	Dusche	

(to) **get things ready** ['redi]	Dinge fertig machen, Dinge vorbereiten	In the evening I **get my things ready** for school.
ready	bereit, fertig	Are you **ready**? Can we go? Dan, Jo! Breakfast is **ready**.
again [ə'gen]	wieder; noch einmal	Look, there's that little dog **again**. Can you say that **again**, please?
(to) **do homework**	die Hausaufgabe(n) machen, die Schularbeiten machen	I **do** my **homework** in the afternoon. **!** **Hausaufgaben sind** langweilig. = **Homework is** boring. *(kein Plural)*
interesting ['ɪntrəstɪŋ]	interessant	This book is great. It's very **interesting**.
other ['ʌðə]	andere(r, s)	Jo is at home. The **other** children are at school.
country ['kʌntri]	Land	Germany is a big **country**.
spy [spaɪ]	Spion/in	
(to) **wear** [weə]	tragen, anhaben *(Kleidung)*	Can I **wear** your blue T-shirt, Dan? – Yes, OK.
sunglasses ['sʌnglɑ:sɪz]	(eine) Sonnenbrille	**!** **glasses** und **sunglasses** sind Pluralwörter: I need my **glasses**. Where **are they**? Ich brauche meine **Brille**. Wo **ist sie**?
glasses ['glɑ:sɪz]	(eine) Brille	
us [əs, ʌs]	uns	We're here. Can you see **us**?
(to) **fit** [fɪt]	passen	The T-shirt is too big. It doesn't **fit**.
story ['stɔ:ri]	Geschichte, Erzählung	

Der Plural von Wörtern auf „-y"

-y nach **Konsonant** wird im Plural zu **-ies**:

one	count**ry**	fami**ly**	hob**by**	s**py**	sto**ry**
lots of	count**ries**	fami**lies**	hob**bies**	s**pies**	sto**ries**

-y nach **Vokal** bleibt:

one	bo**y**	da**y**	essa**y**
lots of	bo**ys**	da**ys**	essa**ys**

p. 49 **difficult** ['dɪfɪkəlt]	schwierig, schwer	difficult ◄► easy
silly ['sɪli]	albern, dumm	

Topic 2: My dream house

p. 50 **dream** [dri:m]	Traum
downstairs [ˌdaʊn'steəz]	unten; nach unten
upstairs [ˌʌp'steəz]	oben; nach oben
stairs *(pl)* [steəz]	Treppe; Treppenstufen

armchair ['ɑ:mtʃeə]	Sessel
sofa ['səʊfə]	Sofa
dining room ['daɪnɪŋ ru:m]	Esszimmer
cooker ['kʊkə]	Herd
cupboard ['kʌbəd]	Schrank
dishwasher ['dɪʃwɒʃə]	Geschirrspülmaschine
fridge [frɪdʒ]	Kühlschrank
sink [sɪŋk]	Spüle, Spülbecken

bath [bɑːθ]	Badewanne	
stereo ['steriəʊ]	Stereoanlage	
washing machine ['wɒʃɪŋ məˌʃiːn]	Waschmaschine	
I don't know. [ˌaɪ dəʊnt 'nəʊ]	Ich weiß es nicht.	
p. 51 **tour (of the house)** [tʊə]	Rundgang, Tour (durch das Haus)	**!** ein **Rundgang durch** Bristol = a **tour of** Bristol
visitor ['vɪzɪtə]	Besucher/in, Gast	
(to) **look different/great/old**	anders/toll/alt aussehen	Ananda has got a new school bag. It **looks great**.
a lot [ə 'lɒt]	viel	
(to) **happen (to)** ['hæpən]	geschehen, passieren (mit)	Tell me what **happens to** Prunella in the story.

Unit 3: Sports and hobbies

Remember?

p. 52 **My hobbies** (Meine Hobbys)

On Mondays I go swimming.

On Tuesdays I play football.

On Wednesdays I ride my bike.

On Thursdays I play hockey.

On Fridays I play computer games.

And you?

sport [spɔːt]	Sport; Sportart	I like **sport**. What are your favourite **sports**?
free [friː]	frei	
free time [ˌfriː 'taɪm]	Freizeit, freie Zeit	
p. 53 (to) **collect** [kə'lekt]	sammeln	
stamp [stæmp]	Briefmarke	
card [kɑːd]	(Spiel-, Post-)Karte	
(to) **go riding** ['raɪdɪŋ]	reiten gehen	
(to) **ride** [raɪd]	reiten	**!** (to) **ride** = reiten – (to) **ride a bike** = Rad fahren
dancing lessons ['dɑːnsɪŋ lesnz]	Tanzstunden, Tanzunterricht	
(to) **dance** [dɑːns]	tanzen	
model ['mɒdl]	Modell*(-flugzeug, -schiff usw.)*	I make **models** in my free time.
guitar [gɪ'tɑː]	Gitarre	**!** Mike **spielt Gitarre**. = Mike **plays the guitar**.
(to) **be right**	Recht haben	**!** Ananda **hat Recht**. = Ananda **is right**.
I like swimming/dancing/...	ich schwimme/tanze/... gern	I **like swimming**. And you? – I **don't like swimming**, but I **like riding**.

stamps **cards**

Sports

American football [əˌmerɪkən 'fʊtbɔːl]	Football
badminton ['bædmɪntən]	Badminton, Federball
baseball ['beɪsbɔːl]	Baseball
basketball ['bɑːskɪtbɔːl]	Basketball
dancing ['dɑːnsɪŋ]	Tanzen
football ['fʊtbɔːl]	Fußball
hockey ['hɒki]	Hockey
judo ['dʒuːdəʊ]	Judo
riding ['raɪdɪŋ]	Reiten, Reitsport
swimming ['swɪmɪŋ]	Schwimmen
table tennis ['teɪbl tenɪs]	Tischtennis
tennis ['tenɪs]	Tennis
volleyball ['vɒlibɔːl]	Volleyball

! Verschiedene Sportarten – verschiedene Verben:

You **play** football, badminton, hockey, … .
You **do** judo. / You **do** sport. („Sport treiben“)
You **go** riding, swimming, … .

Remember?

p. 54

p. 54/A 1

shop assistant ['ʃɒp‿əˌsɪstənt]	Verkäufer, Verkäuferin	
Good afternoon.	Guten Tag. *(nachmittags)*	**!** **Guten Tag.** = **Hello. / Good morning. / Good afternoon.**
size [saɪz]	Größe	
(to) **try on** [ˌtraɪ‿'ɒn]	anprobieren *(Kleidung)*	Can I **try on** your new dress? – Not now. You can **try** it **on** tomorrow.
these [ðiːz]	diese, die (hier)	
…, you know. [nəʊ]	…, wissen Sie. / …, weißt du.	He's really good at football, **you know**.
(to) **know**	wissen	Do you **know** where Jack is? – He's at school. **!** Aussprache: (to) **know** [nəʊ] – **now** [naʊ]
them [ðəm, ðem]	sie; ihnen	Look, the twins. Can you see **them**? Let's help **them**.
(to) **want** [wɒnt]	(haben) wollen	I don't **want** these shoes. I **want** the red boots.
We'll take them. [wiːl 'teɪk‿ðəm]	Wir nehmen sie.	Do you like the boots? – Yes, I do. – OK, **we'll take them**.

p. 54/A 2	**top** [tɒp]	Top, Oberteil	
p. 55/A 3	**project (about, on)** ['prɒdʒekt]	Projekt (über, zu)	
	(to) **ask** [ɑ:sk]	fragen	
	piano [pi'ænəʊ]	Klavier, Piano	! Sie **spielt Klavier**. = She **plays the piano**.
	alone [ə'ləʊn]	allein	Does Prunella play tennis **alone**?
	head [hed]	Kopf	
	always ['ɔ:lweɪz]	immer	Prunella **always** plays tennis with her uncle.
	(to) **win** [wɪn]	gewinnen	
	neighbour ['neɪbə]	Nachbar, Nachbarin	
	anyway ['eniweɪ]	sowieso	I don't like that shirt. And it doesn't fit **anyway**.
p. 56/A 5	**often** ['ɒfn]	oft, häufig	I **often** ride my bike to school.
	Dear Jay ... [dɪə]	Lieber Jay, ...	
	quick [kwɪk]	schnell	
	some [səm, sʌm]	einige, ein paar	There are **some** apples for you in the kitchen.
	question ['kwestʃn]	Frage	You ask lots of **questions**. ! Fragen stellen = (to) ask questions
	(to) **answer** ['ɑ:nsə]	antworten; beantworten	
	answer (to) ['ɑ:nsə]	Antwort (auf)	Here's a quick **answer to** your question.
	match [mætʃ]	Spiel, Wettkampf	Football **matches** are often on Saturdays.
	Love ... [lʌv]	Liebe Grüße, ... *(Briefschluss)*	
	the next morning/day [nekst]	am nächsten Morgen/Tag	
	never ['nevə]	nie, niemals	never ◂▸ always
	usually ['ju:ʒuəli]	meistens, gewöhnlich, normalerweise	**never** – **sometimes** – **often** – **usually** – **always**
	(to) **walk** [wɔ:k]	(zu Fuß) gehen	I never ride my bike to school. I always **walk**.
	Say hi to Dilip **for me.**	Grüß Dilip von mir.	
p. 57/A 8	(to) **hate** [heɪt]	hassen, gar nicht mögen	(to) hate ◂▸ (to) like
	(to) **have to** do ['hæv tə, 'hæf tə]	tun müssen	I can't help you, I **have to** feed the rabbits.
	at least [ət 'li:st]	zumindest, wenigstens	These shoes aren't cool, but **at least** they fit.
	most people [məʊst]	die meisten Leute	**Most** children like hamsters and rabbits. ! **die meisten** Kinder = **most** children
	(to) **understand** [ˌʌndə'stænd]	verstehen, begreifen	In English, please. I don't **understand** German.
	(to) **lay the table** [leɪ]	den Tisch decken	
	dinner ['dɪnə]	Abendessen, Abendbrot	We usually have **dinner** at 7 o'clock.
p. 57/A 9	**right now** [raɪt 'naʊ]	jetzt sofort; jetzt gerade	I need your help **right now**. Sorry, I can't help you **right now**.
	(to) **teach** [ti:tʃ]	unterrichten, lehren	Mr Kingsley is a teacher. He **teaches** English.

	(to) **learn** [lɜːn]	lernen	
p. 58/P 2	**snake** [sneɪk]	Schlange	
p. 60/P 8	(to) **know** [nəʊ]	kennen	**!** (to) **know** = **1.** wissen; **2.** kennen
	appointment [əˈpɔɪntmənt]	Termin, Verabredung	
	(to) **meet** [miːt]	sich treffen	**!** (to) **meet**: **1.** Can **we meet** at 8 o'clock? (Können **wir uns** ... **treffen**?) **2.** Can **you meet us** after school? (Kannst **du uns** ... **treffen**?)
p. 61/P 11	**under** [ˈʌndə]	unter	Oh, there's my book – **under** the desk.
	sentence [ˈsentəns]	Satz	
p. 62/P 12	(to) **skate** [skeɪt]	Inliner/Skateboard fahren	
	skates [skeɪts]	Inliner	
p. 62/P 13	**on the radio** [ˈreɪdiəʊ]	im Radio	
p. 62/P 14	**opposite** [ˈɒpəzɪt]	Gegenteil	What's the **opposite** of 'full'? – 'Empty'.
p. 63/P 16	(to) **link** [lɪŋk]	verbinden, verknüpfen	Can you **link** the words and the pictures?
p. 63/P 17	**car** [kɑː]	Auto	a **car** 
p. 64/P 19	**part** [pɑːt]	Teil	

The SHoCK Team

p. 65	**man** [mæn], *pl* **men** [men]	Mann	
	woman [ˈwʊmən], *pl* **women** [ˈwɪmɪn]	Frau	
	the only guest [ˈəʊnli]	der einzige Gast	Dan and Jo are **the only** twins in 7PK.
	suddenly [ˈsʌdnli]	plötzlich, auf einmal	**Suddenly** everything was quiet.
	noise [nɔɪz]	Geräusch; Lärm	Listen! There's a **noise** at the window. What's all that **noise**? I can't do my homework.
	outside his room [ˌaʊtˈsaɪd]	vor seinem Zimmer; außerhalb seines Zimmers	Sophie's rabbits live **outside** the house – in a hutch in the garden.
	scary [ˈskeəri]	unheimlich; gruselig	
	(to) **run** [rʌn]	laufen, rennen	
	out of ... [ˈaʊt_əv]	aus ... (heraus/hinaus)	
	into ... [ˈɪntə, ˈɪntʊ]	in ... (hinein)	**into** the house **out of** the house
	(to) **call** [kɔːl]	rufen; anrufen; nennen	Please **call** your dog. It's in our garden. **Call** me tomorrow. Here's my phone number. Her name is Elizabeth, but we **call** her Liz.
	police *(pl)* [pəˈliːs]	Polizei	**!** **police** ist immer Plural: Where **are** the **police**? (Wo ist die Polizei?)
	maybe [ˈmeɪbi]	vielleicht	**Maybe** Mr Green is a bank robber?
	This is about Mr Green.	Es geht um Mr Green.	**This is about** the SHoCK Team, not about Jack.
	(to) **find out (about)** [ˌfaɪnd_ˈaʊt]	herausfinden (über)	

detective [dɪ'tektɪv]	Detektiv, Detektivin	! Deutsch: Detektiv – Englisch: detective
p. 66 **a piece of paper** [ˌpiːs_əv 'peɪpə]	ein Stück Papier	**a piece of paper** 
(to) **add (to)** [æd]	hinzufügen, ergänzen, addieren (zu)	**Add** blue **to** yellow and you've got green.
(to) **start** [stɑːt]	starten, anfangen, beginnen (mit)	
watch [wɒtʃ]	Armbanduhr	! **watch** = **1.** *(verb)* beobachten, sich ansehen **2.** *(noun)* Armbanduhr  **watches**  **clocks**
They **plan to** watch ... [plæn]	Sie planen, ... zu beobachten	

Topic 3: An English jumble sale

p. 67 **jumble sale** ['dʒʌmbl seɪl]	Wohltätigkeitsbasar	
pound (£) [paʊnd]	Pfund *(britische Währung)*	
pence (p) *(pl)* [pens]	Pence *(Mehrzahl von „penny")*	10**p** [piː] = 10 **pence**
penny ['peni]	*kleinste britische Münze*	1**p** [piː] = 1 **penny**
euro (€) ['jʊərəʊ]	Euro	
cent (c) [sent]	Cent	
What about ...?	Wie wär's mit ...?	
too much [tuː 'mʌtʃ]	zu viel	! **too** = **1.** auch – The flat is big, and the garden is big **too**. („auch groß") **2.** zu – The house is **too** big. („zu groß")
How much is/are ...? [ˌhaʊ 'mʌtʃ]	Was kostet/kosten ...? / Wie viel kostet/kosten ...?	**How much is** the felt tip? And **how much are** the pencils?
It's £1.	Er/Sie/Es kostet 1 Pfund.	The felt tip **is** £1.25, and the pencils **are** 35p.
only ['əʊnli]	nur, bloß	There aren't two books on the desk, there's **only** one. 
(to) **take** 10c **off** [ˌteɪk_'ɒf]	10 Cent abziehen	£3? That's too much. Can you **take 50p off**?
change [tʃeɪndʒ]	Wechselgeld	

Unit 4: Party, party!

pp. 68/69 (to) **have ... for breakfast**	... zum Frühstück essen/ trinken	I usually **have** toast and orange juice **for breakfast**.
chips *(pl)* [tʃɪps]	Pommes frites	
biscuit ['bɪskɪt]	Keks, Plätzchen	
crisps *(pl)* [krɪsps]	Kartoffelchips	! **crisps** = Kartoffelchips – **chips** = Pommes frites

fruit salad ['fruːt ˌsæləd]	Obstsalat	
sausage ['sɒsɪdʒ]	(Brat-, Bock-)Würstchen, Wurst	**sausages** and **chips**
sweets *(pl)* [swiːts]	Süßigkeiten	
sweet [swiːt]	süß	

Remember?

Food and drink

bottle ['bɒtl]	Flasche	a milk **bottle**  a **bottle** of milk 
glass [glɑːs]	Glas	
jug [dʒʌg]	Krug	

a bottle of ..., a glass of ...

a bottle of milk · a glass of water · a jug of orange juice · a bowl of cornflakes · a plate of chips · a packet of crisps · a basket of apples · a piece of pizza

	Would you like ...? [wəd, wʊd]	Möchtest du ...? / Möchten Sie ...?	**Would you like** a piece of pizza? – Yes, please.
	Would you like some?	Möchtest du etwas/ein paar? / Möchten Sie etwas/ein paar?	**!** **some** = **1.** einige, ein paar – **some** apples/chips **2.** etwas – **some** cheese/juice
	I'd like ... (= I would like ...)	Ich hätte gern ... / Ich möchte gern ...	What would you like? – **I'd like** a hamburger, please.
p. 70/A 1	**invitation (to)** [ˌɪnvɪ'teɪʃn]	Einladung (zu)	
	(to) **invite (to)** [ɪn'vaɪt]	einladen (zu)	Can I **invite** all my friends to my party?
	long [lɒŋ]	lang	Ananda's essay is very **long**.
	short [ʃɔːt]	kurz	Dan's essay is very **short**. short ◂▸ long
	(to) **want to** do [wɒnt]	tun wollen	Do you really **want to** invite all your friends? **!** (to) **want** = haben wollen: Prunella **wants** an invitation. (to) **want to do** = tun wollen: Prunella **wants to** go to Sophie's party.
	both [bəʊθ]	beide	I like **both** T-shirts. Can we take **both**?
	real [rɪəl]	echt, wirklich	It's a party for **real** people, not for poltergeists.

p. 71/A 4	**present** ['preznt]	Geschenk	! **present** = **1.** Gegenwart; **2.** Geschenk
	still [stɪl]	(immer) noch	After dinner Jo was **still** hungry.
	(to) **buy** [baɪ]	kaufen	
	soap [səʊp]	Seife	a piece of **soap** 
	funny ['fʌni]	witzig, komisch	
	expensive [ɪk'spensɪv]	teuer	£60 for a T-shirt? That's very **expensive**.
	any ...? ['eni]	(irgend)welche ...?	! Gibt es Apfelsinen? = Are there **any** oranges**?**
	earring ['ɪərɪŋ]	Ohrring	
	not (...) any	kein, keine	There is**n't any** milk in the fridge. We have**n't** got **any** pets. What about you?
	(to) **be in a hurry** ['hʌri]	in Eile sein, es eilig haben	! **hurry**: **1. I'm in a hurry**. (= Ich habe es eilig.) **2. Hurry up**, please. (= Beeil dich, bitte.)
	(to) **follow** ['fɒləʊ]	folgen; verfolgen	My dog always **follows** me. The police **are following** the man to his house.
p. 71/A 5	**key word** ['kiː wɜːd]	Stichwort, Schlüsselwort	
	another [ə'nʌðə]	ein(e) andere(r, s); noch ein(e)	I can't write with this pen. I need **another** pen. The pizza is good. Can I have **another** piece?
p. 72/A 7	(to) **get ready (for)** ['redi]	sich fertig machen (für), sich vorbereiten (auf)	We have to **get ready for** dinner. Can you lay the table, please?
	(to) **tidy** ['taɪdi]	aufräumen	On Saturdays I **tidy** my room.
	(to) **make a mess** [mes]	alles durcheinanderbringen, alles in Unordnung bringen	Prunella often **makes a mess**.
	away [ə'weɪ]	weg, fort	Go **away**, Prunella. I have to do my homework.
	(to) **take** [teɪk]	(weg-, hin)bringen	Please **take** the plates into the kitchen, Sophie.
	up [ʌp]	hinauf, herauf, nach oben	Go **up** to your room, Toby.
	down [daʊn]	hinunter, herunter, nach unten	down ◄► up
	to Jenny's	zu Jenny	Let's go **to Jenny's** now. (= to Jenny's house/flat)
	later ['leɪtə]	später	
p. 73/A 9	**at the station** ['steɪʃn]	am Bahnhof	Ananda sees Mr Green **at the station**.
	in front of [ɪn 'frʌnt‿əv]	vor	**in front of** the box 
	(to) **hear** [hɪə]	hören	! (to) **hear** = hören (können) (to) **listen (to)** = zuhören, horchen **Listen**. Can you **hear** the dogs in the park?
	train [treɪn]	Zug	! There was a funny man **on the train**. (= **im Zug**)
	(to) **wait (for)** ['weɪt fɔː]	warten (auf)	Don't **wait for** Prunella – she's always late.
	somebody ['sʌmbədi]	jemand	Mr Green is talking to **somebody**.
	(to) **get off (the train/bus)** [ˌget‿'ɒf] **(-tt-)**[1]	(aus dem Zug/Bus) aussteigen	This is where I live. We have to **get off** here.
	(to) **get on (the train/bus)** [ˌget‿'ɒn] **(-tt-)**	(in den Zug/Bus) einsteigen	! in den Bus **einsteigen** = (to) **get on** the bus aus dem Bus **aussteigen** = (to) **get off** the bus

[1] Die Angabe **(-tt-)** zeigt, dass der Endkonsonant bei der Bildung der *-ing*-Form verdoppelt wird: **get** – **getting**.

	parcel ['pɑːsl]	Paket	
	(to) **look round** [ˌlʊk 'raʊnd]	sich umsehen	Mr Green **looks round**, then he starts to run.
	(to) **hide** [haɪd]	sich verstecken; *(etwas)* verstecken	Prunella often **hides** in the wardrobe. Can you **hide** this parcel for me, please?
p. 74/A 10	**Which** picture ...? [wɪtʃ]	Welches Bild ...?	**Which** cake would you like? The chocolate cake?

Remember?

p. 80/P 13 **My body**[1] (Mein Körper)

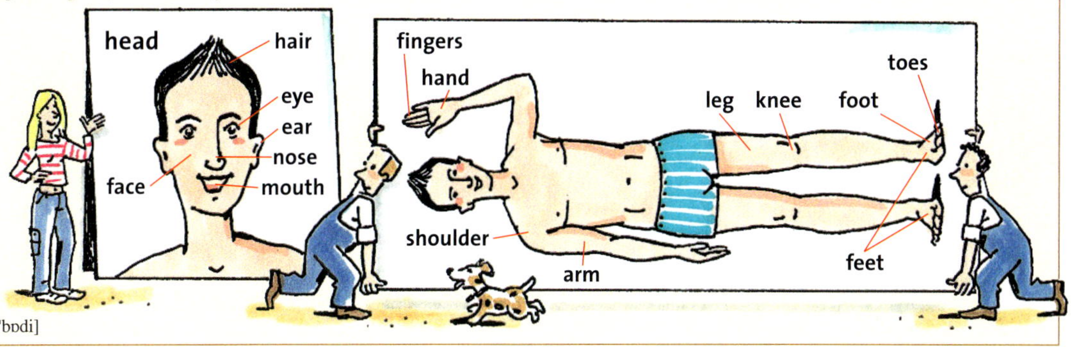

[1] ['bɒdi]

p. 80/P 15	**roll** [rəʊl]	Brötchen	

Sophie's party – a play

p. 81	**play** [pleɪ]	Theaterstück	**!** **play** = **1.** *(verb)* spielen; **2.** *(noun)* Theaterstück
	scene [siːn]	Szene	
	... pm [ˌpiː‿'em]	... Uhr nachmittags/abends	**!** Man verwendet **am** oder **pm** nicht mit **o'clock**. Also nur: **at two pm** (nicht: ~~at two o'clock pm~~)
	... am [ˌeɪ‿'em]	... Uhr morgens/vormittags	
	Don't worry. ['wʌri]	Mach dir keine Sorgen.	
	(to) **worry (about)**	sich Sorgen machen (wegen, um)	When I come home late my mum always **worries about** me.
	minute ['mɪnɪt]	Minute	It's three **minutes** to six. 
	doorbell ['dɔːbel]	Türklingel	
	door [dɔː]	Tür	
	front door [ˌfrʌnt 'dɔː]	Wohnungstür, Haustür	
	inside [ˌɪn'saɪd]	innen (drin), drinnen	Sophie isn't in the garden. She's **inside**.
	outside [ˌaʊt'saɪd]	draußen	Where's Sheeba? – She's **outside**, in the garden.
	fantastic [fæn'tæstɪk]	fantastisch, toll	
	so sweet [səʊ]	so süß	
	(to) **be afraid (of)** [ə'freɪd]	Angst haben (vor)	My brother **is afraid of** big dogs. I**'m afraid of** mice.
	(to) **pass** [pɑːs]	(herüber)reichen, weitergeben	Can you **pass** me the milk, please? You have to **pass** the parcel to the next student.
	(to) **pass round** [ˌpɑːs 'raʊnd]	herumgeben	Now Sophie **is passing round** the party food.
	no more music	keine Musik mehr	
	no	kein, keine	I can't do my homework now. I've got **no** time.

p. 82	**note** [nəʊt]	Mitteilung, Notiz	Here's a **note** from Jack. Can you read it? I can't.
	(to) **take notes**	sich Notizen machen	
	(to) **choose** [tʃuːz]	(sich) aussuchen, (aus)wählen	We have to **choose** a name for our new dog.
	prize [praɪz]	Preis, Gewinn	There's a **prize** for the best story.
	(to) **be over**	vorbei sein, zu Ende sein	
	What are you talking about?	Wovon redest du?	
	(to) **get** [get] **(-tt-)**	gelangen, (hin)kommen	How can we **get** to Cotham School?
	title ['taɪtl]	Titel, Überschrift	

Unit 5: School: not just lessons

pp. 84/85	(to) **finish** ['fɪnɪʃ]	enden; beenden, zu Ende machen	Lessons **finish** at 3.30 pm. Let's **finish** the exercise and read the text again. (to) finish ◄► (to) start
	notice board ['nəʊtɪs bɔːd]	Anschlagtafel, schwarzes Brett	
	programme ['prəʊgræm]	Programm	
	(to) **paint** [peɪnt]	malen, anmalen	Let's **paint** our faces for the party!
	ship [ʃɪp]	Schiff	
	rehearsal [rɪ'hɜːsl]	Probe *(am Theater)*	
	(to) **rehearse** [rɪ'hɜːs]	proben *(am Theater)*	
	spring [sprɪŋ]	Frühling	
	autumn ['ɔːtəm]	Herbst	
	winter ['wɪntə]	Winter	

	show [ʃəʊ]	Show, Vorstellung	
	(to) **show**	zeigen	Can you **show** me your new computer?

	(to) **bring** [brɪŋ]	(mit-, her)bringen	! **Bring** me the newspaper. („herbringen") — Now **take** it to Dad. („hinbringen")
	(to) **use** [juːz]	benutzen, verwenden	Can I **use** your phone, please?
	result [rɪ'zʌlt]	Ergebnis, Resultat	
	junior ['dʒuːniə]	Junioren-, Jugend-	
	choir ['kwaɪə]	Chor	! Schreibung: ch**oir** – Aussprache: ['kwaɪə]
	pirate ['paɪrət]	Pirat, Piratin	! Betonung auf der 1. Silbe: **pirate** ['paɪrət]
	(to) **practise** ['præktɪs]	üben; trainieren	
	exciting [ɪk'saɪtɪŋ]	aufregend, spannend	
p. 86/A 1	(we/you/they) **were** [wə, wɜː]	*Vergangenheitsform von „be"*	I was at home last night. Where **were** you?
	Miss White [mɪs]	Frau White *(unverheiratet)*	

Tipps zum Wörterlernen → S. 122–123 • Englische Laute → S. 149 • Alphabetische Wörterverzeichnisse → S. 179–191 / S. 192–200

	group [gru:p]	Gruppe	
	(to) **sound** [saʊnd]	klingen, sich *(gut usw.)* anhören	A party in the park? That **sounds** very nice.
	sound	Laut; Klang	
	kid [kɪd]	Kind, Jugendliche(r)	
	ticket ['tɪkɪt]	Eintrittskarte	**Tickets** for the party are £2.50.
p. 86/A 2	**yesterday** ['jestədeɪ, 'jestədi]	gestern	**Yesterday** I was home late.
	cinema ['sɪnəmə]	Kino	
	swimming pool ['swɪmɪŋ pu:l]	Schwimmbad, Schwimmbecken	
	sports centre ['spɔ:ts ˌsentə]	Sportzentrum	
p. 87/A 3	**terrible** ['terəbl]	schrecklich, furchtbar	
	mistake [mɪ'steɪk]	Fehler	There are three **mistakes** in your essay.
	I can't wait to see ...	ich kann es kaum erwarten, ... zu sehen	The band is great. **I can't wait to** see their next show.
	a minute **ago** [ə'gəʊ]	vor einer Minute	Where's Dan? – He was here **a minute ago**. ! **ago** steht hinter dem Nomen.
p. 87/A 5	(to) **phone** [fəʊn]	telefonieren, anrufen	! **phone** = **1.** Telefon; **2.** telefonieren, anrufen
p. 88/A 6	**king** [kɪŋ]	König	
p. 88/A 7	**diary** ['daɪəri]	Tagebuch; Terminkalender	
	had [hæd]	*Vergangenheitsform von „have" und von „have got"*	Yesterday I **had** breakfast at 6 o'clock. In 1998 we **had** a dog. Now we've got two cats. ! Nie: ... we ~~had got~~ a dog.
	said [sed]	*Vergangenheitsform von „say"*	'Be quiet,' the teacher **said**.
	(to) **be cross (with)** [krɒs]	böse, sauer sein (auf)	My mum **was cross with** me because I was late.
	saw [sɔ:]	*Vergangenheitsform von „see"*	Dan laughed when he **saw** his brother.

Unregelmäßige Vergangenheitsformen

(to) come	**came** [keɪm]	kommen	(to) run	**ran** [ræn]	laufen, rennen
(to) do	**did** [dɪd]	tun, machen	(to) sit	**sat** [sæt]	sitzen; sich setzen
(to) get up	**got up** [gɒt]	aufstehen	(to) take	**took** [tʊk]	nehmen; (weg-, hin)bringen
(to) go	**went** [went]	gehen	(to) tell	**told** [təʊld]	sagen; erzählen
(to) make	**made** [meɪd]	machen, bauen, bilden			

	this morning/afternoon/evening	heute Morgen/Nachmittag/Abend	I can meet you at two o'clock **this afternoon**.
p. 89/A 9	we **didn't sing** ['dɪdnt]	wir sangen nicht / wir haben nicht gesungen	Ananda **didn't sing** but she made the programmes.
	(to) **stay** [steɪ]	bleiben	Prunella didn't go to the Spring Show – she **stayed** at home.
	city ['sɪti]	(Groß-)Stadt	
	museum [mju'zi:əm]	Museum	
	Did you go ...?	Bist du / Seid ihr ... gegangen?	
p. 89/A 10	a **special** day ['speʃl]	ein besonderer Tag	My birthday is always a **special** day for me.

p. 90/P 3	**phone call** ['fəʊn kɔːl]	Anruf, Telefongespräch	
p. 91/P 5	your **best** friends [best]	deine besten Freunde/ Freundinnen	
p. 92/P 8	**extra** ['ekstrə]	zusätzlich	Oh, here's Sophie. We need an **extra** plate.
	syllable ['sɪləbl]	Silbe	There are two **syllables** in *mistake*: *mis* and *take*.
p. 92/P 9	**report (on)** [rɪ'pɔːt]	Bericht, Reportage (über)	There was a **report on** the Spring Show on the radio.
p. 95/P 17	**elephant** ['elɪfənt]	Elefant	

A pirate story

p. 96	**dark** [dɑːk]	dunkel	It's very **dark** in here. I can't find my pen.
	windy ['wɪndi]	windig	
	wind [wɪnd]	Wind	
	young [jʌŋ]	jung	young ◄► old
	many ['meni]	viele	Poor Peter. He hasn't got **many** friends.
	how many ...?	wie viele ...?	**How many** kids are in the SHoCK Team? – Five.

„viel", „viele"

viel **How much** orange juice have we got? – We haven't got **much** orange juice, but we've got **lots of** milk.
Wie viel Orangensaft ...? – ... nicht **viel** Orangensaft, ... **viel** Milch.

viele **How many** CDs have you got? – I haven't got **many** CDs, but I've got **lots of** computer games.
Wie viele CDs ...? – ... nicht **viele** CDs, ... **viele** Computerspiele.

	(to) **kill** [kɪl]	töten	
	tonight [tə'naɪt]	heute Nacht, heute Abend	! heute Morgen = **this morning** heute Nachmittag = **this afternoon** heute Abend = **this evening** heute Nacht = **tonight**
p. 97	**for** three **days**	drei Tage (lang)	Sophie was in London **for five days** last year.
	that [ðət, ðæt]	dass	Prunella says **that** she never sleeps. Do you think **that** Mr Green is a spy?
	(to) **be scared (of)** [skeəd]	Angst haben (vor)	My little brother is **scared of** poltergeists.
	at last [ət 'lɑːst]	endlich, schließlich	Jack waited for a long time. **At last** Ananda came.
	tired ['taɪəd]	müde	
	soon [suːn]	bald	It's my birthday **soon**. Let's have a party.
	(to) **be asleep** [ə'sliːp]	schlafen	
	when	als	

when

wann	**When**'s your birthday?	**Wann** hast du Geburtstag?
wenn	We can play cards **when** you come home.	Wir können Karten spielen, **wenn** du nach Hause kommst.
als	Jonah was scared **when** Mr Bonny saw him.	Jonah hatte Angst, **als** Mr Bonny ihn sah.

	beautiful ['bjuːtɪfl]	schön	Ann Bonny was a **beautiful** woman.
	clear [klɪə]	klar, deutlich	Is that **clear**? – Yes, I understand now.
	sea [siː]	Meer, *(die)* See	
p. 98	(to) **be cold** [kəʊld]	frieren	It was very windy, and I **was cold**. (= Ich fror. / Mir war kalt.)
	cold	kalt	cold ◂▸ hot
	floor [flɔː]	Fußboden	Jo, put your books on the desk, not on the **floor**.

Unit 6: Great places for kids

p. 100	**town** [taʊn]	(Klein-)Stadt	
	village ['vɪlɪdʒ]	Dorf	
	church [tʃɜːtʃ]	Kirche	
	near [nɪə]	in der Nähe von, nahe (bei)	
	tower ['taʊə]	Turm	
	(to) **have a picnic** ['pɪknɪk]	ein Picknick machen	
	free	kostenlos	
	bridge [brɪdʒ]	Brücke	

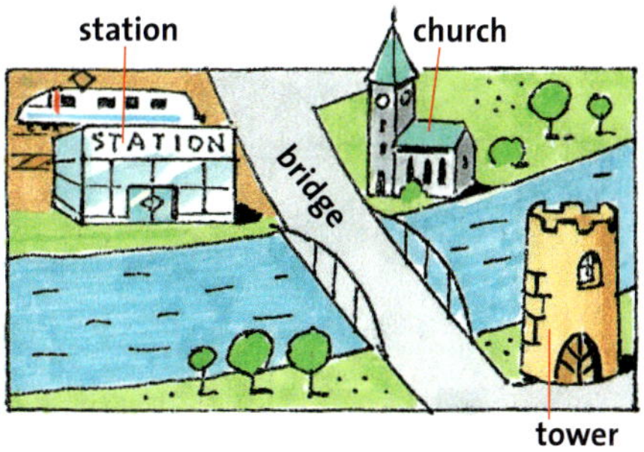

The church is **near** the station.
! in der Nähe (von) = **near** (nicht: ~~in the near of~~)

p. 101	(to) **explore** [ɪk'splɔː]	erkunden, erforschen	It's very interesting to **explore** new places.
	fun [fʌn]	Spaß	

fun

Riding **is fun**. (*Nicht:* ... ~~makes fun~~.)	Reiten **macht Spaß**.
Prunella **has fun** with Sophie.	Prunella **hat viel Spaß / amüsiert sich** mit Sophie.
Have fun!	**Viel Spaß!**
Just **for fun**.	Nur **zum Spaß**.

	cheap [tʃiːp]	billig	expensive ◂▸ cheap
	price [praɪs]	(Kauf-)Preis	
p. 102/A 1	**each** [iːtʃ]	jeder, jede, jedes (einzelne)	There are six guests at the party, so we need six little presents – one for **each** of them.
	must [mʌst]	müssen	**!** **müssen** = **1.** have to; **2.** must (*have to* wird häufiger verwendet als *must*.)
	corner ['kɔːnə]	Ecke	
	(to) **agree (on)** [ə'griː]	sich einigen (auf)	We have to **agree on** a day for our party.
	middle (of) ['mɪdl]	Mitte	
	library ['laɪbrəri]	Bibliothek, Bücherei	
p. 102/A 2	**step** [step]	Schritt	The first **step** is to choose an interesting place.
p. 103/A 3	(to) **whisper** ['wɪspə]	flüstern	
	loud [laʊd]	laut	loud ◂▸ quiet
p. 103/A 5	(to) **take photos**	Fotos machen, fotografieren	Learn to **take photos** at the camera club!

	over there [ˌəʊvə ˈðeə]	da drüben, dort drüben	
	better [ˈbetə]	besser	Your essay is good, but my essay is **better**.
	(to) **be/look the same** [seɪm]	gleich sein/aussehen	All the cars in this museum **look the same**. the same ◄► different
	the same ...	der-/die-/dasselbe ...; dieselben ...	Sophie and her friends are at **the same** school.
	those [ðəʊz]	die (da), jene (dort)	

this, that – these, those

Wenn etwas **näher beim Sprecher** ist, verwendet man eher **this** und **these**.

Wenn etwas **weiter entfernt** ist, verwendet man eher **that** und **those**.

	(to) **smile** [smaɪl]	lächeln	
p. 104/A 7	**glue** [gluː]	Klebstoff	
	(to) **grumble** [ˈgrʌmbl]	murren, nörgeln	
	presentation [ˌpreznˈteɪʃn]	Präsentation, Vorstellung	
p. 104/A 8	**city centre** [ˌsɪti ˈsentə]	Stadtzentrum, Innenstadt	
p. 105/A 9	**for lots of reasons**	aus vielen Gründen	I ride my bike **for lots of reasons** – it's quick, it's fun, and it isn't expensive.
	I'd like to talk about ...	ich möchte über ... reden / ich würde gern über ... reden	Today **I'd like to** talk about great places for kids in Bristol.

The Mr Green mystery

p. 110	**hall** [hɔːl]	Flur, Diele	
	How do you know ...?	Woher weißt/kennst du ...?	**How do you know** my phone number?
	(to) **hurt** [hɜːt], *simple past:* **hurt**	wehtun; verletzen	Poor Ananda. She **hurt** her leg in a hockey match yesterday.

Irregular verbs (Unregelmäßige Verben)

Infinitive	Simple past	
(to) **be**	**was/were**	sein
(to) **come**	**came**	kommen
(to) **do**	**did**	tun, machen
(to) **get up**	**got up**	aufstehen
(to) **go**	**went**	gehen
(to) **have** (**have got**)	**had**	haben
(to) **hurt**	**hurt**	wehtun; verletzen

Infinitive	Simple past	
(to) **make**	**made**	machen; bauen; bilden
(to) **run**	**ran**	laufen, rennen
(to) **say**	**said**	sagen
(to) **see**	**saw**	sehen
(to) **sit**	**sat**	sitzen; sich setzen
(to) **take**	**took**	nehmen; (weg-, hin)bringen
(to) **tell**	**told**	sagen; erzählen

Tipps zum Wörterlernen → S. 122–123 · Englische Laute → S. 149 · Alphabetische Wörterverzeichnisse → S. 179–191 / S. 192–200

Das Dictionary besteht aus zwei alphabetischen Wörterlisten:

Englisch – Deutsch (S. 179–191)
Deutsch – Englisch (S. 192–200).

Das **English – German Dictionary** enthält den gesamten Wortschatz dieses Bandes.
Wenn du wissen möchtest, was ein Wort bedeutet, wie man es ausspricht, wie es genau geschrieben wird oder wo es zum ersten Mal in *English G 21* vorkommt, kannst du hier nachschlagen.

Im **English – German Dictionary** werden folgende **Abkürzungen** und **Symbole** verwendet:

jm.	= jemandem	pl	= plural *(Mehrzahl)*
jn.	= jemanden	no pl	= no plural

° Mit diesem Kringel sind Wörter markiert, die nicht zum Lernwortschatz gehören.
► Der Pfeil verweist auf Kästchen im Vocabulary (S. 150–178), in denen du weitere Informationen zu diesem Wort findest.

Die **Fundstellenangaben** zeigen, wo ein Wort zum ersten Mal vorkommt.
Die Ziffern in Klammern bezeichnen Seitenzahlen:

Welc (8)	= 'Hello' and 'Welcome', Seite 8
Welc (8/150)	= 'Hello' and 'Welcome', Seite 150 (im Vocabulary, zu Seite 8)
1 (33)	= Unit 1, Seite 33
1 (18/156)	= Unit 1, Seite 156 (im Vocabulary, zu Seite 18)
TOP 2 (51)	= Topic 2, Seite 51
TOP 2 (50/165)	= Topic 2, Seite 165 (im Vocabulary, zu Seite 50)

Tipps zur Arbeit mit dem English – German Dictionary findest du im Skills File auf Seite 126.

A

a [ə] ein, eine Welc (8/150) • **a lot** viel TOP 2 (51) • **He likes her a lot.** Er mag sie sehr. 1 (32)

about [ə'baʊt] über Welc (8) • **ask about** nach *etwas* fragen 5 (87) **This is about Mr Green.** Es geht um Mr Green. 3 (65) • **What about ...?** **1.** Was ist mit ...? / Und ...? Welc (6); **2.** Wie wär's mit ...? TOP 3 (67) **What are you talking about?** Wovon redest du? 4 (82)

act [ækt] aufführen, spielen 2 (38) **°Act out ...** Spiele/Spielt ... vor.

activity [æk'tɪvəti] Aktivität, Tätigkeit (3)

add (to) [æd] hinzufügen, ergänzen, addieren (zu) 3 (66)

afraid [ə'freɪd]**: be afraid (of)** Angst haben (vor) 4 (81)

after ['ɑːftə] nach *(zeitlich)* 1 (23) **after that** danach 2 (39)

afternoon [ˌɑːftə'nuːn] Nachmittag 2 (38) • **in the afternoon** nachmittags, am Nachmittag 2 (38/162) **on Friday afternoon** freitagnachmittags, am Freitagnachmittag 2 (38/162)

again [ə'gen] wieder; noch einmal 2 (48)

ago [ə'gəʊ]**: a minute ago** vor einer Minute 5 (87)

agree (on) [ə'griː] sich einigen (auf) 6 (102)

°ahoy [ə'hɔɪ]**: Ship ahoy!** Schiff ahoi!

°alarm clock [ə'lɑːm klɒk] Wecker

°algebra ['ældʒɪbrə] Algebra

all [ɔːl] alle; alles 1 (24) • **all day** den ganzen Tag (lang) 2 (39) • **all the time** die ganze Zeit 2 (39) **This is all wrong.** Das ist ganz falsch. 2 (40)

alone [ə'ləʊn] allein 3 (55)

alphabet ['ælfəbet] Alphabet 1 (22)

°alphabetical [ˌælfə'betɪkl] alphabetisch

°also ['ɔːlsəʊ] auch

always ['ɔːlweɪz] immer 3 (55)

am [ˌeɪ_'em]**: 7 am** 7 Uhr morgens/vormittags 4 (81/173)

American football [əˌmerɪkən 'fʊtbɔːl] Football 3 (53/167)

an [ən] ein, eine 1 (18/156)

and [ənd, ænd] und Welc (8/150)

another [ə'nʌðə] ein(e) andere(r, s); noch ein(e) 4 (71)

answer ['ɑːnsə] **1.** antworten; beantworten 3 (56); **2. answer (to)** Antwort (auf) 3 (56/168)

any ['eni]**: any ...?** (irgend)welche ...? 4 (71) • **not (...) any** kein, keine 4 (71)

anyway ['eniweɪ] sowieso 3 (55)

apple ['æpl] Apfel Welc (8/150)

appointment [ə'pɔɪntmənt] Termin, Verabredung 3 (60)

April ['eɪprəl] April TOP 1 (34/160)

are [ɑː] bist; sind; seid Welc (8/150) **The pencils are 35p.** Die Bleistifte kosten 35 Pence. TOP 3 (67/170)

argue ['ɑːgjuː] sich streiten, sich zanken 2 (40)

arm [ɑːm] Arm 4 (80/173)

armchair ['ɑːmtʃeə] Sessel TOP 2 (50)

art [ɑːt] Kunst 1 (23/158)

°article ['ɑːtɪkl] (Zeitungs-)Artikel

ask [ɑːsk] fragen 3 (55) • **ask about** nach *etwas* fragen 5 (87) **ask questions** Fragen stellen 3 (56/168)

asleep [ə'sliːp]**: be asleep** schlafen 5 (97)

at [ət, æt]**: at 7 Hamilton Street** in der Hamiltonstraße 7 Welc (12) • **at 8.45** um 8.45 1 (23) • **at home** daheim, zu Hause 2 (36) • **at last** endlich, schließlich 5 (97) • **at least** zumindest, wenigstens 3 (57) **at night** nachts, in der Nacht 2 (40/163) • **at school** in der Schule Welc (12/153) • **at that table** an dem Tisch (dort) / an den Tisch (dort) 1 (24/159) • **at the end (of)** am Ende (von) 5 (86) • **at the Shaws' house**

im Haus der Shaws / bei den Shaws zu Hause 2 (41) • **at the station** am Bahnhof 4 (73) • **at the top (of)** oben, am oberen Ende, an der Spitze (von) 2 (41) • **at the weekend** am Wochenende 2 (38/162) **at work** bei der Arbeit / am Arbeitsplatz Welc (16)
°**audience** ['ɔːdɪəns] Zuschauer/innen, Zuhörer/innen, Publikum
August ['ɔːgəst] August TOP 1 (34/160)
aunt [ɑːnt] Tante 2 (41)
autumn ['ɔːtəm] Herbst 5 (84/85/174)
°**avocado** [ˌævə'kɑːdəʊ] Avocado
away [ə'weɪ] weg, fort 4 (72)

B

baby ['beɪbi] Baby Welc (11)
back (to) [bæk] zurück (nach) Welc (17)
bad [bæd] schlecht, schlimm 1 (22) °**bad luck** Pech
badminton ['bædmɪntən] Badminton, Federball 1 (22)
bag [bæg] Tasche, Beutel, Tüte Welc (12/153)
ball [bɔːl] Ball 1 (22/157)
banana [bə'nɑːnə] Banane Welc (8/150)
band [bænd] Band, (Musik-)Gruppe Welc (9/151)
°**Bang!** [bæŋ] Peng!
bank [bæŋk] Bank, Sparkasse 1 (24) **bank robber** ['bæŋk ˌrɒbə] Bankräuber/in 1 (24)
°**barbecue** ['bɑːbɪkjuː] Grillparty
baseball ['beɪsbɔːl] Baseball 3 (53/167)
basket ['bɑːskɪt] Korb 2 (37) • **a basket of apples** ein Korb Äpfel 4 (69/171)
basketball ['bɑːskɪtbɔːl] Basketball 1 (22)
bath [bɑːθ] Badewanne TOP 2 (50)
bathroom ['bɑːθruːm] Badezimmer 2 (36/161)
be [biː] sein 1 (21)
beautiful ['bjuːtɪfl] schön 5 (97)
because [bɪ'kɒz] weil 2 (41)
bed [bed] Bett Welc (16) • **Bed and Breakfast (B&B)** [ˌbed‿ən 'brekfəst] Frühstückspension (*wörtlich:* Bett und Frühstück) Welc (16) • **go to bed** ins Bett gehen 2 (38)
bedroom ['bedruːm] Schlafzimmer 2 (36/161)
before [bɪ'fɔː] **1.** vor *(zeitlich)* 1 (20); °**2.** bevor
°**below** [bɪ'ləʊ] unten
°**bend** [bend] beugen
best [best]**: the best ...** der/die/das beste ...; die besten 5 (91)
better ['betə] besser 6 (103)
big [bɪg] groß Welc (9/151)
bike [baɪk] Fahrrad 3 (52/166) • **ride a bike** Rad fahren 3 (52/166)
biology [baɪ'ɒlədʒi] Biologie 1 (23/158)
bird [bɜːd] Vogel 2 (37/161)
birthday ['bɜːθdeɪ] Geburtstag TOP 1 (34) • **Happy birthday.** Herzlichen Glückwunsch zum Geburtstag. 4 (77) • **My birthday is in May.** Ich habe im Mai Geburtstag. TOP 1 (34/160) • **My birthday is on 13th June.** Ich habe am 13. Juni Geburtstag. TOP 1 (34/161) • **When's your birthday?** Wann hast du Geburtstag? TOP 1 (34/161)
► S. 161 birthdays
biscuit ['bɪskɪt] Keks, Plätzchen 4 (69)
°**bit** [bɪt]**: a bit** ein bisschen
black [blæk] schwarz Welc (13/154)
blue [bluː] blau Welc (13/154)
board [bɔːd] **1.** (Wand-)Tafel 1 (22/157) • **on the board** an der/die Tafel 1 (22/157) • **notice board** Anschlagtafel, schwarzes Brett 5 (84/85) °**2.** Brett
boat [bəʊt] Boot, Schiff Welc (9/151)
body ['bɒdi] Körper 4 (80/173)
book [bʊk] Buch Welc (12)
boot [buːt] Stiefel 3 (54/167)
boring ['bɔːrɪŋ] langweilig 1 (24)
both [bəʊθ] beide 4 (70)
bottle ['bɒtl] Flasche 4 (69) • **a bottle of milk** eine Flasche Milch 4 (69/171)
°**bottom** ['bɒtəm] Grund, Boden
°**bough of holly** [ˌbaʊ‿əv 'hɒlɪ] Stechpalmenast
bowl [bəʊl] Schüssel 2 (39) • **a bowl of cornflakes** eine Schale Cornflakes 4 (69/171)
box [bɒks] Kasten, Kästchen, Kiste 1 (19/157) • **sandwich box** Brotdose 1 (19)
boy [bɔɪ] Junge Welc (9/151)
bread *(no pl)* [bred] Brot 4 (69/171)
break [breɪk] Pause 1 (23)
breakfast ['brekfəst] Frühstück Welc (15) • **have breakfast** frühstücken Welc (15)
bridge [brɪdʒ] Brücke 6 (100)
bring [brɪŋ] (mit-, her)bringen 5 (84/85)
brother ['brʌðə] Bruder Welc (8/150)
brown [braʊn] braun Welc (13/154)
budgie ['bʌdʒi] Wellensittich 2 (37)
°**buffet** ['bʊfeɪ] Büfett
bus [bʌs] Bus 2 (38)
but [bət, bʌt] aber Welc (10)
°**butter** ['bʌtə] Butter
buy [baɪ] kaufen 4 (71)
by [baɪ] von 2 (48)
Bye. [baɪ] Tschüs! 1 (32)

C

°**cabin boy** ['kæbɪn bɔɪ] Schiffsjunge
cage [keɪdʒ] Käfig 2 (37)
cake [keɪk] Kuchen, Torte 4 (69/171)
calendar ['kælɪndə] Kalender TOP 1 (34)
call [kɔːl] **1.** rufen; anrufen; nennen 3 (65); **2.** Anruf, Telefongespräch 5 (90)
came [keɪm] *Vergangenheitsform von „come"* 5 (88/175)
camera ['kæmərə] Kamera, Fotoapparat 5 (84/85)
can [kən, kæn] **1.** können Welc (8/150) **I can't ...** [kɑːnt] ich kann nicht ... Welc (8/150) • **Can I help you?** Kann ich Ihnen helfen? / Was kann ich für Sie tun? *(im Geschäft)* 3 (54) **2.** dürfen 1 (22/133)
°**captain** ['kæptɪn] Kapitän/in
car [kɑː] Auto 3 (63)
°**caravan** ['kærəvæn] Wohnwagen
card [kɑːd] (Spiel-, Post-)Karte 3 (53)
°**Caribbean** [ˌkærə'biːən]**: in the Caribbean** in der Karibik
carrot ['kærət] Möhre, Karotte 2 (39)
cat [kæt] Katze Welc (12/153)
CD [ˌsiː'diː] CD 1 (19) • **CD player** CD-Spieler 4 (78)
cent (c) [sent] Cent TOP 3 (67)
centre ['sentə] Zentrum, Mitte 5 (86) / 6 (104) • **city centre** Stadtzentrum, Innenstadt 6 (104) **sports centre** Sportzentrum 5 (86)
chair [tʃeə] Stuhl 1 (18/156)
champion ['tʃæmpiən] Meister/in, Champion 6 (106)
change [tʃeɪndʒ] Wechselgeld TOP 3 (67)
°**chant** [tʃɑːnt] Sprechchor *(z.B. von Fußballfans)*
°**character** ['kærəktə] Figur, Person *(in Film, Theaterstück)*
°**charity** ['tʃærəti] Wohltätigkeitsorganisation
°**chart** [tʃɑːt] Schaubild, Diagramm, Tabelle
°**chase** [tʃeɪs] jagen
cheap [tʃiːp] billig 6 (101)

check [tʃek] (über)prüfen, kontrollieren 1 (30)
checkpoint ['tʃekpɔɪnt] Kontrollpunkt *(hier: zur Selbstüberprüfung)* (3)
°**Cheers.** [tʃɪəz] Prost!
cheese [tʃi:z] Käse 4 (69/171)
chicken ['tʃɪkɪn] Huhn; (Brat-)Hähnchen 4 (69/171)
child [tʃaɪld], *pl* **children** ['tʃɪldrən] Kind 2 (41)
chips *(pl)* [tʃɪps] Pommes frites 4 (69)
chocolate ['tʃɒklət] Schokolade 4 (69/171)
choir ['kwaɪə] Chor 5 (84/85)
choose [tʃu:z] (sich) aussuchen, (aus)wählen 4 (82)
°**chorus** ['kɔ:rəs] Refrain
Christmas ['krɪsməs] Weihnachten TOP 1 (34) • °**Father Christmas** der Weihnachtsmann • °**Merry Christmas.** Frohe Weihnachten.
church [tʃɜ:tʃ] Kirche 6 (100)
°**chutney** ['tʃʌtni] Chutney *(Paste aus Früchten und Gewürzen)*
cinema ['sɪnəmə] Kino 5 (86)
°**circle** ['sɜ:kl] Kreis
city ['sɪti] (Groß-)Stadt 5 (89)
city centre Stadtzentrum, Innenstadt 6 (104)
°**clap (-pp-)** [klæp]: **Clap your hands.** Klatsch(t) in die Hände.
°**clarinet** [ˌklærə'net] Klarinette
class [klɑ:s] (Schul-)Klasse 1 (24)
class teacher Klassenlehrer/in 1 (24)
classmate ['klɑ:smeɪt] Klassenkamerad/in, Mitschüler/in 1 (31)
classroom ['klɑ:sru:m] Klassenzimmer Welc (12/153)
clean [kli:n] sauber machen, putzen 2 (38) • **I clean my teeth.** Ich putze mir die Zähne. 2 (38)
clear [klɪə] klar, deutlich 5 (97)
clever ['klevə] schlau, klug 1 (20)
climb [klaɪm] klettern; hinaufklettern (auf) 1 (22) • **Climb a tree.** Klettere auf einen Baum. 1 (22)
clock [klɒk] (Wand-, Stand-, Turm-)Uhr 1 (19)
close [kləʊz] schließen, zumachen Welc (10)
°**clothes** *(pl)* [kləʊðz] Kleidung, Kleidungsstücke
club [klʌb] Klub; Verein 5 (84/85)
°**cocktail stick** ['kɒkteɪl stɪk] Cocktailspieß(chen)
cola ['kəʊlə] Cola 4 (69)
cold [kəʊld] kalt 5 (98) • **be cold** frieren 5 (98)
collect [kə'lekt] sammeln 3 (53)
colour ['kʌlə] Farbe Welc (8/150)
What colour is ...? Welche Farbe hat ...? Welc (13)
°**combine** [kəm'baɪn] kombinieren, verbinden
come [kʌm] kommen 1 (20) • **come home** nach Hause kommen 2 (36/161) • **come in** hereinkommen 1 (31)
comic ['kɒmɪk] Comic-Heft 1 (18)
°**compare** [kəm'peə] vergleichen
°**complete** [kəm'pli:t] vervollständigen, ergänzen
computer [kəm'pju:tə] Computer 1 (22/157)
°**context** ['kɒntekst]: **from the context** aus dem Zusammenhang, aus dem Kontext
cooker ['kʊkə] Herd TOP 2 (50)
cool [ku:l] cool 4 (82)
°**copy** ['kɒpi] kopieren, übertragen, abschreiben
corner ['kɔ:nə] Ecke 6 (102)
cornflakes ['kɔ:nfleɪks] Cornflakes 1 (19)
°**correct** [kə'rekt] **1.** korrigieren, verbessern; **2.** richtig, korrekt
country ['kʌntri] Land 2 (48)
course: of course [əv 'kɔ:s] natürlich, selbstverständlich 2 (40)
cousin ['kʌzn] Cousin, Cousine 2 (41)
cover ['kʌvə] (CD-)Hülle 5 (89)
°**Crash.** [kræʃ] Krach!
crisps *(pl)* [krɪsps] Kartoffelchips 4 (69)
°**cross** [krɒs] Kreuz
cross [krɒs]: **be cross (with)** böse, sauer sein (auf) 5 (88)
°**cucumber** ['kju:kʌmbə] (Salat-)Gurke
cupboard ['kʌbəd] Schrank TOP 2 (50)
°**cut (-tt-)** [kʌt] schneiden

D

dad [dæd] Papa, Vati; Vater Welc (8/150)
dance [dɑ:ns] **1.** tanzen 3 (53/166); **2.** Tanz 5 (84/85) • °**dancer** Tänzer/in • **dancing** Tanzen 3 (53/166) • **dancing lessons** Tanzstunden, Tanzunterricht 3 (53)
dark [dɑ:k] dunkel 5 (96)
date [deɪt] Datum TOP 1 (34)
daughter ['dɔ:tə] Tochter 2 (41)
day [deɪ] Tag Welc (12) • **one day** eines Tages 6 (109) • **days of the week** Wochentage Welc (14/154)
dead [ded] tot 2 (41)
dear [dɪə] **1.** Schatz, Liebling 4 (72); **2. Dear Jay ...** Lieber Jay, ... 3 (56)
December [dɪ'sembə] Dezember TOP 1 (34/160)
°**decide (on)** [dɪ'saɪd] sich entscheiden (für), beschließen
°**deck** [dek] Deck
°**deck** [dek] schmücken
°**decorations** *(pl)* [ˌdekə'reɪʃnz] (Fest-)Schmuck
°**design** [dɪ'saɪn] **1.** entwerfen; **2.** Entwurf
desk [desk] Schreibtisch 1 (28/159)
detective [dɪ'tektɪv] Detektiv/in 3 (65)
°**dialogue** ['daɪəlɒg] Dialog
diary ['daɪəri] Tagebuch; Terminkalender 5 (88)
dictionary ['dɪkʃənri] Wörterbuch, *(alphabetisches)* Wörterverzeichnis (3)
did [dɪd] *Vergangenheitsform von „do“* 5 (88/175) • **Did you go ...?** Bist du ... gegangen? / Seid ihr ... gegangen? 5 (89) • **we didn't sing** ['dɪdnt] wir sangen nicht / wir haben nicht gesungen 5 (89)
different (from) ['dɪfrənt] verschieden, unterschiedlich; anders (als) 1 (25)
difficult ['dɪfɪkəlt] schwierig, schwer 2 (49)
dining room ['daɪnɪŋ ru:m] Esszimmer TOP 2 (50)
dinner ['dɪnə] Abendessen, Abendbrot 3 (57) • **have dinner** Abendbrot essen 3 (57/168)
disco ['dɪskəʊ] Disko 4 (70)
°**discuss** [dɪ'skʌs] besprechen; diskutieren (über)
dishwasher ['dɪʃwɒʃə] Geschirrspülmaschine TOP 2 (50)
divorced [dɪ'vɔ:st] geschieden 2 (41)
do [du:] tun, machen 1 (22) • **Do what I do.** Tue, was ich tue. 1 (22) **Do you like ...?** Magst du ...? 1 (18/156) • **do sport** Sport treiben 3 (53/167)
dog [dɒg] Hund Welc (12/153)
don't [dəʊnt]: **Don't listen to Dan.** Hör/Hört nicht auf Dan. 1 (20) **I don't know.** Ich weiß es nicht. TOP 2 (50) • **I don't like ...** Ich mag ... nicht. / Ich mag kein(e) ... Welc (8/150)
door [dɔ:] Tür 4 (81)
doorbell ['dɔ:bel] Türklingel 4 (81)
°**doorstopper** ['dɔ:stɒpə] Türstopper; *hier:* mehrschichtiges Sandwich
dossier ['dɒsieɪ] Mappe, Dossier *(des Sprachenportfolios)* (3)
°**dot** [dɒt] Pünktchen

double ['dʌbl] zweimal, doppelt, Doppel- Welc (15)
down [daʊn] hinunter, herunter, nach unten 4 (72/172)
downstairs [ˌdaʊn'steəz] unten; nach unten TOP 2 (50)
drama ['drɑːmə] Schauspiel, darstellende Kunst 1 (23/158)
°**draw** [drɔː] zeichnen
dream [driːm] Traum TOP 2 (50)
dream house Traumhaus TOP 2 (50)
dress [dres] Kleid 3 (54/167)
dressed [drest]: **get dressed** sich anziehen 2 (39)
°**dress rehearsal** ['dres rɪˌhɜːsl] Generalprobe, Kostümprobe
drink [drɪŋk] **1.** trinken 2 (39); **2.** Getränk 4 (69)
drop (-pp-) [drɒp] fallen lassen Welc (10)
°**drum** [drʌm] Trommel
DVD [ˌdiː viː' diː] DVD 4 (71)

E

each [iːtʃ] jeder, jede, jedes (einzelne) 6 (102)
ear [ɪə] Ohr 4 (80/173)
early ['ɜːli] früh 2 (38)
earring ['ɪərɪŋ] Ohrring 4 (71)
easy ['iːzi] leicht, einfach 2 (38)
eat [iːt] essen 1 (18/156)
elephant ['elɪfənt] Elefant 5 (95)
e-mail ['iːmeɪl] E-Mail 2 (42)
empty ['empti] leer Welc (10)
end [end] Ende 1 (31) • **at the end (of)** am Ende (von) 5 (86)
English ['ɪŋglɪʃ] Englisch; englisch Welc (8/150)
enough [ɪ'nʌf] genug 1 (22)
essay (about, on) ['eseɪ] Aufsatz (über) 2 (38)
°**etc.** [et'setərə] usw.
euro (€) ['jʊərəʊ] Euro TOP 3 (67)
evening ['iːvnɪŋ] Abend 2 (38/162)
in the evening abends, am Abend 2 (38/162) • **on Friday evening** freitagabends, am Freitagabend 2 (38/162)
every ['evri] jeder, jede, jedes 2 (38)
°**everybody** ['evriˌbɒdi] jede, jeder
everything ['evriθɪŋ] alles 1 (31)
°**example** [ɪg'zɑːmpl] Beispiel
°**for example** zum Beispiel
exciting [ɪk'saɪtɪŋ] aufregend, spannend 5 (84/85)
Excuse me, ... [ɪk'skjuːz miː] Entschuldigung, ... / Entschuldigen Sie, ... Welc (17)
► S. 155 „Entschuldigung"

exercise ['eksəsaɪz] Übung, Aufgabe Welc (12/154) • **exercise book** Schulheft, Übungsheft Welc (12)
expensive [ɪk'spensɪv] teuer 4 (71)
explore [ɪk'splɔː] erkunden, erforschen 6 (101)
°**explosive** [ɪk'spləʊsɪv] Sprengstoff
extra ['ekstrə] zusätzlich 5 (92)
eye [aɪ] Auge 4 (80/173)

F

face [feɪs] Gesicht 1 (22/157)
family ['fæməli] Familie Welc (12/153)
family tree (Familien-)Stammbaum 2 (41)
fan [fæn] Fan 6 (106)
°**fancy-dress party** [ˌfænsi'dres] Kostümfest
fantastic [fæn'tæstɪk] fantastisch, toll 4 (81)
°**far** [fɑː]: **so far** bis jetzt, bis hierher
°**Fast away the old year passes.** [fɑːst] *etwa:* Schnell vergeht das alte Jahr.
father ['fɑːðə] Vater Welc (12/153)
°**Father Christmas** der Weihnachtsmann
favourite ['feɪvərɪt] Lieblings- Welc (8/150) • **my favourite colour** meine Lieblingsfarbe Welc (8/150)
February ['februəri] Februar TOP 1 (34/160)
feed [fiːd] füttern 2 (39)
feet [fiːt] *Plural von „foot"* 4 (80/173)
felt tip ['felt tɪp] Filzstift Welc (12/153)
file [faɪl]: **grammar file** *Grammatikanhang* (3/130) • **skills file** *Anhang mit Lern- und Arbeitstechniken* (3/122)
°**fill in** [ˌfɪl_'ɪn] einsetzen
film [fɪlm] Film 2 (48) • **film star** Filmstar 2 (48)
find [faɪnd] finden Welc (10) • **find out (about)** herausfinden (über) 3 (65) • **finder** Finder 5 (90)
finger ['fɪŋgə] Finger 4 (80/173)
finish ['fɪnɪʃ] beenden, zu Ende machen; enden 5 (84/85)
first [fɜːst] **1.** erste(r, s) Welc (14)
the first day der erste Tag Welc (14)
be first der/die Erste sein 6 (105)
2. zuerst, als Erstes 1 (20)
fish, *pl* **fish** [fɪʃ] Fisch 2 (37/161)
fit (-tt-) [fɪt] passen 2 (48)
flat [flæt] Wohnung Welc (14)
floor [flɔː] Fußboden 5 (98)
follow ['fɒləʊ] folgen; verfolgen 4 (71)
food [fuːd] **1.** Essen; Lebensmittel 1 (24); **2.** Futter 2 (39)

foot [fʊt], *pl* **feet** [fiːt] Fuß 4 (80/173)
football ['fʊtbɔːl] Fußball Welc (9/151) • **football boots** Fußballschuhe, -stiefel 3 (54/167)
for [fə, fɔː] **1.** für Welc (12) • **for breakfast/lunch/dinner** zum Frühstück/Mittagessen/Abendbrot 4 (69) • °**for example** zum Beispiel **for lots of reasons** aus vielen Gründen 6 (105) • **for three days** drei Tage (lang) 5 (97) • **just for fun** nur zum Spaß 6 (101/177) • **What's for homework?** Was haben wir als Hausaufgabe auf? 1 (28/159) • °**for a long time** eine lange Zeit, lange °**2.** denn
forget (-tt-) [fə'get] vergessen 1 (28/159)
form [fɔːm] **1.** (Schul-)Klasse 1 (22)
form teacher Klassenlehrer/in 1 (22)
°**2.** Form
free [friː] **1.** frei 3 (52) • **free time** Freizeit, freie Zeit 3 (52)
2. kostenlos 6 (100)
°**freeze** [friːz] einfrieren, gefrieren; *hier:* stillstehen, erstarren
French [frentʃ] Französisch 1 (23/158)
Friday ['fraɪdeɪ, 'fraɪdi] Freitag Welc (14/154)
fridge [frɪdʒ] Kühlschrank TOP 2 (50)
friend [frend] Freund/in Welc (12/153)
from [frəm, frɒm] **1.** aus Welc (8/150); **2.** von 2 (44) • **I'm from ...** Ich komme aus ... / Ich bin aus ... Welc (8/150) • **Where are you from?** Wo kommst du her? Welc (8/150)
front [frʌnt]: **in front of** vor *(räumlich)* 4 (73) • **front door** [ˌfrʌnt 'dɔː] Wohnungstür, Haustür 4 (81)
fruit [fruːt] Obst, Früchte; Frucht 4 (69) • **fruit salad** ['fruːt ˌsæləd] Obstsalat 4 (69)
full [fʊl] voll Welc (10)
fun [fʌn] Spaß 6 (101) • **have fun** Spaß haben, sich amüsieren 6 (101/177) • **Have fun!** Viel Spaß! 6 (101/177) • **just for fun** nur zum Spaß 6 (101/177) • **Riding is fun.** Reiten macht Spaß. 6 (101/177)
► S. 177 fun
funny ['fʌni] witzig, komisch 4 (71)

G

°**galleon** ['gæliən] Galeone
game [geɪm] Spiel (3)
garden ['gɑːdn] Garten 2 (36)
geography [dʒi'ɒgrəfi] Geografie, Erdkunde 1 (23/158)

German ['dʒɜːmən] Deutsch; deutsch; Deutsche(r) 1 (23/158)
Germany ['dʒɜːməni] Deutschland Welc (17)
get (-tt-) [get] **1.** gelangen, (hin-)kommen 4 (82) • **get home** nach Hause kommen 6 (106)
2. get dressed sich anziehen 2 (39) °**Get washed.** Wasch dich.
3. get off (the train/bus) (aus dem Zug/Bus) aussteigen 4 (73) • **get on (the train/bus)** (in den Zug/Bus) einsteigen 4 (73/172)
°**4. Get on with your work.** Sieh zu, dass du mit deiner Arbeit vorankommst.
5. get ready (for) sich fertig machen (für), sich vorbereiten (auf) 4 (72) • **get things ready** Dinge fertig machen, vorbereiten 2 (48)
6. get up aufstehen 2 (38)
getting by in English [ˌgetɪŋ 'baɪ] *etwa:* auf Englisch zurechtkommen (3)
girl [gɜːl] Mädchen Welc (9/151)
give [gɪv] geben 2 (39)
glass [glɑːs] Glas 4 (69) • **a glass of water** ein Glas Wasser 4 (69/171)
glasses *(pl)* ['glɑːsɪz] (eine) Brille 2 (48/165)
°**glorious** ['glɔːriəs] herrlich; ruhmreich
glue [gluː] **1.** Klebstoff 6 (104)
glue stick ['gluː stɪk] Klebestift Welc (12/153)
°**2.** kleben
go (to) [gəʊ] gehen (zu, nach) Welc (14) • **go home** nach Hause gehen 2 (36/161) • **go on** weitermachen 1 (32) • **Go on.** Mach weiter. / Erzähl weiter. 1 (32) • °**go out** weg-, raus-, ausgehen • **go riding** reiten gehen 3 (53) • **go shopping** einkaufen gehen 3 (63) **go swimming** schwimmen gehen 3 (52/166) • **go to bed** ins Bett gehen 2 (38) • **Let's go.** Auf geht's! *(wörtlich:* Lass uns gehen.) Welc (12) • °**go with** passen zu
°**gold** [gəʊld] Gold
good [gʊd] gut Welc (14/154)
Good afternoon. Guten Tag. *(nachmittags)* 3 (54) • **Good luck (with ...)!** Viel Glück (bei/mit ...)! Welc (17) • **Good morning.** Guten Morgen. Welc (14/154)
Goodbye. [ˌgʊd'baɪ] Auf Wiedersehen. Welc (14/154) • **say goodbye** sich verabschieden Welc (17)
got [gɒt]**: I've got ...** Ich habe ... Welc (8/150) • **I haven't got a chair.** Ich habe keinen Stuhl. 1 (24)
got up [ˌgɒt‿'ʌp] *Vergangenheitsform von „get up"* 5 (88/175)
grammar ['græmə] Grammatik (3)
grammar file *Grammatikanhang* (3/130)
grandchild ['græntʃaɪld], *pl* **grandchildren** ['-tʃɪldrən] Enkel/in 2 (41)
grandfather ['grænfɑːðə] Großvater 2 (41/164)
grandma ['grænmɑː] Oma 2 (41)
grandmother ['grænmʌðə] Großmutter 2 (41/164)
grandpa ['grænpɑː] Opa 2 (41)
grandparents ['grænpeərənts] Großeltern 2 (41)
great [greɪt] großartig, toll Welc (9)
green [griːn] grün Welc (13/154)
group [gruːp] Gruppe 5 (86)
grumble ['grʌmbl] murren, nörgeln 6 (104)
°**guess** [ges] raten, erraten
guest [gest] Gast 2 (47)
guinea pig ['gɪni pɪg] Meerschweinchen 2 (37/161)
guitar [gɪ'tɑː] Gitarre 3 (53) • **play the guitar** Gitarre spielen 3 (53/166)

H

had [hæd] *Vergangenheitsform von „have" und von „have got"* 5 (88)
°**hail** [heɪl] *(das neue Jahr)* begrüßen
hair *(no pl)* [heə] Haar, Haare 4 (80/173)
half [hɑːf]**: half past 11** halb zwölf (11.30 / 23.30) Welc (16/155)
hall [hɔːl] Flur, Diele 6 (110)
°**Halloween** [ˌhæləʊ'iːn] *der 31. Oktober (Tag vor Allerheiligen), an dem man sich als Monster, Hexe oder Geist verkleidet*
°**ham** [hæm] Schinken
hamburger ['hæmbɜːgə] Hamburger 4 (69/171)
hamster ['hæmstə] Hamster 2 (37/161)
hand [hænd] Hand 2 (38)
happen (to) ['hæpən] geschehen, passieren (mit) TOP 2 (51)
happy ['hæpi] glücklich, froh Welc (9/151) • **Happy birthday.** Herzlichen Glückwunsch zum Geburtstag. 4 (77)
°**harbour** ['hɑːbə] Hafen
°**hat** [hæt] Hut
hate [heɪt] hassen, gar nicht mögen 3 (57)
have [hæv]**: have a picnic** ein Picknick machen 6 (100) • **have a shower** (sich) duschen 2 (48) **have breakfast** frühstücken Welc (15) • **have dinner** Abendbrot essen 3 (57/168) • **have ... for breakfast** ... zum Frühstück essen/trinken 4 (69) • **have fun** Spaß haben, sich amüsieren 6 (101/177) **Have fun!** Viel Spaß! 6 (101/177) **have to do** tun müssen 3 (57)
have got: I've got ... [aɪv 'gɒt] Ich habe ... Welc (8/150) • **I haven't got a chair.** ['hævnt gɒt] Ich habe keinen Stuhl. 1 (24)
°**hay** [heɪ] Heu
he [hiː] er Welc (8)
head [hed] Kopf 3 (55)
°**heading** ['hedɪŋ] Überschrift, Titel
hear [hɪə] hören 4 (73)
°**heat** [hiːt] Hitze
Hello. [hə'ləʊ] Hallo. / Guten Tag. Welc (8/150)
help [help] **1.** helfen Welc (11)
Can I help you? Kann ich Ihnen helfen? / Was kann ich für Sie tun? *(im Geschäft)* 3 (54)
2. Hilfe 2 (40)
her [hə, hɜː] **1.** ihr, ihre 1 (21); **2.** sie; ihr 1 (32)
here [hɪə] **1.** hier Welc (11); **2.** hierher 2 (42/164) • **Here you are.** Bitte sehr. / Hier bitte. 2 (40)
▶ S.163 „bitte"
Hi! [haɪ] Hallo! Welc (8/150) • **Say hi to Dilip for me.** Grüß Dilip von mir. 3 (56)
hide [haɪd] sich verstecken; *(etwas)* verstecken 4 (73)
°**highlight** ['haɪlaɪt] Höhepunkt
him [hɪm] ihn; ihm 1 (24)
his [hɪz] sein, seine Welc (8)
history ['hɪstri] Geschichte 1 (23/158)
hobby ['hɒbi] Hobby 3 (52/162)
hockey ['hɒki] Hockey 1 (22)
hockey shoes Hockeyschuhe 3 (54/167)
°**hold** [həʊld]**: hold hands** sich an den Händen halten • **hold up** hochhalten
°**hole** [həʊl] Loch
holidays ['hɒlədeɪz] Ferien Welc (12)
home [həʊm] Heim, Zuhause 2 (36)
at home daheim, zu Hause 2 (36)
come home nach Hause kommen 2 (36/161) • **get home** nach Hause kommen 6 (106) • **go home** nach Hause gehen 2 (36/161)
homework *(no pl)* ['həʊmwɜːk] Hausaufgabe(n) 1 (28/159) • **do homework** die Hausaufgabe(n) machen 2 (48) • **What's for homework?** Was haben wir als Hausaufgabe auf? 1 (28/159)
°**Hooray!** [hu'reɪ] Hurra!
horse [hɔːs] Pferd 2 (37/161)

°**hospital** ['hɒspɪtl] Krankenhaus
hot [hɒt] heiß 4 (69/171) • **hot chocolate** heiße Schokolade 4 (69/171)
house [haʊs] Haus Welc (9/151)
at the Shaws' house im Haus der Shaws / bei den Shaws zu Hause 2 (41)
how [haʊ] wie Welc (8/150) • **How do you know ...?** Woher weißt/kennst du ...? 6 (110) • **how many?** wie viele? 5 (96/176) • **how much?** wie viel? 5 (96/176) • **How much is/are ...?** Was kostet/kosten ...? / Wie viel kostet/kosten ...? TOP 3 (67)
How old are you? Wie alt bist du? Welc (8/150) • **How was ...?** Wie war ...? 1 (32)
hundred ['hʌndrəd] hundert Welc (15)
°**hungry** ['hʌŋgri] hungrig • °**be hungry** Hunger haben, hungrig sein
°**hurrah** [hə'rɑː] hurra
hurry ['hʌri]: **1. hurry up** sich beeilen 1 (31); **2. be in a hurry** in Eile sein, es eilig haben 4 (71)
hurt [hɜːt] **1.** wehtun; verletzen 6 (110); **2.** *Vergangenheitsform von „hurt"* 6 (110)
hutch [hʌtʃ] (Kaninchen-)Stall 2 (37)

I

I [aɪ] ich Welc (8/150) • **I'm** [aɪm] ich bin Welc (8/150) • **I'm from ...** Ich komme aus ... / Ich bin aus ... Welc (8/150) • **I'm ... years old.** Ich bin ... Jahre alt. Welc (8/150) • **I'm sorry.** Entschuldigung. / Tut mir leid. 1 (21)
ice: ice cream [ˌaɪs 'kriːm] (Speise-)Eis 4 (69/171) • °**ice rink** ['aɪs rɪŋk] Schlittschuhbahn
idea [aɪ'dɪə] Idee, Einfall 1 (24)
°**if** [ɪf] falls, wenn • °**if you're happy** wenn du glücklich bist
in [ɪn] in Welc (8/150) • **in ... Street** in der ...straße Welc (8/150) • **in English** auf Englisch Welc (8/150)
in front of vor *(räumlich)* 4 (73)
in here hier drinnen Welc (11) • **in the afternoon** nachmittags, am Nachmittag 2 (38/162) • **in the evening** abends, am Abend 2 (38/162) • **in the morning** am Morgen, morgens 1 (19) • **in the photo** auf dem Foto Welc (9/152)
in the picture auf dem Bild Welc (11/152)
°**Indian** ['ɪndiən] indisch
°**industrial museum** [ɪnˌdʌstriəl mju'ziːəm] Industriemuseum
°**infinitive** [ɪn'fɪnətɪv] Infinitiv *(Grundform des Verbs)*
°**information** *(no pl)* [ˌɪnfə'meɪʃn] Information(en)
°**ingredient** [ɪn'griːdiənt] Zutat *(beim Kochen)*
inside [ˌɪn'saɪd] innen (drin), drinnen 4 (81)
interesting ['ɪntrəstɪŋ] interessant 2 (48)
interview ['ɪntəvjuː] **1.** Interview 3 (61); °**2.** interviewen, befragen
into ['ɪntə, 'ɪntʊ] in ... (hinein) 3 (65/169)
invitation (to) [ˌɪnvɪ'teɪʃn] Einladung (zu) 4 (70)
invite (to) [ɪn'vaɪt] einladen (zu) 4 (70/171)
is [ɪz] ist Welc (8/150)
it [ɪt] er/sie/es Welc (9) • **It's £1.** Er/Sie/Es kostet 1 Pfund. TOP 3 (67)
its [ɪts] sein/seine; ihr/ihre 2 (41/138)

J

January ['dʒænjuəri] Januar TOP 1 (34/160)
jeans *(pl)* [dʒiːnz] Jeans 3 (54/167)
job [dʒɒb] Aufgabe, Job 5 (93)
joke [dʒəʊk] Witz 1 (22)
°**jolly** ['dʒɒli] fröhlich
judo ['dʒuːdəʊ] Judo 2 (40) • **do judo** Judo machen 2 (40)
jug [dʒʌg] Krug 4 (69) • **a jug of orange juice** ein Krug Orangensaft 4 (69/171)
juice [dʒuːs] Saft 4 (69/171)
July [dʒu'laɪ] Juli TOP 1 (34/160)
°**jumble** ['dʒʌmbl] gebrauchte Sachen, Trödel
jumble sale ['dʒʌmbl seɪl] Wohltätigkeitsbasar TOP 3 (67)
°**jump** [dʒʌmp] springen
June [dʒuːn] Juni TOP 1 (34/160)
junior ['dʒuːniə] Junioren-, Jugend- 5 (84/85)
just [dʒʌst] (einfach) nur, bloß 2 (41)

K

key word ['kiː wɜːd] Stichwort, Schlüsselwort 4 (71)
kid [kɪd] Kind, Jugendliche(r) 5 (86)
kill [kɪl] töten 5 (96)
king [kɪŋ] König 5 (88)
kitchen ['kɪtʃɪn] Küche 2 (36/161)
kite [kaɪt] Drachen Welc (9)
knee [niː] Knie 4 (80/173)
°**knife** [naɪf], *pl* **knives** [naɪvz] Messer
know [nəʊ] **1.** wissen 3 (54/167); **2.** kennen 3 (60) • **How do you know ...?** Woher weißt du ...? / Woher kennst du ...? 6 (110)
I don't know. Ich weiß es nicht. TOP 2 (50) • **..., you know.** ..., wissen Sie. / ..., weißt du. 3 (54) • **You know what, Sophie?** Weißt du was, Sophie? 6 (104)

L

°**label** ['leɪbl] beschriften, etikettieren
°**lads and lasses** [ˌlædz‿ənd 'læsəz] *(umgangssprachlich)* Jungs und Mädels
lamp [læmp] Lampe 1 (19)
language ['læŋgwɪdʒ] Sprache (3)
lasagne [lə'zænjə] Lasagne 1 (24)
last [lɑːst] letzte(r, s) Welc (12)
the last day der letzte Tag Welc (12)
at last endlich, schließlich 5 (97)
late [leɪt] spät; zu spät Welc (12)
be late zu spät sein/kommen Welc (12) • **Sorry, I'm late.** Entschuldigung, dass ich zu spät bin/komme. Welc (12)
later ['leɪtə] später 4 (72)
laugh [lɑːf] lachen Welc (10)
lay the table [leɪ] den Tisch decken 3 (57)
°**lazy** ['leɪzi] faul
learn [lɜːn] lernen 3 (57)
least: at least [ət 'liːst] zumindest, wenigstens 3 (57)
°**leave** [liːv] verlassen
°**leaves** *(pl)* [liːvz] Laub, Blätter
leg [leg] Bein 4 (80/173)
lemonade [ˌlemə'neɪd] Limonade 4 (69/171)
lesson ['lesn] (Unterrichts-)Stunde 1 (20) • **lessons** *(pl)* ['lesnz] Unterricht 1 (20)
Let's ... [lets] Lass uns ... / Lasst uns ... Welc (12) • **Let's go.** Auf geht's! *(wörtlich:* Lass uns gehen.) Welc (12)
Let's look at the list. Sehen wir uns die Liste an. / Lasst uns die Liste ansehen. Welc (12)
letter ['letə] Buchstabe 2 (40)
°**lettuce** ['letɪs] (grüner) Salat
library ['laɪbrəri] Bibliothek, Bücherei 6 (102)
life [laɪf], *pl* **lives** [laɪvz] Leben 2 (38)
like [laɪk] wie 1 (24) • °**like this** so
like [laɪk] mögen, gernhaben Welc (8/150) • **I like ...** Ich mag ...

Welc (8/150) • **I don't like ...** Ich mag ... nicht. / Ich mag kein(e) ... Welc (8/150) • **Do you like ...?** Magst du ...? 1 (18/156) • **Dilip likes ...** Dilip mag ... 1 (32) • **I like swimming/dancing.** Ich schwimme/tanze gern. 3 (53) • **I'd like ... (= I would like ...)** Ich hätte gern ... / Ich möchte gern ... 4 (69) • **I'd like to talk about ... (= I would like to talk about ...)** Ich möchte/würde gern über ... reden 6 (105) • **Would you like ...?** Möchtest du ...? / Möchten Sie ...? 4 (69) • **Would you like some?** Möchtest du etwas/ein paar? / Möchten Sie etwas/ein paar? 4 (69)

°**line** [laɪn] Linie

link [lɪŋk] verbinden, verknüpfen 3 (63)

list [lɪst] Liste Welc (12)

listen (to) ['lɪsn] zuhören; sich *etwas* anhören Welc (9/151)

little ['lɪtl] klein 1 (32)

live [lɪv] leben, wohnen Welc (8/150)

lives [laɪvz] *Plural von „life"* 2 (38)

living room ['lɪvɪŋ ru:m] Wohnzimmer 2 (36/161)

°**local** ['ləʊkl] lokal, örtlich, Lokal-

°**locked** [lɒkt] abgeschlossen, verschlossen

long [lɒŋ] lang 4 (70)

look [lʊk] schauen, gucken Welc (10) • **look at** ansehen, anschauen Welc (12/153) • **Look at the board.** Sieh/Seht an die Tafel. 1 (24/159) • **look different/great/old** anders/toll/alt aussehen TOP 2 (51) **look round** sich umsehen 4 (73) °**look for** suchen • °**look up words** Wörter nachschlagen

▸ S.163 (to) look – (to) see – (to) watch

°**look-out** ['lʊkaʊt] Ausguck

lot: a lot [ə 'lɒt] viel TOP 2 (51) **Thanks a lot!** Vielen Dank! 3 (56) **He likes her a lot.** Er mag sie sehr. 1 (32) • **lots more** [lɒts] viel mehr 6 (101) • **lots of ...** eine Menge ..., viele ..., viel ... 1 (18)

loud [laʊd] laut 6 (103)

°**love** [lʌv] lieben

Love ... [lʌv] Liebe Grüße, ... *(Briefschluss)* 3 (56)

luck [lʌk]: **Good luck (with ...)!** Viel Glück (bei/mit ...)! Welc (17) • °**bad luck** Pech

°**luggage van** ['lʌgɪdʒ væn] Gepäckwagen

lunch [lʌntʃ] Mittagessen 1 (23) **lunch break** Mittagspause 1 (23)

M

mad [mæd] verrückt 1 (20)

made [meɪd] *Vergangenheitsform von „make"* 5 (88/175)

magazine [ˌmægə'zi:n] Zeitschrift, Magazin 5 (89)

make [meɪk] machen; bauen TOP 1 (34) • **make a mess** alles durcheinander bringen, alles in Unordnung bringen 4 (72)

man [mæn], *pl* **men** [men] Mann 3 (65)

many ['meni] viele 5 (96) • **how many?** wie viele? 5 (96/176)

▸ S.176 „viel", „viele"

March [mɑ:tʃ] März TOP 1 (34/160)

°**mark** [mɑ:k] markieren, kennzeichnen

marmalade ['mɑ:məleɪd] (Orangen-)Marmelade 1 (18)

married (to) ['mærɪd] verheiratet (mit) 2 (41)

match [mætʃ] Spiel, Wettkampf 3 (56)

°**match** [mætʃ] **1.** passen zu; **2.** zuordnen • °**Match the letters and numbers.** Ordne die Buchstaben den Zahlen zu.

maths [mæθs] Mathematik 1 (23/158)

May [meɪ] Mai TOP 1 (34/160)

°**may** [meɪ] dürfen

maybe ['meɪbi] vielleicht 3 (65)

me [mi:] mir; mich Welc (10) • **Me too.** Ich auch. Welc (12) • **That's me.** Das bin ich. Welc (10) • **Why me?** Warum ich? Welc (14)

meat [mi:t] Fleisch 2 (39)

meet [mi:t] **1.** treffen; kennenlernen Welc (8); **2.** sich treffen 3 (60)

men [men] *Plural von „man"* 3 (65)

°**Merry Christmas.** [ˌmeri 'krɪsməs] Frohe Weihnachten.

mess [mes]: **make a mess** alles durcheinanderbringen, alles in Unordnung bringen 4 (72)

°**miaow** [mi'aʊ] miauen

mice [maɪs] *Plural von „mouse"* 2 (37/161)

middle (of) ['mɪdl] Mitte 6 (102)

milk [mɪlk] Milch 1 (19)

°**mime** [maɪm] **1.** vorspielen, pantomimisch darstellen; **2.** Pantomime

mind map ['maɪnd mæp] Mindmap („Gedankenkarte", „Wissensnetz") 2 (38)

mints *(pl)* [mɪnts] Pfefferminzbonbons 1 (32)

minute ['mɪnɪt] Minute 4 (81)

Miss White [mɪs] Frau White *(unverheiratet)* 5 (86)

°**missing** ['mɪsɪŋ]: **be missing** fehlen **the missing information/words** die fehlenden Informationen/Wörter

mistake [mɪ'steɪk] Fehler 5 (87)

°**mix (with)** [mɪks] sich vermischen (mit) • °**mix up** durcheinanderbringen

°**mobile** ['məʊbaɪl] Mobile

mobile (phone) ['məʊbaɪl] Mobiltelefon, Handy 1 (19)

model ['mɒdl] Modell*(-flugzeug, -schiff usw.)* 3 (53)

Monday ['mʌndeɪ, 'mʌndi] Montag Welc (14/154) • **Monday morning** Montagmorgen Welc (14/154)

money ['mʌni] Geld 1 (19)

month [mʌnθ] Monat TOP 1 (34/160)

more [mɔ:] mehr 1 (32) • **lots more** viel mehr 6 (101) • **no more music** keine Musik mehr 4 (81)

morning ['mɔ:nɪŋ] Morgen, Vormittag Welc (14/154) • **in the morning** morgens, am Morgen 2 (38/162) • **Monday morning** Montagmorgen Welc (14/154) • **on Friday morning** freitagmorgens, am Freitagmorgen 2 (38/162)

most [məʊst]: **most people** die meisten Leute 3 (57)

mother ['mʌðə] Mutter Welc (12/153)

mouse [maʊs], *pl* **mice** [maɪs] Maus 2 (37/161)

mouth [maʊθ] Mund 4 (80/173)

°**mozzarella** [ˌmɒtsə'relə] Mozzarella

MP3 player [ˌempi:'θri: ˌpleɪə] MP3-Spieler Welc (12)

Mr ... ['mɪstə] Herr ... Welc (12/153)

Mrs ... ['mɪsɪz] Frau ... Welc (12/153)

°**Ms ...** [mɪz, məz] Frau ...

much [mʌtʃ] viel TOP 3 (67) • **how much?** wie viel? 5 (96/176) • **How much is/are ...?** Was kostet/kosten ...? / Wie viel kostet/kosten ...? TOP 3 (67)

▸ S.176 „viel", „viele"

mum [mʌm] Mama, Mutti; Mutter Welc (8/150)

museum [mju'zi:əm] Museum 5 (89)

music ['mju:zɪk] Musik 1 (23/158)

musical ['mju:zɪkl] **1.** Musical 5 (86); °**2.** musikalisch

must [mʌst] müssen 6 (102)

my [maɪ] mein/e Welc (8/150) • **My name is ...** Ich heiße ... / Mein Name ist ... Welc (8/150)

°**mystery** ['mɪstri] Rätsel, Geheimnis

N

name [neɪm] Name Welc (8/150)
My name is ... Ich heiße ... / Mein Name ist ... Welc (8/150) • **What's your name?** Wie heißt du? Welc (8/150)
near [nɪə] in der Nähe von, nahe (bei) 6 (100)
°**necklace** ['nekləs] Halskette
need [ni:d] brauchen, benötigen Welc (12)
neighbour ['neɪbə] Nachbar/in 3 (55)
nervous ['nɜ:vəs] nervös, aufgeregt 1 (20)
°**network** ['netwɜ:k] (Wörter-)Netz
never ['nevə] nie, niemals 3 (56)
new [nju:] neu Welc (8)
°**news** [nju:z]: **no news** keine Neuigkeiten
newspaper ['nju:speɪpə] Zeitung Welc (15)
next [nekst]: **be next** der/die Nächste sein 6 (105) • **the next morning/day** am nächsten Morgen/Tag 3 (56) • **What have we got next?** Was haben wir als Nächstes? 1 (24)
°**next to** [nekst] neben
nice [naɪs] schön, nett Welc (11)
°**nickname** ['nɪkneɪm] Spitzname
night [naɪt] Nacht, später Abend 2 (40) • **at night** nachts, in der Nacht 2 (40/163) • **on Friday night** freitagnachts, Freitagnacht 2 (40/163)
no [nəʊ] **1.** nein Welc (8/150); **2.** kein, keine 4 (81/173) • **no more music** keine Musik mehr 4 (81) • °**no news** keine Neuigkeiten
noise [nɔɪz] Geräusch; Lärm 3 (65)
nose [nəʊz] Nase 4 (80/173)
not [nɒt] nicht Welc (9/151) • **not (...) any** kein, keine 4 (71)
note [nəʊt] Mitteilung, Notiz 4 (82)
take notes sich Notizen machen 4 (82/174)
°**notice** ['nəʊtɪs] Notiz, Mitteilung
notice board Anschlagtafel, schwarzes Brett 5 (84/85)
November [nəʊ'vembə] November TOP 1 (34/160)
now [naʊ] nun, jetzt Welc (8)
number ['nʌmbə] Zahl, Ziffer, Nummer Welc (9/151)

O

o [əʊ] null Welc (15)
o'clock [ə'klɒk]: **eleven o'clock** elf Uhr Welc (16/155)
October [ɒk'təʊbə] Oktober TOP 1 (34/160)
°**odd** [ɒd]: **What word is the odd one out?** Welches Wort passt nicht dazu / gehört nicht dazu?
°**ode** [əʊd] Ode *(feierliches Gedicht)*
of [əv, ɒv] von 2 (38) • **of the summer holidays** der Sommerferien Welc (12)
of course [əv 'kɔ:s] natürlich, selbstverständlich 2 (40)
off [ɒf]: **take 10c off** 10 Cent abziehen TOP 3 (67)
often ['ɒfn] oft, häufig 3 (56)
Oh well ... [əʊ 'wel] Na ja ... / Na gut ... Welc (13)
OK [əʊ'keɪ] okay, gut, in Ordnung Welc (12)
old [əʊld] alt Welc (8/150)
on [ɒn] auf 1 (23/158) • **on 13th June** am 13. Juni TOP 1 (34/161) • **on Friday** am Freitag 1 (23) • **on Friday afternoon** freitagnachmittags, am Freitagnachmittag 2 (38/162) • **on Friday evening** freitagabends, am Freitagabend 2 (38/162) • **on Friday morning** freitagmorgens, am Freitagmorgen 2 (38/162) • **on Friday night** freitagnachts, Freitagnacht 2 (40/163)
on the board an die Tafel 1 (22/157)
on the phone am Telefon 4 (78)
on the radio im Radio 3 (62)
°**on the right** rechts, auf der rechten Seite • **on the train** im Zug 4 (73/172) • °**on the way (upstairs)** auf dem Weg (nach oben) • **on TV** im Fernsehen 2 (39/163) • **What page are we on?** Auf welcher Seite sind wir? 1 (28/159)
one [wʌn] eins, ein, eine Welc (14)
one day eines Tages 6 (109)
only ['əʊnli] **1.** nur, bloß TOP 3 (67); **2. the only guest** der einzige Gast 3 (65)
°**onto** ['ɒntə, 'ɒntu] auf (... hinauf)
open ['əʊpən] **1.** öffnen, aufmachen Welc (10); **2.** geöffnet 6 (110)
opposite ['ɒpəzɪt] Gegenteil 3 (62)
or [ɔ:] oder 1 (22)
orange ['ɒrɪndʒ] **1.** orange(farben) Welc (13/154); **2.** Orange, Apfelsine 4 (69/171) • **orange juice** ['ɒrɪndʒ dʒu:s] Orangensaft 4 (69/171)
°**order** ['ɔ:də] **1.** Reihenfolge • **in the right order** in der richtigen Reihenfolge • °**word order** Wortstellung
2. Befehl
other ['ʌðə] andere(r, s) 2 (48)
the others die anderen 3 (66)
Ouch! [aʊtʃ] Autsch! 4 (82)
our ['aʊə] unser, unsere 1 (21)
out of ... ['aʊt‿əv] aus ... (heraus/hinaus) 1 (28/159) / 3 (65)
outside [,aʊt'saɪd] draußen 4 (81/173) • **outside his room** vor seinem Zimmer; außerhalb seines Zimmers 3 (65)
over ['əʊvə] **1.** über, oberhalb von Welc (14) • **over there** da drüben, dort drüben 6 (103)
2. be over vorbei sein, zu Ende sein 4 (82)
°**own** [əʊn]: **your own ideas** deine eigenen Ideen
°**Oxfam** ['ɒksfæm] *bekannteste Wohltätigkeitsorganisation Großbritanniens mit einer Kette von Gebrauchtwarengeschäften*

P

packet ['pækɪt] Päckchen, Packung, Schachtel 1 (32) • **a packet of mints** ein Päckchen/eine Packung Pfefferminzbonbons 1 (32)
page [peɪdʒ] (Buch-, Heft-)Seite Welc (8) • **What page are we on?** Auf welcher Seite sind wir? 1 (28/159)
paint [peɪnt] (an)malen 5 (84/85)
°**pair** [peə]: **nine pairs of opposites** neun Gegenteil-Paare
paper ['peɪpə] Papier 3 (66)
parcel ['pɑ:sl] Paket 4 (73)
parents ['peərənts] Eltern 2 (41/164)
park [pɑ:k] Park Welc (10)
parrot ['pærət] Papagei Welc (16)
part [pɑ:t] Teil 3 (64)
partner ['pɑ:tnə] Partner/in Welc (8)
party ['pɑ:ti] Party 4 (68)
pass [pɑ:s] (herüber)reichen, weitergeben 4 (81) • **pass round** herumgeben 4 (81)
°**past** [pɑ:st] Vergangenheit
past [pɑ:st]: **half past 11** halb zwölf (11.30 / 23.30) Welc (16/155)
quarter past 11 Viertel nach 11 (11.15 / 23.15) Welc (16/155)
PE [,pi:‿'i:], **Physical Education** [,fɪzɪkəl‿edʒu'keɪʃn] Turnen, Sportunterricht 1 (23/158)
pen [pen] Kugelschreiber, Füller Welc (12/153)
pence (p) *(pl)* [pens] Pence *(Plural von „penny")* TOP 3 (67)
pencil ['pensl] Bleistift Welc (12/153)
pencil case ['pensl keɪs] Federmäppchen Welc (12/153) • **pencil sharpener** ['pensl ʃɑ:pnə] Bleistiftanspitzer Welc (12)
penny ['peni] *kleinste britische Münze* TOP 3 (67/170)

people ['pi:pl] Menschen, Leute 2 (36)
°**pepper** ['pepə] Pfeffer
°**person** ['pɜ:sn] Person
pet [pet] Haustier Welc (12/153)
pet shop Tierhandlung 2 (44)
phone [fəʊn] **1.** Telefon 1 (19) • **on the phone** am Telefon 4 (78)
phone call Anruf, Telefongespräch 5 (90) • **phone number** Telefonnummer Welc (15)
2. telefonieren, anrufen 5 (87)
photo ['fəʊtəʊ] Foto Welc (9) • **in the photo** auf dem Foto Welc (9/152) • **take photos** Fotos machen, fotografieren 6 (103)
°**phrase** [freɪz] Ausdruck, (Rede-)Wendung
piano [pi'ænəʊ] Klavier, Piano 3 (55)
play the piano Klavier spielen 3 (55/168)
picnic ['pɪknɪk] Picknick 6 (100)
have a picnic ein Picknick machen 6 (100)
picture ['pɪktʃə] Bild Welc (11) • **in the picture** auf dem Bild Welc (11/152)
piece [pi:s]: **a piece of** ein Stück 3 (66) • **a piece of paper** ein Stück Papier 3 (66)
pink [pɪŋk] pink(farben), rosa Welc (13/154)
pirate ['paɪrət] Pirat, Piratin 5 (84/85)
°**pistol** ['pɪstl] Pistole
pizza ['pi:tsə] Pizza 1 (24)
place [pleɪs] Ort, Platz Welc (9)
°**placemat** ['pleɪsmæt] Set, Platzdeckchen
plan [plæn] **1.** Plan 2 (38); **2. plan to do (-nn-)** planen zu tun 3 (66)
°**plank** [plæŋk] Brett, Planke
°**plastic explosive** [ˌplæstɪk ɪk'spləʊsɪv] Plastiksprengstoff
plate [pleɪt] Teller Welc (13) • **a plate of chips** ein Teller Pommes frites 4 (69/171)
play [pleɪ] **1.** spielen Welc (9/151)
play football Fußball spielen Welc (9/151) • **play the guitar** Gitarre spielen 3 (53/166) • **play the piano** Klavier spielen 3 (55/168)
player Spieler/in 6 (106)
2. Theaterstück 4 (81)
please [pli:z] bitte *(in Fragen und Aufforderungen)* Welc (12/153)
▸ S.163 „bitte"
pm [ˌpi:_'em]: **7 pm** 7 Uhr nachmittags/abends 4 (81)
poem ['pəʊɪm] Gedicht Welc (14)
°**poetry** ['pəʊətri] *hier:* Gedichte
°**point** [pɔɪnt] **1.** Punkt; **2. point to** zeigen auf, deuten auf
police *(pl)* [pə'li:s] Polizei 3 (65)
poltergeist ['pəʊltəgaɪst] Poltergeist Welc (10)
poor [pɔ:, pʊə] arm 1 (31) • **poor Sophie** (die) arme Sophie 1 (31)
poster ['pəʊstə] Poster 1 (24)
potato [pə'teɪtəʊ], *pl* **potatoes** Kartoffel 4 (69/171)
pound (£) [paʊnd] Pfund *(britische Währung)* TOP 3 (67)
practice ['præktɪs] *hier:* Übungsteil (3)
practise ['præktɪs] üben; trainieren 5 (84/85)
°**prepare** [prɪ'peə] vorbereiten
present ['preznt] **1.** Gegenwart 4 (71/172); **2.** Geschenk 4 (71)
°**present (to)** [prɪ'zent] *(jm. etwas)* präsentieren, vorstellen
presentation [ˌprezn'teɪʃn] Präsentation, Vorstellung 6 (104)
pretty ['prɪti] hübsch Welc (6)
price [praɪs] (Kauf-)Preis 6 (101)
prize [praɪz] Preis, Gewinn 4 (82)
programme ['prəʊgræm] Programm 5 (84/85)
project (about, on) ['prɒdʒekt] Projekt (über, zu) 3 (55)
pronunciation [prəˌnʌnsi'eɪʃn] Aussprache (3)
pull [pʊl] ziehen Welc (10)
purple ['pɜ:pl] violett; lila Welc (13/154)
push [pʊʃ] drücken, schieben, stoßen Welc (10)
put (-tt-) [pʊt] legen, stellen, *(etwas wohin)* tun 2 (39) • °**Put up your hand.** Heb deine Hand. / Hebt eure Hand.

Q

quarter ['kwɔ:tə]: **quarter past 11** Viertel nach 11 (11.15 / 23.15) Welc (16/155) • **quarter to 12** Viertel vor 12 (11.45 / 23.45) Welc (16/155)
question ['kwestʃn] Frage 3 (56)
ask questions Fragen stellen 3 (56/168) • °**question word** Fragewort
quick [kwɪk] schnell 3 (56)
quiet ['kwaɪət] leise, still, ruhig 1 (22)
quiz [kwɪz], *pl* **quizzes** ['kwɪzɪz] Quiz, Ratespiel 2 (45)

R

rabbit ['ræbɪt] Kaninchen 2 (37/161)
°**racket** ['rækɪt] (Tennis-, Federball-, Squash-)Schläger
radio ['reɪdiəʊ] Radio 3 (62) • **on the radio** im Radio 3 (62)
°**ram (-mm-)** [ræm] rammen
ran [ræn] *Vergangenheitsform von „run"* 5 (88/175)
rap [ræp] Rap *(rhythmischer Sprechgesang)* 1 (22)
RE [ˌɑ:r_'i:], **Religious Education** [rɪˌlɪdʒəs_edʒu'keɪʃn] Religion, Religionsunterricht 1 (23/158)
read [ri:d] lesen 2 (38) • °**read out** vorlesen • °**Read out loud.** Lies laut vor. • °**Read the poem to a partner.** Lies das Gedicht einem Partner/einer Partnerin vor.
ready ['redi] bereit, fertig 2 (48)
get ready (for) sich fertig machen (für), sich vorbereiten (auf) 4 (72)
get things ready Dinge fertig machen, vorbereiten 2 (48)
real [rɪəl] echt, wirklich 4 (70)
really ['rɪəli] wirklich 1 (24)
reason ['ri:zn] Grund, Begründung 6 (105) • **for lots of reasons** aus vielen Gründen 6 (105)
red [red] rot Welc (13/154)
rehearsal [rɪ'hɜ:sl] Probe *(am Theater)* 5 (84/85)
rehearse [rɪ'hɜ:s] proben *(am Theater)* 5 (84/85/174)
remember [rɪ'membə] **1.** sich erinnern (an) 2 (45); **2.** sich *etwas* merken 1 (22) • **Can you remember that?** Kannst du dir das merken? 1 (22)
report (on) [rɪ'pɔ:t] Bericht, Reportage (über) 5 (92)
result [rɪ'zʌlt] Ergebnis, Resultat 5 (84/85)
revision [rɪ'vɪʒn] Wiederholung *(des Lernstoffs)* (3)
°**rhythm** ['rɪðəm] Rhythmus
ride [raɪd] reiten 3 (53/166) • **go riding** ['raɪdɪŋ] reiten gehen 3 (53)
ride a bike Rad fahren 3 (52/166)
right [raɪt] **1.** richtig Welc (11) • **be right** Recht haben 3 (53) • **That's right.** Das ist richtig. / Das stimmt. Welc (11) • **You need a school bag, right?** Du brauchst eine Schultasche, stimmt's? / nicht wahr? Welc (12)
°**2. on the right** rechts, auf der rechten Seite
3. right now jetzt sofort; jetzt gerade 3 (57)
road [rəʊd] Straße Welc (10) • **Park Road** [ˌpɑ:k 'rəʊd] Parkstraße Welc (10)
roll [rəʊl] Brötchen 4 (80)
°**roll up** [ˌrəʊl_'ʌp] aufrollen

room [ru:m, rʊm] Raum, Zimmer Welc (9/151)

rubber ['rʌbə] Radiergummi Welc (12/153)

ruler ['ru:lə] Lineal Welc (12/153)

run (-nn-) [rʌn] laufen, rennen 3 (65)

S

said [sed] *Vergangenheitsform von „say"* 5 (88)

°**sail** [seɪl] segeln

°**sailor** ['seɪlə] Seemann, Matrose

salad ['sæləd] Salat *(als Gericht oder Beilage)* 4 (69)

°**salami** [sə'lɑ:mi] Salami

°**salt** [sɔ:lt] Salz

same [seɪm]: **the same ...** der-/die-/dasselbe ...; dieselben ... 6 (103/178) **be/look the same** gleich sein/aussehen 6 (103)

sandwich ['sænwɪtʃ, 'sænwɪdʒ] Sandwich, *(zusammengeklapptes)* belegtes Brot 1 (19) • **sandwich box** Brotdose 1 (19)

sat [sæt] *Vergangenheitsform von „sit"* 5 (88/175)

Saturday ['sætədeɪ, 'sætədi] Samstag, Sonnabend Welc (14/154)

sausage ['sɒsɪdʒ] (Brat-, Bock-)Würstchen, Wurst 4 (69)

saw [sɔ:] *Vergangenheitsform von „see"* 5 (88)

say [seɪ] sagen Welc (12) • **say goodbye** sich verabschieden Welc (17) • **Say hi to Dilip for me.** Grüß Dilip von mir. 3 (56)

°**scare away** [ˌskeər_ə'weɪ] verscheuchen, verjagen

scared [skeəd]: **be scared (of)** Angst haben (vor) 5 (97)

scary ['skeəri] unheimlich; gruselig 3 (65)

scene [si:n] Szene 4 (81)

school [sku:l] Schule Welc (12/153) **at school** in der Schule Welc (12/153) **school bag** Schultasche Welc (12/153) **school subject** Schulfach 1 (23/158)
► S.158 School subjects

science ['saɪəns] Naturwissenschaft 1 (23/158)

sea [si:] Meer, *(die)* See 5 (97)

°**season** ['si:zn] Jahreszeit

second ['sekənd] zweite(r, s) TOP 1 (34)

°**secret** ['s[illegible] Geheimnis

see [si:] [illegible]en Welc (9) • **See?** Siehst [illegible] 4 (81) • **See you.** Tsch[illegible] bis bald. 1 (32)
► S.163 (to) look – (to) see – (to) watch

°**sell** [sel] verkaufen

sentence ['sentəns] Satz 3 (61)

September [sep'tembə] September TOP 1 (34/160)

°**shadow** ['ʃædəʊ] Schatten

°**shake** [ʃeɪk] schütteln

share (with) [ʃeə] sich *etwas* teilen (mit) 2 (36)

she [ʃi:] sie Welc (8)

shelf [ʃelf], *pl* **shelves** [ʃelvz] Regal(brett) 2 (36/161)

ship [ʃɪp] Schiff 5 (84/85)

shirt [ʃɜ:t] Hemd 3 (54/167)

shoe [ʃu:] Schuh 3 (54/167)

shop [ʃɒp] **1.** Laden, Geschäft Welc (14); **2. (-pp-)** einkaufen (gehen) 4 (72) • **shop assistant** ['ʃɒp_əˌsɪstənt] Verkäufer/in 3 (54) °**shop window** [ˌʃɒp 'wɪndəʊ] Schaufenster • **shopping** ['ʃɒpɪŋ] (das) Einkaufen Welc (12) • **go shopping** einkaufen gehen 3 (63) **shopping list** Einkaufsliste Welc (12)

short [ʃɔ:t] kurz 4 (70/171)

shorts *(pl)* [ʃɔ:ts] Shorts, kurze Hose 3 (54/167)

shoulder ['ʃəʊldə] Schulter 4 (80/173)

shout [ʃaʊt] schreien, rufen 1 (28/159) °**shout at** *jn.* anschreien

show [ʃəʊ] **1.** zeigen 5 (84/85/174); **2.** Show, Vorstellung 5 (84/85)

shower ['ʃaʊə] Dusche 2 (48) • **have a shower** (sich) duschen 2 (48)

°**Shut up.** ['ʃʌt_ʌp] Halt den Mund.

°**signal** ['sɪgnəl] Signal, Zeichen

silly ['sɪli] albern, dumm 2 (49)

°**silver** ['sɪlvə] Silber

sing [sɪŋ] singen Welc (8/150)

single ['sɪŋgl] ledig, alleinstehend 2 (41)

sink [sɪŋk] Spüle, Spülbecken TOP 2 (50)

°**Sir** [sɜ:] Sir

sister ['sɪstə] Schwester Welc (8/150)

sit (-tt-) [sɪt] sitzen; sich setzen 1 (20) • °**Sit down.** Setz dich. • **Sit with me.** Setz dich zu mir. / Setzt euch zu mir. 1 (20)

size [saɪz] Größe 3 (54)

skate [skeɪt] Inliner/Skateboard fahren 3 (62) • **skates** [skeɪts] Inliner 3 (62/169)

skateboard ['skeɪtbɔ:d] Skateboard Welc (9/151)

sketch [sketʃ] Sketch 5 (86)

skills file ['skɪlz faɪl] *Anhang mit Lern- und Arbeitstechniken* (3/122)

sleep [sli:p] schlafen 2 (38)

°**sleepover** ['sli:pəʊvə] Schlafparty

°**sleet** [sli:t] Schneeregen

small [smɔ:l] klein 2 (36)

smile [smaɪl] lächeln 6 (103)

snake [sneɪk] Schlange 3 (58)

°**snow** [snəʊ] Schnee

so [səʊ] **1.** also; deshalb, daher 2 (41); **2. so sweet** so süß 4 (81) • °**so far** bis jetzt, bis hierher

soap [səʊp] Seife 4 (71)

sock [sɒk] Socke, Strumpf 3 (54/167)

sofa ['səʊfə] Sofa TOP 2 (50)

some [səm, sʌm] einige, ein paar 3 (56) • **some cheese/juice** etwas Käse/Saft 4 (69/171)

somebody ['sʌmbədi] jemand 4 (73)

sometimes ['sʌmtaɪmz] manchmal 2 (40)

son [sʌn] Sohn 2 (41)

song [sɒŋ] Lied, Song Welc (8/150)

soon [su:n] bald 5 (97)

sorry ['sɒri]: **(I'm) sorry.** Entschuldigung. / Tut mir leid. 1 (21) **Sorry, I'm late.** Entschuldigung, dass ich zu spät bin/komme. Welc (12) • **Sorry?** Wie bitte? 1 (21/157)
► S.155 „Entschuldigung" / S.157 sorry

sound [saʊnd] **1.** klingen, sich *(gut usw.)* anhören 5 (86); **2.** Laut; Klang 5 (86/175)

°**Spanish** ['spænɪʃ] spanisch

°**speak** [spi:k] sprechen

special ['speʃl]: **a special day** ein besonderer Tag 5 (89)

°**speech bubble** ['spi:tʃ bʌbl] Sprechblase

spell [spel] buchstabieren 1 (22)

sport [spɔ:t] Sport; Sportart 3 (52) **do sport** Sport treiben 3 (53/167) **sports centre** Sportzentrum 5 (86)
► S.167 Sports

spring [sprɪŋ] Frühling 5 (84/85)

spy [spaɪ] Spion/in 2 (48)

stairs *(pl)* [steəz] Treppe; Treppenstufen TOP 2 (50)

stamp [stæmp] Briefmarke 3 (53)

star [stɑ:] (Film-, Pop-)Star 2 (48)

start [stɑ:t] starten, anfangen, beginnen (mit) 3 (66)

°**statement** ['steɪtmənt] Aussage

station ['steɪʃn] Bahnhof 4 (73) **at the station** am Bahnhof 4 (73)

°**statue** ['stætʃu:] Statue

stay [steɪ] bleiben 5 (89) • °**stay with** wohnen bei

step [step] Schritt 6 (102) • °**take a step** einen Schritt tun

stereo ['steriəʊ] Stereoanlage TOP 2 (50)

still [stɪl] (immer) noch 4 (71)

stop (-pp-) [stɒp] **1.** aufhören Welc (14) • **Stop that!** Hör auf damit! / Lass das! Welc (14) **2.** anhalten 1 (30)

story ['stɔ:ri] Geschichte, Erzählung 2 (48)
street [stri:t] Straße Welc (12) • **at 7 Hamilton Street** in der Hamiltonstraße 7 Welc (12)
°**stretch** [stretʃ] strecken, dehnen
student ['stju:dənt] Schüler/in; Student/in 1 (20)
study skills *(pl)* ['stʌdi skɪlz] Lern- und Arbeitstechniken (3)
subject ['sʌbdʒɪkt] Schulfach 1 (23/158)
► S.158 School subjects
suddenly ['sʌdnli] plötzlich, auf einmal 3 (65)
summer ['sʌmə] Sommer Welc (12)
Sunday ['sʌndeɪ, 'sʌndi] Sonntag Welc (14/154)
sunglasses *(pl)* ['sʌnglɑ:sɪz] (eine) Sonnenbrille 2 (48)
°**sure** [ʃʊə, ʃɔ:] sicher
°**swap (-pp-)** [swɒp] tauschen
sweatshirt ['swetʃɜ:t] Sweatshirt 3 (54/167)
sweet [swi:t] süß 4 (69/171)
sweets *(pl)* Süßigkeiten 4 (69)
swim (-mm-) [swɪm] schwimmen 3 (52/166) • **go swimming** schwimmen gehen 3 (52/166) • **swimming pool** ['swɪmɪŋ pu:l] Schwimmbad, Schwimmbecken 5 (86)
°**sword** [sɔ:d] Schwert
°**swordfish** ['sɔ:dfɪʃ] Schwertfisch
syllable ['sɪləbl] Silbe 5 (92)
°**synchronize watches** ['sɪŋkrənaɪz] Uhren gleichstellen

T

table ['teɪbl] Tisch 1 (18/152) • **table tennis** ['teɪbl tenɪs] Tischtennis 3 (53/167)
take [teɪk] **1.** nehmen Welc (11); **2.** (weg-, hin)bringen 4 (72) • **take 10c off** 10 Cent abziehen TOP 3 (67)
take notes sich Notizen machen 4 (82/174) • **take out** herausnehmen 1 (23) • **take photos** Fotos machen, fotografieren 6 (103)
°**take a step** einen Schritt tun
°**Take turns.** Wechselt euch ab.
We'll take them. [wi:l 'teɪk_ðəm] *(beim Einkaufen)* Wir nehmen sie. 3 (54)
talk [tɔ:k]: **talk (about)** reden (über), sich unterhalten (über) Welc (8)
talk (to) reden (mit), sich unterhalten (mit) Welc (8)
°**tavern** ['tævən] Schenke, Kneipe
tea [ti:] Tee; *(auch:) leichte Nachmittags- oder Abendmahlzeit* 1 (31)
teach [ti:tʃ] unterrichten, lehren 3 (57) • **teacher** ['ti:tʃə] Lehrer/in 1 (21)
team [ti:m] Team, Mannschaft 2 (40)
teeth [ti:θ] *Plural von „tooth"* 2 (38)
telephone ['telɪfəʊn] Telefon Welc (15) • **telephone number** Telefonnummer Welc (15) • **What's your telephone number?** Was ist deine Telefonnummer? Welc (15)
television (TV) ['telɪvɪʒn] Fernsehen 2 (39/163)
tell (about) [tel] erzählen (von), berichten (über) 1 (22/158) • **Tell me your names.** Sagt mir eure Namen. 1 (22)
tennis ['tenɪs] Tennis 1 (22)
terrible ['terəbl] schrecklich, furchtbar 5 (87)
°**test** [test] Test, (Klassen-)Arbeit
text [tekst] Text (3)
Thank you. ['θæŋk ju:] Danke (schön). Welc (12/153) • **Thanks.** [θæŋks] Danke. 2 (40) • **Thanks a lot!** Vielen Dank! 3 (56)
that [ðət, ðæt] **1.** das (dort) Welc (11); **2.** jene(r, s) 1 (24) • **That's me.** Das bin ich. Welc (10) • **That's right.** Das ist richtig. / Das stimmt. Welc (11)
3. dass 5 (97)
► S.178 this, that – these, those
the [ðə, ði] der, die, das; die Welc (9/151)
°**theatre** ['θɪətə] Theater
their [ðeə] ihr, ihre *(Plural)* Welc (12)
them [ðəm, ðem] sie; ihnen 3 (54)
then [ðen] dann, danach Welc (10)
there [ðeə] **1.** da, dort Welc (11); **2.** dahin, dorthin 2 (42/164) • **over there** da drüben, dort drüben 6 (103) • **there are** es sind (vorhanden); es gibt 1 (18) • **there's** es ist (vorhanden); es gibt 1 (18) • **there isn't a ...** es ist kein/e ...; es gibt kein/e ... 1 (18/156)
► S.156 There's ... / There are ...
these [ði:z] diese, die (hier) 3 (54)
► S.178 this, that – these, those
they [ðeɪ] sie *(Plural)* Welc (8)
thing [θɪŋ] Ding, Sache Welc (10)
think [θɪŋk] glauben, meinen, denken Welc (11) • °**think of** sich ausdenken
third [θɜ:d] dritte(r, s) TOP 1 (34)
°**thirsty** ['θɜ:sti] durstig • °**be thirsty** Durst haben, durstig sein
this [ðɪs] **1.** dies (hier) Welc (8); **2.** diese(r, s) 1 (33) • **this morning/afternoon/evening** heute Morgen/Nachmittag/Abend 5 (88) • °**This is the way ...** So ... / Auf diese Weise ...
► S.178 this, that – these, those
those [ðəʊz] die (da), jene (dort) 6 (103)
► S.178 this, that – these, those
thousand ['θaʊznd] tausend TOP 1 (34)
throw [θrəʊ] werfen 1 (22)
°**Thud!** [θʌd] Rums!
Thursday ['θɜ:zdeɪ, 'θɜ:zdi] Donnerstag Welc (14/154)
°**tick** [tɪk] **1.** Häkchen; **2.** ankreuzen, ein Häkchen machen
ticket ['tɪkɪt] Eintrittskarte 5 (86)
°**ticket inspector** ['tɪkɪt_ɪn,spektə] Fahrkartenkontrolleur/in
tidy ['taɪdi] aufräumen 4 (72)
°**tie** [taɪ] zusammenbinden
till [tɪl] bis *(zeitlich)* 2 (40)
time [taɪm] Zeit; Uhrzeit Welc (16/155) • **What's the time?** Wie spät ist es? Welc (16/155) • °**The Times** *britische Tageszeitung*
timetable ['taɪmteɪbl] Stundenplan 1 (23)
tired ['taɪəd] müde 5 (97)
°**Tis** [tɪz] *= It is*
title ['taɪtl] Titel, Überschrift 4 (82)
to [tə, tu] **1.** zu, nach Welc (14) • **to Jenny's** zu Jenny 4 (72)
2. an e-mail to eine E-Mail an 3 (56)
write to schreiben an 3 (56)
3. quarter to 12 Viertel vor 12 (11.45 / 23.45) Welc (16/155)
4. try to help/to play/... versuchen, zu helfen/zu spielen/... 2 (39)
°**5.** um zu
toast [təʊst] Toast(brot) 2 (38)
today [tə'deɪ] heute Welc (12)
toe [təʊ] Zeh 4 (80/173)
together [tə'geðə] zusammen 1 (21)
toilet ['tɔɪlət] Toilette 1 (28/159)
told [təʊld] *Vergangenheitsform von „tell"* 5 (88/175)
°**tomato** [tə'mɑ:təʊ], *pl* **tomatoes** Tomate
tomorrow [tə'mɒrəʊ] morgen Welc (14)
°**tongue-twister** ['tʌŋtwɪstə] Zungenbrecher
tonight [tə'naɪt] heute Nacht, heute Abend 5 (96)
too [tu:]: **1. from Bristol too** auch aus Bristol Welc (8) • **Me too.** Ich auch. Welc (12)
2. too much zu viel TOP 3 (67)
took [tʊk] *Vergangenheitsform von „take"* 5 (88/175)
tooth [tu:θ], *pl* **teeth** [ti:θ] Zahn 2 (38)

top [tɒp] **1.** Spitze, oberes Ende 2 (41) • **at the top (of)** oben, am oberen Ende, an der Spitze (von) 2 (41)
2. Top, Oberteil 3 (54)
topic ['tɒpɪk] Thema, Themenbereich (3)
°**tornado** [tɔː'neɪdəʊ] Tornado, Wirbelsturm
tortoise ['tɔːtəs] Schildkröte 2 (37)
tour (of the house) [tʊə] Rundgang, Tour (durch das Haus) TOP 2 (51)
tower ['taʊə] Turm 6 (100)
town [taʊn] (Klein-)Stadt 6 (100)
°**toy** [tɔɪ] Spielzeug
train [treɪn] Zug 4 (73) • **on the train** im Zug 4 (73/172)
°**train** [treɪn] trainieren • °**trainer** ['treɪnə] Trainer/in
°**translate (into)** [træns'leɪt] übersetzen (in)
tree [triː] Baum Welc (9/151)
trick [trɪk] (Zauber-)Kunststück, Trick Welc (15) • **do tricks** (Zauber-) Kunststücke machen Welc (15)
trip [trɪp] Reise; Ausflug Welc (17)
°**true** [truː] wahr
try [traɪ] **1.** versuchen 2 (39); **2.** probieren, kosten 4 (76) • **try and do / try to do** versuchen, zu tun 2 (39)
try on anprobieren *(Kleidung)* 3 (54)
T-shirt ['tiːʃɜːt] T-Shirt 2 (46)
Tuesday ['tjuːzdeɪ, 'tjuːzdi] Dienstag Welc (14/154)
turn [tɜːn]: **It's your turn.** Du bist dran / an der Reihe. 1 (28) • °**Take turns.** Wechselt euch ab.
°**turn around** [ˌtɜːn‿ə'raʊnd] sich umdrehen
TV [tiː'viː] Fernsehen 2 (39/163)
on TV im Fernsehen 2 (39/163)
watch TV fernsehen 2 (39/163)
twin [twɪn]: **twin brother** Zwillingsbruder Welc (8) • **twins** *(pl)* Zwillinge Welc (8/151)

U

°**unchanging** [ˌʌn'tʃeɪndʒɪŋ] gleich bleibend
uncle ['ʌŋkl] Onkel 2 (41)
under ['ʌndə] unter 3 (61)
understand [ˌʌndə'stænd] verstehen, begreifen 3 (57)
uniform ['juːnɪfɔːm] Uniform Welc (14)
unit ['juːnɪt] Lektion, Kapitel (3)
up [ʌp] hinauf, herauf, nach oben 4 (72)
upstairs [ˌʌp'steəz] oben; nach oben TOP 2 (50/165)
us [əs, ʌs] uns 2 (48)
use [juːz] benutzen, verwenden 5 (84/85) • °**used** [juːzd] gebraucht
usually ['juːʒuəli] meistens, gewöhnlich, normalerweise 3 (56)

V

°**Valentine's Day** ['væləntaɪnz deɪ] Valentinstag
very ['veri] sehr Welc (11)
village ['vɪlɪdʒ] Dorf 6 (100)
visitor ['vɪzɪtə] Besucher/in, Gast TOP 2 (51)
vocabulary [və'kæbjələri] Vokabelverzeichnis, Wörterverzeichnis (3)
°**voice** [vɔɪs] Stimme
volleyball ['vɒlibɔːl] Volleyball 3 (53/167)

W

wait (for) ['weɪt fɔː] warten (auf) 4 (73) • **I can't wait to see ...** ich kann es kaum erwarten, ... zu sehen 5 (87)
walk [wɔːk] (zu Fuß) gehen 3 (56)
°**wall** [wɔːl] Wand
°**Wallop!** ['wɒləp] Schepper!
want [wɒnt] (haben) wollen 3 (54)
want to do tun wollen 4 (70)
°**wanted** ['wɒntɪd] *(polizeilich)* gesucht
wardrobe ['wɔːdrəʊb] Kleiderschrank 2 (36/161)
was [wəz, wɒz]: **(I/he/she/it) was** *Vergangenheitsform von „be"* 1 (32)
How was ...? Wie war ...? 1 (32)
wash [wɒʃ] waschen 2 (38) • **I wash my face.** Ich wasche mir das Gesicht. 2 (38) • °**Get washed.** Wasch dich.
washing machine ['wɒʃɪŋ məˌʃiːn] Waschmaschine TOP 2 (50)
watch [wɒtʃ] beobachten, sich *etwas* ansehen; zusehen 2 (39)
watch TV fernsehen 2 (39/163)
► S.163 (to) look – (to) see – (to) watch
watch [wɒtʃ] Armbanduhr 3 (66)
water ['wɔːtə] Wasser Welc (9/151)
°**way** [weɪ]: **on the way (upstairs)** auf dem Weg (nach oben)
°**way** [weɪ]: **This is the way ...** So ... / Auf diese Weise ...
we [wiː] wir Welc (8/150)
wear [weə] tragen, anhaben *(Kleidung)* 2 (48)
Wednesday ['wenzdeɪ, 'wenzdi] Mittwoch Welc (14/154)
week [wiːk] Woche Welc (14)
days of the week Wochentage Welc (14/154)
weekend [ˌwiːk'end] Wochenende 2 (36) • **at the weekend** am Wochenende 2 (38/162)
welcome ['welkəm]: **1. welcome (to)** *jn.* begrüßen, willkommen heißen (in) Welc (16) • **They welcome you to ...** Sie heißen dich in ... willkommen Welc (16)
2. Welcome (to Bristol). Willkommen (in Bristol). Welc (8);
3. You're welcome. Gern geschehen. / Nichts zu danken. Welc (17)
► S.156 welcome
well [wel]: **Well, ...** Nun, ... / Also, ... Welc (14) • **Oh well ...** Na ja ... / Na gut ... Welc (13)
went [went] *Vergangenheitsform von „go"* 5 (88/175)
were [wə, wɜː]: **(we/you/they) were** *Vergangenheitsform von „be"* 5 (86)
°**wet** [wet] nass
what [wɒt] **1.** was Welc (8/150);
2. welche(r, s) Welc (13) • **What about ...?** **1.** Was ist mit ...? / Und ...? Welc (6); **2.** Wie wär's mit ...? TOP 3 (67) • **What are you talking about?** Wovon redest du? 4 (82)
What colour is ...? Welche Farbe hat ...? Welc (13) • **What have we got next?** Was haben wir als Nächstes? 1 (24) • **What page are we on?** Auf welcher Seite sind wir? 1 (28/159) • **What's for homework?** Was haben wir als Hausaufgabe auf? 1 (28/159) • **What's the time?** Wie spät ist es? Welc (16/155)
What's your name? Wie heißt du? Welc (8/150) • **What's your telephone number?** Was ist deine Telefonnummer? Welc (15)
wheelchair ['wiːltʃeə] Rollstuhl Welc (16)
when [wen] **1.** wann TOP 1 (34)
When's your birthday? Wann hast du Geburtstag? TOP 1 (34/161)
2. wenn Welc (10); **3.** als 5 (97)
where [weə] **1.** wo Welc (8/150);
2. wohin 2 (42/164) • **Where are you from?** Wo kommst du her? Welc (8/150)
which [wɪtʃ]: **Which picture ...?** Welches Bild ...? 4 (74)
whisper ['wɪspə] flüstern 6 (103)
white [waɪt] weiß Welc (13/154)
who [huː] wer Welc (11) • **Who are you?** Wer bist du? Welc (11)

why [waɪ] warum Welc (14) • **Why me?** Warum ich? Welc (14)
win (-nn-) [wɪn] gewinnen 3 (55)
wind [wɪnd] Wind 5 (96/176)
window ['wɪndəʊ] Fenster 1 (28/159)
windy ['wɪndi] windig 5 (96)
winter ['wɪntə] Winter 5 (84/85/174)
with [wɪð] **1.** mit Welc (8); **2.** bei 1 (23) • **Sit with me.** Setz dich zu mir. / Setzt euch zu mir. 1 (20)
without [wɪ'ðaʊt] ohne 2 (41)
woman ['wʊmən], *pl* **women** ['wɪmɪn] Frau 3 (65/169)
°**wonder** ['wʌndə] sich fragen
°**wonderful** ['wʌndəfəl] wunderbar
word [wɜ:d] Wort 1 (19) • °**word order** Wortstellung
work [wɜ:k] **1.** arbeiten 1 (28/159)
work on an *etwas* arbeiten 5 (92)
2. Arbeit Welc (16) • **at work** bei der Arbeit / am Arbeitsplatz Welc (16)
worksheet ['wɜ:kʃi:t] Arbeitsblatt 1 (28/159)
world [wɜ:ld] Welt 1 (32)
worry (about) ['wʌri] sich Sorgen machen (wegen, um) 4 (81)
Don't worry. Mach dir keine Sorgen. 4 (81)
would [wəd, wʊd]**: I'd like … (= I would like …)** Ich hätte gern … / Ich möchte gern … 4 (69) • **Would you like …?** Möchtest du …? / Möchten Sie …? 4 (69) • **Would you like some?** Möchtest du etwas/ein paar? / Möchten Sie etwas/ein paar? 4 (69) • **I'd like to talk about … (= I would like to talk about …)** Ich möchte über … reden / Ich würde gern über … reden 6 (105)
write [raɪt] schreiben 1 (22)
write down aufschreiben 1 (23)
write to schreiben an 3 (56)
wrong [rɒŋ] falsch, verkehrt 1 (20)

Y

year [jɪə] **1.** Jahr Welc (8/150); **2.** Jahrgangsstufe 5 (84/85) • °**year planner** Jahresplaner
yellow ['jeləʊ] gelb Welc (13/154)
yes [jes] ja Welc (8/150)
yesterday ['jestədeɪ, 'jestədi] gestern 5 (86) • **yesterday morning/afternoon/evening** gestern Morgen/Nachmittag/Abend 5 (87)
°**yet** [jet]**: They aren't here yet.** Sie sind noch nicht da.
yoga ['jəʊgə] Yoga 3 (57)
you [ju:] **1.** du; Sie Welc (8/150)
You're welcome. Gern geschehen. / Nichts zu danken. Welc (17)
2. ihr Welc (10) • **you two** ihr zwei Welc (12)
3. dir; dich; euch Welc (10)
► S.152 you – I/me
young [jʌŋ] jung 5 (96)
your [jɔ:] **1.** dein/e Welc (8/150)
It's your turn. Du bist dran / an der Reihe. 1 (28) • **What's your name?** Wie heißt du? Welc (8/150)
2. Ihr Welc (17); **3.** euer/eure 1 (21)
°**yourself** [jə'self, jɔ:'self]**: about yourself** über dich selbst
°**youth** [ju:θ] Jugend, Jugend-

Z

zero ['zɪərəʊ] null Welc (15)

Das **German – English Dictionary** enthält den **Lernwortschatz** dieses Bandes. Es kann dir eine erste Hilfe sein, wenn du vergessen hast, wie etwas auf Englisch heißt.
Wenn du wissen möchtest, wo das englische Wort zum ersten Mal in *English G 21* vorkommt, dann kannst du im **English – German Dictionary** (S. 179–191) nachschlagen.

► Der Pfeil verweist auf Kästchen im Vocabulary (S. 150–178), in denen du weitere Informationen findest.

A

Abend evening ['i:vnɪŋ]; *(später Abend)* night [naɪt] • **am Abend, abends** in the evening
Abendbrot, Abendessen dinner
Abendbrot essen have dinner
zum Abendbrot for dinner
aber but [bət, bʌt]
abziehen: 10 Cent abziehen take 10c off [ˌteɪk_'ɒf]
addieren (zu) add (to) [æd]
Aktivität activity [æk'tɪvəti]
albern silly
alle *(die ganze Gruppe)* all [ɔ:l]
allein alone [ə'ləʊn]
alleinstehend single ['sɪŋgl]
alles everything ['evriθɪŋ]; all [ɔ:l]
Alphabet alphabet ['ælfəbet]
als *(zeitlich)* when [wen]
also *(daher, deshalb)* so [səʊ]
Also, ... Well, ... [wel]
alt old [əʊld]
am 1. am Bahnhof at the station
am oberen Ende / an der Spitze (von) at the top (of) • **am Telefon** on the phone
2. *(zeitlich)* **am 13. Juni** on 13th June
am Morgen/Nachmittag/Abend in the morning/afternoon/evening
am Ende (von) at the end (of)
am Freitag on Friday • **am Freitagmorgen** on Friday morning
am nächsten Morgen/Tag the next morning/day • **am Wochenende** at the weekend
amüsieren: sich amüsieren have fun [hæv 'fʌn]
an: an dem/den Tisch (dort) at that table • **an der Spitze** at the top (of) • **an der/die Tafel** on the board • **schreiben an** write to
andere(r, s) other ['ʌðə] • **die anderen** the others
anders (als) different (from) ['dɪfrənt]
anfangen (mit) start [stɑ:t]
Angst haben (vor) be afraid (of) [ə'freɪd]; be scared (of) [skeəd]
anhaben *(Kleidung)* wear [weə]
anhalten stop [stɒp]
anhören 1. sich *etwas* **anhören** listen to ['lɪsn]; **2. sich gut anhören** sound good [saʊnd]
anmalen paint [peɪnt]
anprobieren *(Kleidung)* try on [ˌtraɪ_'ɒn]
Anruf call; phone call ['fəʊn kɔ:l]
anrufen call [kɔ:l]; phone [fəʊn]
anschauen look at [lʊk]
Anschlagtafel notice board ['nəʊtɪs bɔ:d]
ansehen: sich *etwas* **ansehen** look at [lʊk]; watch [wɒtʃ]
Antwort (auf) answer (to) ['ɑ:nsə]
antworten answer ['ɑ:nsə]
anziehen: sich anziehen get dressed [get 'drest]
Apfel apple ['æpl]
Apfelsine orange ['ɒrɪndʒ]
April April ['eɪprəl]
Arbeit work [wɜ:k] • **bei der Arbeit/ am Arbeitsplatz** at work
arbeiten (an) work (on) [wɜ:k]
Arbeitsblatt worksheet ['wɜ:kʃi:t]
Arbeits- und Lerntechniken study skills ['stʌdi skɪlz]
arm poor [pɔ:, pʊə]
Arm arm [ɑ:m]
Armbanduhr watch [wɒtʃ]
auch: auch aus Bristol from Bristol too [tu:] • **Ich auch.** Me too.
auf on [ɒn] • **auf dem Bild/Foto** in the picture/photo • **auf einmal** suddenly ['sʌdnli] • **auf Englisch** in English • **Auf geht's!** Let's go.
Auf welcher Seite sind wir? What page are we on? • **Auf Wiedersehen.** Goodbye. [ˌgʊd'baɪ]
aufführen *(Szene, Dialog)* act [ækt]
Aufgabe *(im Schulbuch)* exercise ['eksəsaɪz]; *(Job)* job [dʒɒb]
aufgeregt *(nervös)* nervous ['nɜ:vəs]
aufhören stop [stɒp]
aufmachen open ['əʊpən]
aufräumen tidy ['taɪdi]
aufregend exciting [ɪk'saɪtɪŋ]
Aufsatz essay ['eseɪ]
aufschreiben write down [ˌraɪt 'daʊn]
aufstehen get up [ˌget_'ʌp]
Auge eye [aɪ]
August August ['ɔ:gəst]
aus: Ich komme/bin aus ... I'm from ... [frəm, frɒm] • **aus ... (heraus/hinaus)** out of ... ['aʊt_əv] • **aus dem Zug/Bus aussteigen** get off the train/bus • **aus vielen Gründen** for lots of reasons
Ausflug trip [trɪp]
aussehen: anders/toll/alt aussehen look different/great/old [lʊk]
außerhalb seines Zimmers outside his room [ˌaʊt'saɪd]
Aussprache pronunciation [prəˌnʌnsi'eɪʃn]
aussteigen (aus dem Zug/Bus) get off (the train/bus) [ˌget_'ɒf]
aussuchen: (sich) *etwas* **aussuchen** choose [tʃu:z]
auswählen choose [tʃu:z]
Auto car [kɑ:]
Autsch! Ouch! [aʊtʃ]

B

Baby baby ['beɪbi]
Badewanne bath [bɑ:θ]
Badezimmer bathroom ['bɑ:θru:m]
Badminton badminton ['bædmɪntən]
Bahnhof station ['steɪʃn] • **am Bahnhof** at the station
bald soon [su:n] • **Bis bald.** See you. ['si: ju:]
Ball ball [bɔ:l]
Banane banana [bə'nɑ:nə]
Band *(Musikgruppe)* band [bænd]
Bank *(Sparkasse)* bank [bæŋk]
Bankräuber/in bank robber ['rɒbə]
Baseball baseball ['beɪsbɔ:l]
Basketball basketball ['bɑ:skɪtbɔ:l]
Baum tree [tri:]
beantworten answer ['ɑ:nsə]
beeilen: sich beeilen hurry up [ˌhʌri_'ʌp]
beenden finish ['fɪnɪʃ]
beginnen (mit) start [stɑ:t]
begreifen understand [ˌʌndə'stænd]
Begründung reason ['ri:zn]
bei: bei den Shaws zu Hause at the Shaws' house • **bei der Arbeit** at work • **Englisch bei Mr Kingsley** English with Mr Kingsley
beide both [bəʊθ]
Bein leg [leg]
benötigen need [ni:d]
benutzen use [ju:z]
beobachten watch [wɒtʃ]
bereit ready ['redi]
Bericht (über) report (on) [rɪ'pɔ:t]
berichten (über) tell (about) [tel]
besondere(r, s): ein besonderer Tag a special day ['speʃl]

besser better ['betə]
beste: der/die/das beste ...; die besten ... the best ... [best]
Besucher/in visitor ['vɪzɪtə]
Bett bed [bed] • **ins Bett gehen** go to bed
Beutel bag [bæg]
Bibliothek library ['laɪbrəri]
Bild picture ['pɪktʃə] • **auf dem Bild** in the picture
billig cheap [tʃi:p]
Biologie biology [baɪ'ɒlədʒi]
bis *(zeitlich)* till [tɪl] • **Bis bald.** See you. ['si: ju:]
bitte **1.** *(in Fragen und Aufforderungen)* please [pli:z]; **2. Bitte sehr. / Hier bitte.** Here you are.; **3. Bitte, gern geschehen.** You're welcome. ['welkəm]; **4. Wie bitte?** Sorry? ['sɒri] ► S.163 „bitte"
blau blue [blu:]
bleiben stay [steɪ]
Bleistift pencil ['pensl]
Bleistiftanspitzer pencil sharpener ['pensl ʃɑ:pnə]
bloß just [dʒʌst]; only ['əʊnli]
Boot boat [bəʊt]
böse sein (auf) be cross (with) [krɒs]
brauchen need [ni:d]
braun brown [braʊn]
Briefmarke stamp [stæmp]
Brille: (eine) Brille glasses *(pl)* ['glɑ:sɪz]
bringen: (mit-, her)bringen bring [brɪŋ] • **(weg-, hin)bringen** take [teɪk] • **alles durcheinander-/in Unordnung bringen** make a mess
Brot bread *(no pl)* [bred]
Brötchen roll [rəʊl]
Brotdose sandwich box ['sænwɪtʃ bɒks]
Brücke bridge [brɪdʒ]
Bruder brother ['brʌðə]
Buch book [bʊk]
Bücherei library ['laɪbrəri]
Buchstabe letter ['letə]
buchstabieren spell [spel]
Bus bus [bʌs]

C

CD CD [ˌsi:'di:] • **CD-Spieler** CD player [ˌsi:'di: ˌpleɪə]
Cent cent (c) [sent]
Chor choir ['kwaɪə]
Cola cola ['kəʊlə]
Comic-Heft comic ['kɒmɪk]
Computer computer [kəm'pju:tə]
cool cool [ku:l]
Cornflakes cornflakes ['kɔ:nfleɪks]
Cousin, Cousine cousin ['kʌzn]

D

da, dahin *(dort, dorthin)* there [ðeə]
da drüben over there [ˌəʊvə 'ðeə]
daheim at home [ət 'həʊm]
daher so [səʊ]
danach *(zeitlich)* after that [ˌɑ:ftə 'ðæt]
Danke. Thank you. ['θæŋk ju:]; Thanks.
Vielen Dank! Thanks a lot!
dann then [ðen]
darstellende Kunst drama ['drɑ:mə]
das *(Artikel)* the [ðə, ði]
das (dort) *(Singular)* that [ðət, ðæt]; *(Plural)* those [ðəʊz] • **Das bin ich.** That's me.
dass that [ðət, ðæt]
dasselbe the same [seɪm]
Datum date [deɪt]
decken: den Tisch decken lay the table [ˌleɪ ðə 'teɪbl]
dein(e) your [jɔ:]
denken think [θɪŋk]
der *(Artikel)* the [ðə, ði]
derselbe the same [seɪm]
deshalb so [səʊ]
Detektiv/in detective [dɪ'tektɪv]
deutlich clear [klɪə]
Deutsch; deutsch; Deutsche(r) German ['dʒɜ:mən]
Deutschland Germany ['dʒɜ:məni]
Dezember December [dɪ'sembə]
dich you [ju:]
die *(Artikel)* the [ðə, ði]
die (dort) *(Singular)* that [ðət, ðæt]; *(Plural)* those [ðəʊz] • **die (hier)** *(Singular)* this [ðɪs]; *(Plural)* these [ði:z] ► S.178 this, that – these, those
Diele hall [hɔ:l]
Dienstag Tuesday ['tju:zdeɪ, 'tju:zdi] *(siehe auch unter „Freitag")*
dies (hier); diese(r, s) *(Singular)* this [ðɪs]; *(Plural)* these [ði:z]
dieselbe(n) the same [seɪm]
Ding thing [θɪŋ]
dir you [ju:]
Disko disco ['dɪskəʊ]
Donnerstag Thursday ['θɜ:zdeɪ, 'θɜ:zdi] *(siehe auch unter „Freitag")*
doppelt, Doppel- double ['dʌbl]
Dorf village ['vɪlɪdʒ]
dort, dorthin there [ðeə] • **dort drüben** over there [ˌəʊvə 'ðeə]
Dossier dossier ['dɒsieɪ]
Drachen kite [kaɪt]
dran: Ich bin dran. It's my turn. [tɜ:n]
draußen outside [ˌaʊt'saɪd]
drinnen inside [ˌɪn'saɪd] • **hier drinnen** in here [ˌɪn 'hɪə]
dritte(r, s) third [θɜ:d]
drüben: da/dort drüben over there [ˌəʊvə 'ðeə]
drücken push [pʊʃ]
du you [ju:]
dumm *(albern)* silly ['sɪli]
dunkel dark [dɑ:k]
durcheinander: alles durcheinanderbringen make a mess [ˌmeɪk ə 'mes]
dürfen can [kən, kæn]
Dusche shower ['ʃaʊə]
duschen; sich duschen have a shower ['ʃaʊə]
DVD DVD [ˌdi: vi:' di:]

E

echt real [rɪəl]
Ecke corner ['kɔ:nə]
Eile: in Eile sein be in a hurry ['hʌri]
eilig: es eilig haben be in a hurry ['hʌri]
ein(e) a, an [ə, ən]; one ['wʌn]
ein(e) andere(r, s) ... another ... [ə'nʌðə] • **eine Menge ...** lots of ... ['lɒts_əv] • **ein paar** some [səm, sʌm]
eines Tages one day
einfach *(nicht schwierig)* easy ['i:zi]
einfach nur just [dʒʌst]
Einfall *(Idee)* idea [aɪ'dɪə]
einige some [səm, sʌm]
einigen: sich einigen (auf) agree (on) [ə'gri:]
einkaufen shop [ʃɒp] • **einkaufen gehen** go shopping; shop • **(das) Einkaufen** shopping • **Einkaufsliste** shopping list
einladen (zu) invite (to) [ɪn'vaɪt]
Einladung (zu) invitation (to) [ˌɪnvɪ'teɪʃn]
einmal: auf einmal suddenly ['sʌdnli]
eins, ein, eine one ['wʌn]
einsteigen (in den Zug/Bus) get on (the train/bus) [ˌget_'ɒn]
Eintrittskarte ticket ['tɪkɪt]
einzig: der einzige Gast the only guest ['əʊnli]
Eis *(Speiseeis)* ice cream [ˌaɪs 'kri:m]
Elefant elephant ['elɪfənt]
Eltern parents ['peərənts]
E-Mail (an) e-mail (to) ['i:meɪl]
Ende **1.** end [end] • **am Ende (von)** at the end (of) • **zu Ende machen** finish ['fɪnɪʃ] • **zu Ende sein** be over ['əʊvə]
2. oberes Ende *(Spitze)* top [tɒp]
am oberen Ende at the top
enden finish ['fɪnɪʃ]
endlich at last [ət 'lɑ:st]
Englisch; englisch English ['ɪŋglɪʃ]
Enkel/in grandchild ['græntʃaɪld], *pl* grandchildren ['græntʃɪldrən]
Entschuldigung **1.** *(Tut mir leid)* I'm sorry. ['sɒri] • **Entschuldigung, dass ich zu spät bin/komme.** Sorry, I'm

late.
2. Entschuldigung, ... / Entschuldigen Sie, ... *(Darf ich mal stören?)* Excuse me, ... [ɪk'skjuːz miː]
▸ S.155 „Entschuldigung"
er **1.** *(männliche Person)* he [hiː]; **2.** *(Ding, Tier)* it [ɪt]
Erdkunde geography [dʒi'ɒgrəfi]
erforschen explore [ɪk'splɔː]
ergänzen add (to) [æd]
Ergebnis result [rɪ'zʌlt]
erinnern: sich erinnern (an) remember [rɪ'membə]
erkunden explore [ɪk'splɔː]
erste(r, s) first [fɜːst] • **als Erstes** first • **der erste Tag** the first day **der/die Erste sein** be first
erwarten: ich kann es kaum erwarten, ... zu sehen I can't wait to see ... [weɪt]
erzählen (von) tell (about) [tel]
Erzählung story ['stɔːri]
es it [ɪt] • **es gibt** *(es ist vorhanden)* there's; *(es sind vorhanden)* there are ▸ S.156 There's ... / There are ...
Essen food [fuːd]
essen eat [iːt] • **Abendbrot essen** have dinner • **Toast zum Frühstück essen** have toast for breakfast
Esszimmer dining room ['daɪnɪŋ ruːm]
etwas Käse/Saft some cheese/juice [səm, sʌm]
euch you [juː]
euer, eure your [jɔː]
Euro euro ['jʊərəʊ]

F

fahren: Inliner/Skateboard fahren skate [skeɪt] • **Rad fahren** ride a bike [ˌraɪd ə 'baɪk]
Fahrrad bike [baɪk]
fallen lassen drop [drɒp]
falsch wrong [rɒŋ]
Familie family ['fæməli]
Fan fan [fæn]
fantastisch fantastic [fæn'tæstɪk]
Farbe colour ['kʌlə] • **Welche Farbe hat ...?** What colour is ...?
Februar February ['februəri]
Federball badminton ['bædmɪntən]
Federmäppchen pencil case ['pensl keɪs]
Fehler mistake [mɪ'steɪk]
Fenster window ['wɪndəʊ]
Ferien holidays ['hɒlədeɪz]
Fernsehen television ['telɪvɪʒn]; TV [tiː'viː] • **im Fernsehen** on TV
fernsehen watch TV [ˌwɒtʃ tiː'viː]
fertig *(bereit)* ready ['redi] • **sich fertig machen (für)** *(sich vorbereiten)* get ready (for) • **Dinge fertig machen (für)** *(vorbereiten)* get things ready (for)
Film film [fɪlm]
Filmstar film star ['fɪlm stɑː]
Filzstift felt tip ['felt tɪp]
finden *(entdecken)* find [faɪnd]
Finder finder ['faɪndə]
Finger finger ['fɪŋgə]
Fisch fish, *pl* fish [fɪʃ]
Flasche bottle ['bɒtl] • **eine Flasche Milch** a bottle of milk
Fleisch meat [miːt]
Flur hall [hɔːl]
flüstern whisper ['wɪspə]
folgen follow ['fɒləʊ]
Football American football [əˌmerɪkən 'fʊtbɔːl]
fort away [ə'weɪ]
Foto photo ['fəʊtəʊ] • **auf dem Foto** in the photo • **Fotos machen** take photos
Fotoapparat camera ['kæmərə]
fotografieren take photos [teɪk 'fəʊtəʊz]
Frage question ['kwestʃn] • **Fragen stellen** ask questions
fragen ask [ɑːsk] • **nach** *etwas* **fragen** ask about
Französisch French [frentʃ]
Frau woman ['wʊmən], *pl* women ['wɪmɪn] • **Frau Brown** Mrs Brown ['mɪsɪz] • **Frau White** *(unverheiratet)* Miss White [mɪs]
frei [friː] free • **freie Zeit** free time
Freitag Friday ['fraɪdeɪ, 'fraɪdi] **freitagabends, am Freitagabend** on Friday evening • **freitagnachts, Freitagnacht** on Friday night
Freizeit free time [ˌfriː 'taɪm]
Freund/in friend [frend]
frieren be cold [kəʊld]
froh happy ['hæpi]
Frucht, Früchte fruit [fruːt]
früh early ['ɜːli]
Frühling spring [sprɪŋ]
Frühstück breakfast ['brekfəst] **zum Frühstück** for breakfast
frühstücken have breakfast
Frühstückspension Bed and Breakfast (B&B) [ˌbed_ən 'brekfəst]
Füller pen [pen]
für for [fə, fɔː]
furchtbar terrible ['terəbl]
Fuß foot [fʊt], *pl* feet [fiːt]
Fußball football ['fʊtbɔːl] • **Fußball spielen** play football
Fußballschuhe, -stiefel football boots ['fʊtbɔːl buːts]
Fußboden floor [flɔː]
Futter food [fuːd]
füttern feed [fiːd]

G

ganz: den ganzen Tag (lang) all day **die ganze Zeit** all the time • **Das ist ganz falsch.** This is all wrong.
Garten garden ['gɑːdn]
Gast guest [gest]; *(Besucher/in)* visitor ['vɪzɪtə]
geben give [gɪv] • **es gibt** *(es ist vorhanden)* there's; *(es sind vorhanden)* there are
▸ S.156 There's ... / There are ...
Geburtstag birthday ['bɜːθdeɪ] **Herzlichen Glückwunsch zum Geburtstag.** Happy birthday. **Ich habe im Mai / am 13. Juni Geburtstag.** My birthday is in May / on 13th June. • **Wann hast du Geburtstag?** When's your birthday?
Gedicht poem ['pəʊɪm]
Gegenteil opposite ['ɒpəzɪt]
Gegenwart present ['preznt]
gehen **1. gehen (nach, zu)** go (to) [gəʊ] • **(zu Fuß) gehen** walk [wɔːk] **Auf geht's!** Let's go. • **einkaufen gehen** go shopping; shop [ʃɒp] **ins Bett gehen** go to bed • **nach Hause gehen** go home • **reiten/schwimmen gehen** go riding/swimming
2. Es geht um Mr Green. This is about Mr Green.
gelangen *(hinkommen)* get [get]
gelb yellow ['jeləʊ]
Geld money ['mʌni]
genug enough [ɪ'nʌf]
geöffnet open ['əʊpən]
Geografie geography [dʒi'ɒgrəfi]
gerade: jetzt gerade right now [raɪt 'naʊ]
Geräusch noise [nɔɪz]
gern: Ich hätte gern ... / Ich möchte gern ... I'd like ... (= I would like ...) • **Ich schwimme/tanze/... gern.** I like swimming/dancing/... • **Ich würde gern über ... reden** I'd like to talk about ... • **Gern geschehen.** You're welcome. ['welkəm]
gernhaben like [laɪk]
Geschäft shop [ʃɒp]
geschehen (mit) happen (to) ['hæpən]
Geschenk present ['preznt]
Geschichte **1.** story ['stɔːri]; **2.** *(vergangene Zeiten)* history ['hɪstri]
geschieden divorced [dɪ'vɔːst]
Geschirrspülmaschine dishwasher ['dɪʃwɒʃə]
Gesicht face [feɪs]
gestern yesterday ['jestədeɪ, 'jestədi] **gestern Morgen/Nachmittag/Abend** yesterday morning/afternoon/evening

Getränk drink [drɪŋk]
Gewinn prize [praɪz]
gewinnen win [wɪn]
gewöhnlich usually ['ju:ʒuəli]
Gitarre guitar [gɪ'tɑ:] • **Gitarre spielen** play the guitar
Glas glass [glɑ:s] • **ein Glas Wasser** a glass of water
glauben think [θɪŋk]
gleich sein/aussehen be/look the same [seɪm]
Glück: Viel Glück (bei/mit ...)! Good luck (with ...)! [gʊd 'lʌk]
glücklich happy ['hæpi]
Grammatik grammar ['græmə]
groß big [bɪg]
großartig great [greɪt]
Größe *(Schuhgröße usw.)* size [saɪz]
Großeltern grandparents ['grænpeərənts]
Großmutter grandmother ['grænmʌðə]
Großstadt city ['sɪti]
Großvater grandfather ['grænfɑ:ðə]
grün green [gri:n]
Grund reason ['ri:zn] • **aus vielen Gründen** for lots of reasons
Gruppe group [gru:p]; *(Musikgruppe)* band [bænd]
gruselig scary ['skeəri]
Gruß: Liebe Grüße, ... *(Briefschluss)* Love ... [lʌv]
Grüß Dilip von mir. Say hi to Dilip for me.
gucken look [lʊk]
gut good [gʊd]; *(okay)* OK [əʊ'keɪ] **Guten Morgen.** Good morning. **Guten Tag.** Hello.; *(nachmittags)* Good afternoon.

H

Haar, Haare hair *(no pl)* [heə]
haben have got ['hæv gɒt] • **Ich habe keinen Stuhl.** I haven't got a chair. • **Ich habe am 13. Juni/im Mai Geburtstag.** My birthday is on 13th June/in May. • **Wann hast du Geburtstag?** When's your birthday? • **haben wollen** want [wɒnt] **Was haben wir als Hausaufgabe auf?** What's for homework?
Hähnchen chicken ['tʃɪkɪn]
halb zwölf half past 11 [hɑ:f]
Hallo! Hi! [haɪ]; Hello. [hə'ləʊ]
Hamburger hamburger ['hæmbɜ:gə]
Hamster hamster ['hæmstə]
Hand hand [hænd]
Handy mobile (phone) ['məʊbaɪl]
hassen hate [heɪt]
häufig often ['ɒfn]
Haus house [haʊs] • **im Haus der Shaws / bei den Shaws zu Hause** at the Shaws' house • **nach Hause gehen** go home [həʊm] • **nach Hause kommen** come home; get home • **zu Hause** at home
Hausaufgabe(n) homework *(no pl)* ['həʊmwɜ:k] • **die Hausaufgabe(n) machen** do homework • **Was haben wir als Hausaufgabe auf?** What's for homework?
Haustier pet [pet]
Haustür front door [ˌfrʌnt 'dɔ:]
Heim home [həʊm]
heiß hot [hɒt]
heißen 1. Ich heiße ... My name is ... **Wie heißt du?** What's your name? **2. Sie heißen dich in ... willkommen** They welcome you to ... ['welkəm]
helfen help [help]
Hemd shirt [ʃɜ:t]
herauf up [ʌp]
heraus: aus ... heraus out of ... ['aʊt_əv]
herausfinden find out [ˌfaɪnd_'aʊt]
herausnehmen take out [ˌteɪk_'aʊt]
herbringen bring [brɪŋ]
Herbst autumn ['ɔ:təm]
Herd cooker ['kʊkə]
hereinkommen come in [ˌkʌm_'ɪn]
Herr Brown Mr Brown ['mɪstə]
herumgeben pass round [ˌpɑ:s 'raʊnd]
herunter down [daʊn]
Herzlichen Glückwunsch zum Geburtstag. Happy birthday. [ˌhæpi 'bɜ:θdeɪ]
heute today [tə'deɪ] • **heute Morgen/Nachmittag/Abend** this morning/afternoon/evening **heute Nacht** tonight [tə'naɪt]
hier here [hɪə] • **Hier bitte.** *(Bitte sehr.)* Here you are. • **hier drinnen** in here [ˌɪn 'hɪə]
hierher here [hɪə]
Hilfe help [help]
hinauf up [ʌp]
hinaufklettern (auf) climb [klaɪm] **Klettere auf einen Baum.** Climb a tree.
hinaus: aus ... hinaus out of ... ['aʊt_əv]
hinein: in ... hinein into ... ['ɪntə, 'ɪntʊ]
hinkommen *(gelangen)* get [get]
hinunter down [daʊn]
hinzufügen (zu) add (to) [æd]
Hobby hobby ['hɒbi], *pl* hobbies
Hockey hockey ['hɒki]
Hockeyschuhe hockey shoes ['hɒki ʃu:z]
hören hear [hɪə]
hübsch pretty ['prɪti]
Huhn chicken ['tʃɪkɪn]
Hülle cover ['kʌvə]
Hund dog [dɒg]
hundert hundred ['hʌndrəd]

I

ich I [aɪ] • **Ich auch.** Me too. [ˌmi: 'tu:] • **Das bin ich.** That's me. **Warum ich?** Why me?
Idee idea [aɪ'dɪə]
ihm him; *(bei Dingen, Tieren)* it
ihn him; *(bei Dingen, Tieren)* it
ihnen them [ðəm, ðem]
Ihnen *(höfliche Anrede)* you [ju:]
ihr *(Plural von „du")* you [ju:] • **ihr zwei** you two [ˌju: 'tu:]
ihr: Hilf ihr. Help her. [hə, hɜ:]
ihr(e) *(besitzanzeigend)* *(zu „she")* her [hə, hɜ:]; *(zu „they")* their [ðeə]
Ihr(e) your [jɔ:]
im: im Fernsehen on TV • **im Haus der Shaws** at the Shaws' house **im Mai** in May • **im Radio** on the radio • **im Zug** on the train
immer always ['ɔ:lweɪz] • **immer noch** still [stɪl]
in in • **in ... (hinein)** into ... ['ɪntə, 'ɪntʊ] • **in der ...straße** in ... Street **in der Hamiltonstraße 7** at 7 Hamilton Street • **in der Nacht** at night • **in der Nähe von** near **in der Schule** at school • **in Eile sein** be in a hurry • **in den Zug/Bus einsteigen** get on the train/bus • **ins Bett gehen** go to bed
Inliner skates [skeɪts] • **Inliner fahren** skate
innen (drin) inside [ˌɪn'saɪd]
Innenstadt city centre [ˌsɪti 'sentə]
interessant interesting ['ɪntrəstɪŋ]
Interview interview ['ɪntəvju:]
irgendwelche any ['eni]

J

ja yes [jes]
Jahr year [jɪə]
Jahrgangsstufe year [jɪə]
Januar January ['dʒænjuəri]
Jeans jeans *(pl)* [dʒi:nz]
jede(r, s) ... *(Begleiter)* **1.** every ... ['evri] **2.** *(jeder einzelne)* each ... [i:tʃ]
jemand somebody ['sʌmbədi]
jene(r, s) *(Singular)* that [ðət, ðæt]; *(Plural)* those [ðəʊz]
jetzt now [naʊ] • **jetzt gerade, jetzt sofort** right now
Job job [dʒɒb]
Judo judo ['dʒu:dəʊ] • **Judo machen** do judo

Jugend- junior ['dʒu:niə]
Jugendliche(r) kid [kɪd]
Juli July [dʒu'laɪ]
jung young [jʌŋ]
Junge boy [bɔɪ]
Juni June [dʒu:n]
Junioren- junior ['dʒu:niə]

K

Käfig cage [keɪdʒ]
Kalender calendar ['kælɪndə]
kalt cold [kəʊld]
Kamera camera ['kæmərə]
Kaninchen rabbit ['ræbɪt]
Karotte carrot ['kærət]
Karte *(Post-, Spielkarte)* card [kɑ:d]
Kartoffel potato [pə'teɪtəʊ], *pl* potatoes
Kartoffelchips crisps *(pl)* [krɪsps]
Käse cheese [tʃi:z]
Kästchen, Kasten box [bɒks]
Katze cat [kæt]
kaufen buy [baɪ]
kein(e) no; not a; not (...) any • **Ich habe keinen Stuhl.** I haven't got a chair. • **keine Musik mehr** no more music
Keks biscuit ['bɪskɪt]
kennen know [nəʊ]
kennenlernen meet [mi:t]
Kind child [tʃaɪld], *pl* children ['tʃɪldrən]; kid [kɪd]
Kino cinema ['sɪnəmə]
Kirche church [tʃɜ:tʃ]
Kiste box [bɒks]
Klang sound [saʊnd]
klar clear [klɪə]
Klasse class [klɑ:s]; form [fɔ:m]
Klassenkamerad/in classmate ['klɑ:smeɪt]
Klassenlehrer/in class teacher; form teacher
Klassenzimmer classroom ['klɑ:sru:m]
Klavier piano [pi'ænəʊ] • **Klavier spielen** play the piano
Klebestift glue stick ['glu: stɪk]
Klebstoff glue [glu:]
Kleid dress [dres]
Kleiderschrank wardrobe ['wɔ:drəʊb]
klein little ['lɪtl]; small [smɔ:l]
Kleinstadt town [taʊn]
klettern climb [klaɪm] • **Klettere auf einen Baum.** Climb a tree.
klingen sound [saʊnd]
Klub club [klʌb]
klug clever ['klevə]
Knie knee [ni:]
komisch *(witzig)* funny ['fʌni]
kommen come [kʌm]; *(hinkommen)* get [get] • **Ich komme aus ...** I'm from ... • **Wo kommst du her?** Where are you from? • **nach Hause kommen** come home; get home • **zu spät kommen** be late
König king [kɪŋ]
können can [kən, kæn] • **ich kann nicht ...** I can't ... [kɑ:nt] • **Kann ich Ihnen helfen? / Was kann ich für Sie tun?** *(im Laden)* Can I help you?
kontrollieren *(überprüfen)* check [tʃek]
Kopf head [hed]
Korb basket ['bɑ:skɪt] • **ein Korb Äpfel** a basket of apples
Körper body ['bɒdi]
kosten *(Essen probieren)* try [traɪ]
kosten: Er/Sie/Es kostet 1 Pfund. It's £1. • **Sie kosten 35 Pence.** They are 35p. • **Wie viel kostet/kosten ...?** How much is/are ...?
kostenlos free [fri:]
Krug jug [dʒʌg] • **ein Krug Orangensaft** a jug of orange juice
Küche kitchen ['kɪtʃɪn]
Kuchen cake [keɪk]
Kugelschreiber pen [pen]
Kühlschrank fridge [frɪdʒ]
Kunst art [ɑ:t]
kurz short [ʃɔ:t] • **kurze Hose** shorts *(pl)* [ʃɔ:ts]

L

lächeln smile [smaɪl]
lachen laugh [lɑ:f]
Laden *(Geschäft)* shop [ʃɒp]
Lampe lamp [læmp]
Land country ['kʌntri]
lang long [lɒŋ] • **drei Tage lang** for three days
langweilig boring ['bɔ:rɪŋ]
Lärm noise [nɔɪz]
Lasagne lasagne [lə'zænjə]
lassen: Lass das! Stop that! • **Lass uns ... / Lasst uns ...** Let's ... [lets]
laufen run [rʌn]
laut loud [laʊd]
Laut sound [saʊnd]
leben live [lɪv]
Leben life [laɪf], *pl* lives [laɪvz]
Lebensmittel food [fu:d]
ledig single ['sɪŋgl]
leer empty ['empti]
legen *(hin-, ablegen)* put [pʊt]
lehren teach [ti:tʃ]
Lehrer/in teacher ['ti:tʃə]
leicht *(nicht schwierig)* easy ['i:zi]
leid: Tut mir leid. I'm sorry. ['sɒri]
leise quiet ['kwaɪət]
Lektion *(im Schulbuch)* unit ['ju:nɪt]
lernen learn [lɜ:n]
Lern- und Arbeitstechniken study skills ['stʌdi skɪlz]
lesen read [ri:d]
letzte(r, s) last [lɑ:st]
Leute people ['pi:pl]
Liebe Grüße, ... *(Briefschluss)* Love ... [lʌv]
Lieber Jay, ... Dear Jay ... [dɪə]
Liebling dear [dɪə]
Lieblings-: meine Lieblingsfarbe my favourite colour ['feɪvərɪt]
Lied song [sɒŋ]
lila purple ['pɜ:pl]
Limonade lemonade [,lemə'neɪd]
Lineal ruler ['ru:lə]
Liste list [lɪst]

M

machen do [du:]; make [meɪk] • **die Hausaufgabe(n) machen** do homework • **ein Picknick machen** have a picnic • **Fotos machen** take photos • **Judo machen** do judo • **sich Notizen machen** take notes • **sich Sorgen machen (um, wegen)** worry (about) ['wʌri] • **(Zauber-)Kunststücke machen** do tricks • **Reiten macht Spaß.** Riding is fun.
Mädchen girl [gɜ:l]
Magazin *(Zeitschrift)* magazine [,mægə'zi:n]
Magst du ...? Do you like ...? *(siehe auch unter „mögen")*
Mai May [meɪ]
malen paint [peɪnt]
Mama mum [mʌm]
manchmal sometimes ['sʌmtaɪmz]
Mann man [mæn], *pl* men [men]
Mannschaft team [ti:m]
Mappe *(des Sprachenportfolios)* dossier ['dɒsieɪ]
Marmelade *(Orangenmarmelade)* marmalade ['mɑ:məleɪd]
März March [mɑ:tʃ]
Mathematik maths [mæθs]
Maus mouse [maʊs], *pl* mice [maɪs]
Meer sea [si:]
Meerschweinchen guinea pig ['gɪni pɪg]
mehr more [mɔ:] • **viel mehr** lots more • **keine Musik mehr** no more music
mein(e) my [maɪ]
meinen think [θɪŋk]
meist: die meisten Leute most people [məʊst]
meistens usually ['ju:ʒuəli]
Meister/in *(Champion)* champion ['tʃæmpiən]

Menschen people ['pi:pl]
merken: sich *etwas* **merken** remember [rɪ'membə]
mich me [mi:]
Milch milk [mɪlk]
Mindmap mind map ['maɪnd mæp]
Minute minute ['mɪnɪt]
mir me [mi:]
mit with [wɪð]
mitbringen bring [brɪŋ]
Mitschüler/in classmate ['klɑ:smeɪt]
Mittagessen lunch [lʌntʃ] • **zum Mittagessen** for lunch
Mittagspause lunch break ['lʌntʃ breɪk]
Mitte centre ['sentə]; middle (of) ['mɪdl]
Mitteilung *(Notiz)* note [nəʊt]
Mittwoch Wednesday ['wenzdeɪ, 'wenzdi] *(siehe auch unter „Freitag")*
Mobiltelefon mobile phone [ˌməʊbaɪl 'fəʊn]; mobile ['məʊbaɪl]
möchte: Ich möchte gern ... (haben) I'd like ... (= I would like ...) • **Ich möchte über ... reden** I'd like to talk about ... • **Möchtest du etwas (Saft) / ein paar (Kekse)?** Would you like some (juice/biscuits)?
Modell*(-auto, -schiff)* model ['mɒdl]
mögen like [laɪk] • **Ich mag ...** I like ... • **Ich mag ... nicht. / Ich mag kein(e) ...** I don't like ... • **Magst du ...?** Do you like ...?
Möhre carrot ['kærət]
Monat month [mʌnθ]
Montag Monday ['mʌndeɪ, 'mʌndi] *(siehe auch unter „Freitag")*
morgen tomorrow [tə'mɒrəʊ]
Morgen morning ['mɔ:nɪŋ] • **am Morgen, morgens** in the morning **Guten Morgen.** Good morning. **Montagmorgen** Monday morning
MP3-Spieler MP3 player [ˌempi:'θri: ˌpleɪə]
müde tired ['taɪəd]
Mund mouth [maʊθ]
murren grumble ['grʌmbl]
Museum museum [mju'zi:əm]
Musical musical ['mju:zɪkl]
Musik music ['mju:zɪk]
müssen have to; must [mʌst]
Mutter mother ['mʌðə]
Mutti mum [mʌm]

N

Na ja ... / Na gut ... Oh well ... [əʊ 'wel]
nach 1. *(örtlich)* to [tə, tu] • **nach Hause gehen** go home • **nach Hause kommen** come home; get home • **nach oben** up; *(im Haus)* upstairs [ˌʌp'steəz] • **nach unten** down; *(im Haus)* downstairs [ˌdaʊn'steəz]
2. *(zeitlich)* after ['ɑ:ftə] • **Viertel nach 11** quarter past 11 [pɑ:st]
3. nach *etwas* **fragen** ask about [ə'baʊt]
Nachbar/in neighbour ['neɪbə]
Nachmittag afternoon [ˌɑ:ftə'nu:n] **am Nachmittag, nachmittags** in the afternoon
nächste(r, s): am nächsten Tag the next day [nekst] • **der Nächste sein** be next • **Was haben wir als Nächstes?** What have we got next?
Nacht night [naɪt] • **heute Nacht** tonight [tə'naɪt] • **in der Nacht, nachts** at night
nahe (bei) near [nɪə]
Nähe: in der Nähe von near [nɪə]
Name name [neɪm]
Nase nose [nəʊz]
natürlich of course [əv 'kɔ:s]
Naturwissenschaft science ['saɪəns]
nehmen take [teɪk] • **Wir nehmen es.** *(beim Einkaufen)* We'll take it.
nein no [nəʊ]
nennen call [kɔ:l]
nervös nervous ['nɜ:vəs]
nett nice [naɪs]
neu new [nju:]
nicht not [nɒt] • **Du brauchst eine Schultasche, nicht wahr?** You need a school bag, right? [raɪt] • **Ich weiß es nicht.** I don't know. [ˌdəʊnt 'nəʊ]
Nichts zu danken. You're welcome. ['welkəm]
nie, niemals never ['nevə]
noch: noch ein(e) ... another ... [ə'nʌðə] • **noch einmal** again [ə'gen] • **(immer) noch** still [stɪl]
nörgeln grumble ['grʌmbl]
normalerweise usually ['ju:ʒuəli]
Notiz note [nəʊt] • **sich Notizen machen** take notes
November November [nəʊ'vembə]
null o [əʊ]; zero ['zɪərəʊ]
Nummer number ['nʌmbə]
nun now [naʊ] • **Nun, ...** Well, ... [wel]
nur only ['əʊnli]; just [dʒʌst] • **nur zum Spaß** just for fun

O

oben *(an der Spitze)* at the top (of) [tɒp]; *(im Haus)* upstairs [ˌʌp'steəz] **nach oben** up; *(im Haus)* upstairs
oberhalb von over ['əʊvə]
Oberteil top [tɒp]
Obst fruit [fru:t]
Obstsalat fruit salad ['fru:t ˌsæləd]
oder or [ɔ:]
öffnen open ['əʊpən]
oft often ['ɒfn]
ohne without [wɪ'ðaʊt]
Ohr ear [ɪə]
Ohrring earring ['ɪərɪŋ]
okay OK [əʊ'keɪ]
Oktober October [ɒk'təʊbə]
Oma grandma ['grænmɑ:]
Onkel uncle ['ʌŋkl]
Opa grandpa ['grænpɑ:]
Orange orange ['ɒrɪndʒ]
orange(farben) orange ['ɒrɪndʒ]
Orangenmarmelade marmalade ['mɑ:məleɪd]
Orangensaft orange juice ['ɒrɪndʒ dʒu:s]
Ort place [pleɪs]

P

paar: ein paar some [səm, sʌm]
Päckchen, Packung packet ['pækɪt] **ein Päckchen / eine Packung Pfefferminzbonbons** a packet of mints
Paket parcel ['pɑ:sl]
Papa dad [dæd]
Papagei parrot ['pærət]
Papier paper ['peɪpə]
Park park [pɑ:k]
Partner/in partner ['pɑ:tnə]
Party party ['pɑ:ti]
passen fit [fɪt]
passieren (mit) happen (to) ['hæpən]
Pause break [breɪk]
Pence pence (p) [pens]
Pfefferminzbonbons mints [mɪnts]
Pferd horse [hɔ:s]
Pfund *(britische Währung)* pound (£) [paʊnd] • **Es kostet 1 Pfund.** It's £1.
Piano piano [pi'ænəʊ]
Picknick picnic ['pɪknɪk] • **ein Picknick machen** have a picnic
pink(farben) pink [pɪŋk]
Pirat/in pirate ['paɪrət]
Pizza pizza ['pi:tsə]
Plan plan [plæn]
planen plan [plæn]
Platz *(Ort, Stelle)* place [pleɪs]
Plätzchen biscuit ['bɪskɪt]
plötzlich suddenly ['sʌdnli]
Polizei police *(pl)* [pə'li:s]
Poltergeist poltergeist ['pəʊltəgaɪst]
Pommes frites chips *(pl)* [tʃɪps]
Poster poster ['pəʊstə]
Präsentation presentation [ˌprezn'teɪʃn]
Preis *(Kaufpreis)* price [praɪs]; *(Gewinn)* prize [praɪz]

Probe *(am Theater)* rehearsal [rɪ'hɜ:sl]
proben *(am Theater)* rehearse [rɪ'hɜ:s]
probieren try [traɪ]
Programm programme ['prəʊɡræm]
Projekt (über, zu) project (on, about) ['prɒdʒekt]
prüfen *(überprüfen)* check [tʃek]
putzen clean [kli:n] • **Ich putze mir die Zähne.** I clean my teeth.

Q

Quiz quiz [kwɪz], *pl* quizzes ['kwɪzɪz]

R

Rad fahren ride a bike [ˌraɪd_ə 'baɪk]
Radiergummi rubber ['rʌbə]
Radio radio ['reɪdiəʊ] • **im Radio** on the radio
Rap rap [ræp]
Ratespiel quiz [kwɪz], *pl* quizzes ['kwɪzɪz]
Raum room [ru:m]
Recht haben be right [raɪt]
reden (mit, über) talk (to, about) [tɔ:k] • **Wovon redest du?** What are you talking about?
Regal(brett) shelf [ʃelf], *pl* shelves [ʃelvz]
reichen *(weitergeben)* pass [pɑ:s]
Reihe: Du bist an der Reihe. It's your turn. [tɜ:n]
Reise trip [trɪp]
reiten ride [raɪd] • **reiten gehen** go riding
Religion *(Religionsunterricht)* RE [ˌɑ:r_'i:], Religious Education [rɪˌlɪdʒəs_edʒu'keɪʃn]
rennen run [rʌn]
Reportage (über) report (on) [rɪ'pɔ:t]
Resultat result [rɪ'zʌlt]
richtig right [raɪt]
Rollstuhl wheelchair ['wi:ltʃeə]
rosa pink [pɪŋk]
rot red [red]
rufen call [kɔ:l]; shout [ʃaʊt] • **die Polizei rufen** call the police
ruhig quiet ['kwaɪət]
Rundgang (durch das Haus) tour (of the house) [tʊə]

S

Sache thing [θɪŋ]
Saft juice [dʒu:s]
sagen say [seɪ] • **Sagt mir eure Namen.** Tell me your names. [tel]
Salat *(Gericht, Beilage)* salad ['sæləd]
sammeln collect [kə'lekt]
Samstag Saturday ['sætədeɪ, 'sætədi] *(siehe auch unter „Freitag")*
Sandwich sandwich ['sænwɪtʃ]
Satz sentence ['sentəns]
sauber machen clean [kli:n]
sauer sein (auf) be cross (with) [krɒs]
Schachtel packet ['pækɪt]
Schale bowl [bəʊl] • **eine Schale Cornflakes** a bowl of cornflakes
Schatz dear [dɪə]
schauen look [lʊk]
Schauspiel drama ['drɑ:mə]
schieben push [pʊʃ]
Schiff boat [bəʊt]; ship [ʃɪp]
Schildkröte tortoise ['tɔ:təs]
schlafen sleep [sli:p]; *(nicht wach sein)* be asleep [ə'sli:p]
Schlafzimmer bedroom ['bedru:m]
Schlange snake [sneɪk]
schlau clever ['klevə]
schlecht bad [bæd]
schließen *(zumachen)* close [kləʊz]
schließlich at last [ət 'lɑ:st]
schlimm bad [bæd]
Schlüsselwort key word ['ki: wɜ:d]
schnell quick [kwɪk]
Schokolade chocolate ['tʃɒklət]
schön beautiful ['bju:tɪfl]; *(nett)* nice [naɪs]
Schrank cupboard ['kʌbəd]; *(Kleiderschrank)* wardrobe ['wɔ:drəʊb]
schrecklich terrible ['terəbl]
schreiben (an) write (to) [raɪt]
Schreibtisch desk [desk]
schreien shout [ʃaʊt]
Schritt step [step]
Schuh shoe [ʃu:]
Schule school [sku:l] • **in der Schule** at school
Schüler/in student ['stju:dənt]
Schulfach (school) subject ['sʌbdʒɪkt]
Schulheft exercise book ['eksəsaɪz bʊk]
Schultasche school bag ['sku:l bæɡ]
Schulter shoulder ['ʃəʊldə]
Schüssel bowl [bəʊl]
schwarz black [blæk] • **schwarzes Brett** notice board ['nəʊtɪs bɔ:d]
schwer *(schwierig)* difficult ['dɪfɪkəlt]
Schwester sister ['sɪstə]
schwierig difficult ['dɪfɪkəlt]
Schwimmbad, -becken swimming pool ['swɪmɪŋ pu:l]
schwimmen swim [swɪm]
schwimmen gehen go swimming
See *(die See, das Meer)* sea [si:]
sehen see [si:] • **Siehst du?** See?
sehr very ['veri] • **Er mag sie sehr.** He likes her a lot. [ə 'lɒt]
Seife soap [səʊp]
sein *(Verb)* be [bi:]
sein(e) *(besitzanzeigend)* *(zu „he")* his; *(zu „it")* its
Seite *(Buch-, Heftseite)* page [peɪdʒ]
Auf welcher Seite sind wir? What page are we on?
selbstverständlich of course [əv 'kɔ:s]
September September [sep'tembə]
Sessel armchair ['ɑ:mtʃeə]
setzen: sich setzen sit [sɪt] • **Setz dich / Setzt euch zu mir.** Sit with me.
Shorts shorts *(pl)* [ʃɔ:ts]
Show show [ʃəʊ]
sie **1.** *(weibliche Person)* she [ʃi:]
Frag sie. Ask her. [hə, hɜ:]
2. *(Ding, Tier)* it [ɪt]
3. *(Plural)* they [ðeɪ] • **Frag sie.** Ask them. [ðəm, ðem]
4. Sie *(höfliche Anrede)* you [ju:]
Silbe syllable ['sɪləbl]
singen sing [sɪŋ]
sitzen sit [sɪt]
Skateboard skateboard ['skeɪtbɔ:d]
Skateboard fahren skate [skeɪt]
Sketch sketch [sketʃ]
so süß so sweet [səʊ]
Socke sock [sɒk]
Sofa sofa ['səʊfə]
Sohn son [sʌn]
Sommer summer ['sʌmə]
Song song [sɒŋ]
Sonnabend Saturday ['sætədeɪ, 'sætədi] *(siehe auch unter „Freitag")*
Sonnenbrille: (eine) Sonnenbrille sunglasses *(pl)* ['sʌnɡlɑ:sɪz]
Sonntag Sunday ['sʌndeɪ, 'sʌndi] *(siehe auch unter „Freitag")*
Sorgen: sich Sorgen machen (wegen, um) worry (about) ['wʌri] • **Mach dir keine Sorgen.** Don't worry.
sowieso anyway ['eniweɪ]
spannend exciting [ɪk'saɪtɪŋ]
Spaß fun [fʌn] • **Spaß haben** have fun • **nur zum Spaß** just for fun
Reiten macht Spaß. Riding is fun.
Viel Spaß! Have fun! ► S.177 fun
spät late [leɪt] • **Wie spät ist es?** What's the time? • **zu spät sein/kommen** be late
später later ['leɪtə]
Spiel game [ɡeɪm]; *(Wettkampf)* match [mætʃ]
spielen play [pleɪ]; *(Szene, Dialog)* act [ækt] • **Fußball spielen** play football • **Gitarre/Klavier spielen** play the guitar/the piano
Spieler/in player ['pleɪə]
Spion/in spy [spaɪ]
Spitze *(oberes Ende)* top [tɒp] • **an der Spitze (von)** at the top (of)
Sport; Sportart sport [spɔ:t] • **Sport treiben** do sport ► S.167 Sports

Sportunterricht PE [ˌpiː_ˈiː], Physical Education [ˌfɪzɪkəl_edʒuˈkeɪʃn]
Sportzentrum sports centre [ˈspɔːts ˌsentə]
Sprache language [ˈlæŋgwɪdʒ]
Spülbecken, Spüle sink [sɪŋk]
Stadt *(Großstadt)* city [ˈsɪti]; *(Kleinstadt)* town [taʊn]
Stadtzentrum city centre [ˌsɪti ˈsentə]
Stall *(für Kaninchen)* hutch [hʌtʃ]
Stammbaum family tree [ˈfæməli triː]
Star *(Film-, Popstar)* star [stɑː]
starten start [stɑːt]
stellen *(hin-, abstellen)* put [pʊt] **Fragen stellen** ask questions
Stereoanlage stereo [ˈsteriəʊ]
Stichwort *(Schlüsselwort)* key word [ˈkiː wɜːd]
Stiefel boot [buːt]
still quiet [ˈkwaɪət]
stimmen: Das stimmt. That's right. [raɪt] • **Du brauchst ein Lineal, stimmt's?** You need a ruler, right?
stoßen push [pʊʃ]
Straße road [rəʊd]; street [striːt]
streiten: sich streiten argue [ˈɑːgjuː]
Strumpf sock [sɒk]
Stück piece [piːs] • **ein Stück Papier** a piece of paper
Student/in student [ˈstjuːdənt]
Stuhl chair [tʃeə]
Stunde *(Schulstunde)* lesson [ˈlesn]
Stundenplan timetable [ˈtaɪmteɪbl]
süß sweet [swiːt]
Süßigkeiten sweets *(pl)* [swiːts]
Sweatshirt sweatshirt [ˈswetʃɜːt]
Szene scene [siːn]

T

Tafel *(Wandtafel)* board [bɔːd] • **an der/die Tafel** on the board
Tag day [deɪ] • **drei Tage (lang)** for three days • **eines Tages** one day **Guten Tag.** Hello.; *(nachmittags)* Good afternoon. [gʊd_ɑːftəˈnuːn]
Tagebuch diary [ˈdaɪəri]
Tante aunt [ɑːnt]
Tanz dance [dɑːns]
tanzen dance [dɑːns]
Tanzen dancing [ˈdɑːnsɪŋ]
Tanzstunden, Tanzunterricht dancing lessons [ˈdɑːnsɪŋ ˌlesnz]
Tasche *(Tragetasche, Beutel)* bag [bæg]
Tätigkeit activity [ækˈtɪvəti]
tausend thousand [ˈθaʊznd]
Team team [tiːm]
Tee tea [tiː]
Teil part [pɑːt]
teilen: sich *etwas* teilen (mit) share (with) [ʃeə]
Telefon (tele)phone [ˈtelɪfəʊn] • **am Telefon** on the phone
telefonieren phone [fəʊn]
Telefonnummer (tele)phone number [ˈtelɪfəʊn ˌnʌmbə]
Teller plate [pleɪt] • **ein Teller Pommes frites** a plate of chips
Tennis tennis [ˈtenɪs]
Termin appointment [əˈpɔɪntmənt]
Terminkalender diary [ˈdaɪəri]
teuer expensive [ɪkˈspensɪv]
Text text [tekst]
Theaterstück play [pleɪ]
Thema, Themenbereich topic [ˈtɒpɪk]
Tier *(Haustier)* pet [pet]
Tierhandlung pet shop [ˈpet ʃɒp]
Tisch table [ˈteɪbl]
Tischtennis table tennis [ˈteɪbl tenɪs]
Titel title [ˈtaɪtl]
Toast(brot) toast [təʊst]
Tochter daughter [ˈdɔːtə]
Toilette toilet [ˈtɔɪlət]
toll fantastic [fænˈtæstɪk]; great [greɪt]
Top *(Oberteil)* top [tɒp]
Torte cake [keɪk]
tot dead [ded]
töten kill [kɪl]
Tour (durch das Haus) tour (of the house) [tʊə]
tragen *(Kleidung)* wear [weə]
trainieren practise [ˈpræktɪs]
Traum dream [driːm] • **Traumhaus** dream house
treffen; sich treffen meet [miːt]
Treppe(nstufen) stairs *(pl)* [steəz]
Trick *(Zauberkunststück)* trick [trɪk]
trinken drink [drɪŋk] • **Milch zum Frühstück trinken** have milk for breakfast
Tschüs. Bye. [baɪ]; See you. [ˈsiː juː]
T-Shirt T-shirt [ˈtiːʃɜːt]
tun do [duː] • **Tue, was ich tue.** Do what I do. • **tun müssen** have to do • **tun wollen** want to do [wɒnt] **Tut mir leid.** I'm sorry. [ˈsɒri]
Tür door [dɔː]
Türklingel doorbell [ˈdɔːbel]
Turm tower [ˈtaʊə]
Turnen *(Sportunterricht)* PE [ˌpiː_ˈiː], Physical Education [ˌfɪzɪkəl_edʒuˈkeɪʃn]
Tut mir leid. I'm sorry. [ˈsɒri]
Tüte bag [bæg]

U

üben practise [ˈpræktɪs]
über about [əˈbaʊt]; *(räumlich)* over [ˈəʊvə]
überprüfen check [tʃek]
Überschrift title [ˈtaɪtl]
Übung *(im Schulbuch)* exercise [ˈeksəsaɪz]
Übungsheft exercise book [ˈeksəsaɪz bʊk]
Uhr **1.** *(Armbanduhr)* watch [wɒtʃ]; *(Wand-, Stand-, Turmuhr)* clock [klɒk]
2. elf Uhr eleven o'clock • **7 Uhr morgens/vormittags** 7 am [ˌeɪ_ˈem] **7 Uhr nachmittags/abends** 7 pm [ˌpiː_ˈem] • **um 8 Uhr 45** at 8.45
Uhrzeit time [taɪm]
um: um 8.45 at 8.45 • **Es geht um Mr Green.** This is about Mr Green.
umsehen: sich umsehen look round [ˌlʊk ˈraʊnd]
und and [ənd, ænd]
unheimlich scary [ˈskeəri]
Uniform uniform [ˈjuːnɪfɔːm]
Unordnung: alles in Unordnung bringen make a mess [ˌmeɪk_ə ˈmes]
uns us [əs, ʌs]
unser(e) our [ˈaʊə]
unten *(im Haus)* downstairs [ˌdaʊnˈsteəz] • **nach unten** down [daʊn]; *(im Haus)* downstairs
unter under [ˈʌndə]
unterhalten: sich unterhalten (mit, über) talk (to, about) [tɔːk]
Unterricht lessons *(pl)* [ˈlesnz]
unterrichten teach [tiːtʃ]
unterschiedlich different [ˈdɪfrənt]

V

Vater father [ˈfɑːðə]
Vati dad [dæd]
Verabredung appointment [əˈpɔɪntmənt]
verabschieden: sich verabschieden say goodbye [ˌseɪ gʊdˈbaɪ]
verbinden *(einander zuordnen)* link [lɪŋk]
Verein club [klʌb]
verfolgen follow [ˈfɒləʊ]
vergessen forget [fəˈget]
verheiratet (mit) married (to) [ˈmærɪd]
Verkäufer/in shop assistant [ˈʃɒp_əˌsɪstənt]
verkehrt *(falsch)* wrong [rɒŋ]
verknüpfen *(einander zuordnen)* link [lɪŋk]
verletzen hurt [hɜːt]
verrückt mad [mæd]
verschieden different [ˈdɪfrənt]
verstecken; sich verstecken hide [haɪd]
verstehen understand [ˌʌndəˈstænd]

versuchen try [traɪ] • **versuchen zu tun** try and do / try to do
verwenden use [juːz]
viel a lot [ə 'lɒt]; lots of; much [mʌtʃ] **viele** lots of; many ['meni] • **Viel Glück (bei/mit ...)!** Good luck (with ...)! • **viel mehr** lots more • **Viel Spaß!** Have fun! • **wie viel?** how much? • **wie viele?** how many? **Vielen Dank!** Thanks a lot!
► S.176 „viel", „viele"
vielleicht maybe ['meɪbi]
Viertel: Viertel nach 11 quarter past 11 ['kwɔːtə] • **Viertel vor 12** quarter to 12
violett purple ['pɜːpl]
Vogel bird [bɜːd]
Vokabelverzeichnis vocabulary [və'kæbjələri]
voll full [fʊl]
Volleyball volleyball ['vɒlibɔːl]
von of [əv, ɒv]; from [frəm, frɒm] • **ein Aufsatz von ...** an essay by ... [baɪ]
vor 1. *(räumlich)* in front of [ɪn 'frʌnt‿əv]; 2. *(zeitlich)* **vor dem Abendessen** before dinner [bɪ'fɔː] • **vor einer Minute** a minute ago [ə'gəʊ] **Viertel vor 12** quarter to 12
vorbei sein be over ['əʊvə]
vorbereiten: Dinge vorbereiten get things ready ['redi] • **sich vorbereiten (auf)** get ready (for)
Vormittag morning ['mɔːnɪŋ]
Vorstellung *(Präsentation)* presentation [,prezn'teɪʃn]; *(Show)* show [ʃəʊ]

W

wählen *(auswählen)* choose [tʃuːz]
wann when [wen]
warten (auf) wait (for) [weɪt]
warum why [waɪ] • **Warum ich?** Why me?
was what [wɒt] • **Was haben wir als Hausaufgabe auf?** What's for homework? • **Was haben wir als Nächstes?** What have we got next? • **Was ist mit ...?** What about ...? • **Was kostet/kosten ...?** How much is/are ...?
waschen wash [wɒʃ] • **Ich wasche mir das Gesicht.** I wash my face.
Waschmaschine washing machine ['wɒʃɪŋ mə,ʃiːn]
Wasser water ['wɔːtə]
Wechselgeld change [tʃeɪndʒ]
weg away [ə'weɪ]
wehtun hurt [hɜːt]
Weihnachten Christmas ['krɪsməs]
weil because [bɪ'kɒz]
weiß white [waɪt]
weitergeben pass [pɑːs]
weitermachen go on [,gəʊ‿'ɒn]
welche(r, s) which [wɪtʃ] • **Auf welcher Seite sind wir?** What page are we on? [wɒt] • **Welche Farbe hat ...?** What colour is ...?
Wellensittich budgie ['bʌdʒi]
Welt world [wɜːld]
wenigstens at least [ət 'liːst]
wenn *(zeitlich)* when [wen]
wer who [huː]
werfen throw [θrəʊ]
Wettkampf match [mætʃ]
wie 1. *(Fragewort)* how [haʊ] • **Wie bitte?** Sorry? ['sɒri] • **Wie heißt du?** What's your name? • **Wie spät ist es?** What's the time? **wie viel?** how much? • **wie viele?** how many? • **Wie war ...?** How was ...? • **Wie wär's mit ...?** What about ...? **2. wie ein Filmstar** like a film star [laɪk]
wieder again [ə'gen]
Wiederholung *(des Lernstoffs)* revision [rɪ'vɪʒn]
Wiedersehen: Auf Wiedersehen. Goodbye. [,gʊd'baɪ]
willkommen: Willkommen (in Bristol). Welcome (to Bristol). ['welkəm] • **Sie heißen dich in ... willkommen** They welcome you to ...
Wind wind [wɪnd]
windig windy ['wɪndi]
Winter winter ['wɪntə]
wir we [wiː]
wirklich 1. *(Adverb: tatsächlich)* really ['rɪəli]; 2. *(Adjektiv: echt)* real [rɪəl]
wissen know [nəʊ] • **Ich weiß es nicht.** I don't know. • **..., wissen Sie. / ..., weißt du.** ..., you know. **Weißt du was, Sophie?** You know what, Sophie? • **Woher weißt du ...?** How do you know ...?
Witz joke [dʒəʊk]
witzig funny ['fʌni]
wo where [weə] • **Wo kommst du her?** Where are you from?
Woche week [wiːk]
Wochenende weekend [,wiːk'end] **am Wochenende** at the weekend
Wochentage days of the week
Woher weißt du ...? How do you know ...? [nəʊ]
wohin where [weə]
Wohltätigkeitsbasar jumble sale ['dʒʌmbl seɪl]
wohnen live [lɪv]
Wohnung flat [flæt]
Wohnungstür front door [,frʌnt 'dɔː]
Wohnzimmer living room ['lɪvɪŋ ruːm]
wollen *(haben wollen)* want [wɒnt] **tun wollen** want to do
Wort word [wɜːd]
Wörterbuch dictionary ['dɪkʃənri]
Wörterverzeichnis vocabulary [və'kæbjələri]; *(alphabetisches)* dictionary ['dɪkʃənri]
Wovon redest du? What are you talking about?
Wurst, Würstchen sausage ['sɒsɪdʒ]

Y

Yoga yoga ['jəʊgə]

Z

Zahl number ['nʌmbə]
Zahn tooth [tuːθ], *pl* teeth [tiːθ] • **Ich putze mir die Zähne.** I clean my teeth.
zanken: sich zanken argue ['ɑːgjuː]
Zauberkunststück trick [trɪk] • **Zauberkunststücke machen** do tricks
Zeh toe [təʊ]
zeigen show [ʃəʊ]
Zeit time [taɪm]
Zeitschrift magazine [,mægə'ziːn]
Zeitung newspaper ['njuːspeɪpə]
Zentrum centre ['sentə]
ziehen pull [pʊl]
Ziffer number ['nʌmbə]
Zimmer room [ruːm]
zu 1. *(örtlich)* to [tə, tu] • **zu Jenny** to Jenny's • **zu Hause** at home **Setz dich zu mir.** Sit with me. **2. zum Frühstück/Mittagessen/Abendbrot** for breakfast/lunch/dinner [fə, fɔː] **3. zu viel** too much [tuː] • **zu spät sein/kommen** be late **4. versuchen zu tun** try and do / try to do
zuerst first [fɜːst]
Zug train [treɪn] • **im Zug** on the train
Zuhause home [həʊm]
zuhören listen (to) ['lɪsn]
zumachen close [kləʊz]
zumindest at least [ət 'liːst]
zurück (nach) back (to) [bæk]
zusammen together [tə'geðə]
zusätzlich extra ['ekstrə]
zusehen watch [wɒtʃ]
zweite(r, s) second ['sekənd]
Zwillinge twins *(pl)* [twɪnz]
Zwillingsbruder twin brother ['twɪn ,brʌðə]

First names
(Vornamen)

Ananda [ə'nændə]
Anastacia [ˌænə'steɪʒə]
Ann [æn]
Anna ['ænə]
Anne [æn]
Barnabas ['bɑ:nəbəs]
Becky ['beki]
Bella ['belə]
Ben [ben]
Bill [bɪl]
Bob [bɒb]
Catherine ['kæθrɪn]
Dan [dæn]
Daniel ['dænjəl]
David ['deɪvɪd]
Dennis ['denɪs]
Dilip ['dɪlɪp]
Elizabeth [ɪ'lɪzəbəθ]
Emily ['eməli]
Gyles [dʒaɪlz]
Hannah ['hænə]
Harry ['hæri]
Henry ['henri]
Hip [hɪp]
Hop [hɒp]
Howard ['haʊəd]
Indira [ɪn'dɪərə]
Isabel ['ɪzəbel]
Jack [dʒæk]
James [dʒeɪmz]
Jamie ['dʒeɪmi]
Jane [dʒeɪn]
Jay [dʒeɪ]
Jennifer ['dʒenɪfə]
Jenny ['dʒeni]
Jerry ['dʒeri]
Jim [dʒɪm]
Jo [dʒəʊ]
John [dʒɒn]
Jonah ['dʒəʊnə]
Kelly ['kelɪ]
Larry ['læri]
Laura ['lɔ:rə]
Lee [li:]
Les [lez]
Lisa ['li:sə, 'li:zə]
Liz [lɪz]
Mark [mɑ:k]
Mary ['meəri]
Matt [mæt]
Michael ['maɪkl]
Michelle [mɪ'ʃel]
Mike [maɪk]
Mitsu ['mɪtsu:]
Nicole [nɪ'kəʊl]
Nora ['nɔ:rə]
Pat [pæt]
Patrick ['pætrɪk]
Paul [pɔ:l]
Peter ['pi:tə]
Philip ['fɪlɪp]
Polly ['pɒli]
Prunella [pru'nelə]
Rob [rɒb]
Rosie ['rəʊzi]
Sally ['sæli]
Sanjay ['sændʒeɪ]
Sheeba ['ʃi:bə]
Sheila ['ʃi:lə]
Shirley ['ʃɜ:li]
Simon ['saɪmən]
Sophie ['səʊfi]
Tim [tɪm]
Toby ['təʊbi]
Tom [tɒm]
Wanda ['wɒndə]
Winston ['wɪnstən]
Yoko ['jəʊkəʊ]

Family names
(Familiennamen)

Barker ['bɑ:kə]
Bates [beɪts]
Baxter ['bækstə]
Baynton ['beɪntən]
Bonny ['bɒni]
Brandreth ['brændrɪθ]
Carter-Brown [ˌkɑ:tə 'braʊn]
Cunliffe ['kʌnlɪf]
Green [gri:n]
Gupta ['gʊptə]
Hanson ['hænsn]
Hart [hɑ:t]
Hill [hɪl]
Kapoor [kə'pɔ:, kə'pʊə]
King [kɪŋ]
Kingsley ['kɪŋzli]
Kowalski [kə'wɒlski]
Muller ['mʌlə, 'mʊlə]
Parker ['pɑ:kə]
Rackham ['rækəm]
Robinson ['rɒbɪnsən]
Scott [skɒt]
Shaw [ʃɔ:]
Smith [smɪθ]
Thompson ['tɒmpsən]
Thorpe [θɔ:p]
West [west]
White [waɪt]
Yakahama [ˌjækə'hɑ:mə]

Place names
(Ortsnamen)

Australia [ɒ'streɪliə]
Bath [bɑ:θ]
Bristol ['brɪstl]
Cabot Tower [ˌkæbət 'taʊə]
Clifton Suspension Bridge [ˌklɪftən sə'spenʃn brɪdʒ]
Cooper Street ['ku:pə stri:t]
Cotham ['kɒtəm]
Cotham Park Road [ˌkɒtəm pɑ:k 'rəʊd]
Delhi ['deli]
England ['ɪŋglənd]
Frogmore Street ['frɒgmɔ: stri:t]
Germany ['dʒɜ:məni]
Hamilton Street ['hæməltən stri:t]
The **Hippodrome Theatre** [ˌhɪpədrəʊm 'θɪətə]
India ['ɪndiə]
The **Industrial Museum** [ɪnˌdʌstriəl mju'zi:əm]
London ['lʌndən]
New York [ˌnju: 'jɔ:k]
New Zealand [nju: 'zi:lənd]
Paris ['pærɪs]
Penzance [pen'zæns]
Tokyo ['təʊkiəʊ]
Uganda [ju'gændə]

Other names
(Andere Namen)

Arsenal ['ɑ:snəl]
The **Australian Open** [ɒˌstreɪliən_'əʊpən]
Blackbeard ['blækbɪəd]
Dracula ['drækjʊlə]
Easter ['i:stə]
Frankfurter sausages [ˌfræŋkfɜ:tə 'sɒsɪdʒɪz]
Halloween [ˌhæləʊ'i:n]
Hokey Cokey [ˌhəʊki 'kəʊki]
The **Houston Rockets** [ˌhju:stən 'rɒkɪts]
The **NBA** [ˌen bi:_'eɪ] (National Basketball Association)
The **New York Knicks** [ˌnju: jɔ:k 'nɪks]
Oxfam ['ɒksfæm]
United [ju'naɪtɪd]
Valentine's Day ['væləntaɪnz deɪ]

Classroom English

Zu Beginn und am Ende des Unterrichts

Guten Morgen, Frau ...	**Good morning, Mrs/Ms/Miss ...**	*(bis 12 Uhr)*
Guten Tag, Herr ...	**Good afternoon, Mr ...**	*(ab 12 Uhr)*
Entschuldigung, dass ich zu spät komme.	**Sorry, I'm late.**	
Auf Wiedersehen! / Bis morgen.	**Goodbye. / See you tomorrow.**	

Du brauchst Hilfe

Können Sie mir bitte helfen?	**Can you help me, please?**
Auf welcher Seite sind wir bitte?	**What page are we on, please?**
Was heißt ... auf Englisch/Deutsch?	**What's ... in English/German?**
Können Sie bitte ... buchstabieren?	**Can you spell ..., please?**
Können Sie es bitte an die Tafel schreiben?	**Can you write it on the board, please?**

Hausaufgaben und Übungen

Tut mir leid, ich habe mein Schulheft nicht dabei.	**Sorry, I haven't got my exercise book.**
Ich verstehe diese Übung nicht.	**I don't understand this exercise.**
Ich kann Nummer 3 nicht lösen.	**I can't do number 3.**
Entschuldigung, ich bin noch nicht fertig.	**Sorry, I haven't finished.**
Ich habe ... Ist das auch richtig?	**I've got ... Is that right too?**
Tut mir leid, das weiß ich nicht.	**Sorry, I don't know.**
Was haben wir (als Hausaufgabe) auf?	**What's for homework?**

Wenn es Probleme gibt

Kann ich es auf Deutsch sagen?	**Can I say it in German?**
Können Sie/Kannst du bitte lauter sprechen?	**Can you speak louder, please?**
Können Sie/Kannst du das bitte noch mal sagen?	**Can you say that again, please?**
Kann ich bitte das Fenster öffnen/zumachen?	**Can I open/close the window, please?**
Kann ich bitte zur Toilette gehen?	**Can I go to the toilet, please?**

Partnerarbeit

Kann ich mit Julian arbeiten?	**Can I work with Julian?**
Kann ich bitte dein Lineal/deinen Filzstift/... haben?	**Can I have your ruler/felt tip/..., please?**
Danke. / Vielen Dank.	**Thank you. / Thanks a lot.**
Du bist dran.	**It's your turn.**

Diese Arbeitsanweisungen findest du häufig im Schülerbuch

Act out your dialogue for the class.	Spielt der Klasse euren Dialog vor.
Ask questions (about the pictures).	Stelle Fragen (zu den Bildern).
Answer the questions.	Beantworte die Fragen.
Check your answers.	Überprüfe deine Antworten.
Choose the right word.	Wähle das richtige Wort aus.
Compare with your partner.	Vergleiche mit deinem Partner/deiner Partnerin.
Complete the sentences.	Vervollständige die Sätze.
Copy the chart.	Schreib die Tabelle ab.
Correct the sentences.	Verbessere die Sätze.
Fill in the correct form.	Setze die richtige Form ein.
Find the missing words.	Finde die fehlenden Wörter.
Listen. / Listen again.	Hör zu. / Hör noch einmal zu.
Make a chart/a mind map/a page for your dossier.	Fertige eine Tabelle/Mindmap/Seite für dein Dossier an.
Match the numbers and the letters.	Ordne die Nummern den Buchstaben zu.
Practise the dialogue.	Übt den Dialog.
Prepare a dialogue.	Bereitet einen Dialog vor.
Put the pictures in the right order.	Bring die Bilder in die richtige Reihenfolge.
Read the sentences.	Lies die Sätze.
Right or wrong?	Richtig oder falsch?
Swap charts.	Tauscht die Tabellen.
Take notes.	Mach dir Notizen.
Take turns.	Wechselt euch ab.
Talk to your partner about your picture.	Sprich mit deinem Partner/deiner Partnerin über dein Bild.
Tell your partner about your picture.	Erzähle deinem Partner/deiner Partnerin etwas über dein Bild.
Tick the right box.	Mach einen Haken in das richtige Kästchen.
Use the words from the box.	Verwende die Wörter aus dem Kasten.
What is the odd word out?	Welches Wort passt nicht dazu?
What's different?	Was ist anders?
Work with a partner.	Arbeite mit einem Partner/einer Partnerin zusammen.
Write the sentences.	Schreib die Sätze auf.

Illustrationen

Graham-Cameron Illustration, UK: Fliss Cary, Grafikerin (wenn nicht anders angegeben);
Roland Beier, Berlin (Vignetten vordere Umschlaginnenseite; S. 6/7; 17 unten; 28; 38 oben; 39; 45 oben; 58 Mitte; 62; 64 unten; 71 unten; 76; 88 oben; 92; 95; 99; 103 Mitte; 106; 107; 112/113 unten; 122–178);
Carlos Borrell, Berlin (Karten vordere und hintere Umschlaginnenseite);
Johann Brandstetter, Winhöring/Kronberg (S. 96–98; 128);
Julie Colthorpe, Berlin (S. 17 oben; 19; 48 oben; 52 Bild 5; 53; 88 unten; 109 Bild 2).

Fotos

Rob Cousins, Bristol (wenn im Bildquellenverzeichnis nicht anders angegeben)

Bildquellen

Alamy, Abingdon (S. 41 Grandma Shaw: Eliane Farray Sulle; S. 60 u. 115 Sanjay: David Sanger Photography; S. 89 li.: Phillip Wills; S. 100 Bild 2: Rolf Richardson);
Artquest, London (S. 67 oben re.);
Bank of England, London (S. 67 banknotes, reproduced with kind permission);
Graham Bool Photography, Braintree (S. 53 unten re.);
Britain on View, London (S. 101 Bild 4);
British Heart Foundation, London (S. 113 Mitte);
BTZ Bremer Touristik-Zentrale Gesellschaft für Marketing & Service mbH (S. 129);
Corbis, Düsseldorf (S. 9 Bild 3: Ariel Skelley; S. 52 Bild 4: LWA-Dann Tardif; S. 56 Mitte: RF; S. 60 u. 115 Yoko: Paul Barton);
Corel Library (S. 86, S. 89 re.);
Gareth Evans, Berlin (S. 59; S. 62 unten; S. 70; S. 80 Bild 1 u. 3; S. 84/85 pinboard; S. 118);
Brian Harris Photographer, Saffron Walden (S. 101 Bild 5);
Horse World, Bristol (S. 100 Bild 3: Alex Menhams);
Bernhard Hunger, Dettingen (S. 35 oben, 51);
Ingram Publishing, UK (S. 80 Bild 2);
Juniors Bildarchiv, Ruhpolding (S. 37 Bild E);
Keystone, Hamburg (S. 9 Bild 4: TopFoto.co.uk);
Ling Design Ltd., Kent (S. 112 re.);
Mauritius, Mittenwald (S. 60 u. 115 Britta);
Courtesy of The **Medici Society Limited**, London (S. 112 li.);
Picture-Alliance, Frankfurt/Main (S. 62 hockey: dpa; basketball, tennis, judo, volleyball: dpa/dpaweb; football: PA_WIRE);
PunchStock, Madison (S. 60 u. 115 Lars);
Tobias Schumacher, Kleinfischlingen (S. 21 unten);
Statics Ltd., London: David Wojtowycz (S. 113 re.);
Courtesy of St George's School Archives, Harpenden (S. 91);
Hartmut Tschepe, Berlin (S. 17 unten);
Carita Watts, Sweden (S. 127).

Titelbild

Rob Cousins, Bristol;
IFA-Bilderteam, Ottobrunn (Hintergrund Union Jack: Jon Arnold Images);
mpixel/Achim Meissner, Krefeld (Himmel).

Textquellen

S. 99: *Ode to a Goldfish* by Gyles Brandreth from: "Discovering Poetry. A Poetry Course for Key Stage" by Denise Scott. © Rigby Heinemann 1991. Adaptations © Sue Stewart 1993, Heinemann Educational Publishers, Oxford 1993;
Orders of the Day by John Cunliffe from: "John Cunliffe's Fizzy Whizzy Poetry Book". © John Cunliffe, 1995, Scholastic Children's Books, London 1995;
The Poetry United Chant by Les Baynton from: "The Works". Poems chosen by Paul Cookson. © Paul Cookson 2000, Macmillan Children's Books, London 2000.
